LEADING HOLISTIC IMPROVEMENT WITH LEAN SIX SIGMA 2.0

Second Edition

LEADING HOLISTIC IMPROVEMENT WITH LEAN SIX SIGMA 2.0

Second Edition

Ronald D. Snee

Roger W. Hoerl

Editor-in-Chief: Greg Wiegand
Executive Editor: Laura Norman
Senior Marketing Manager: Stephane Nakib
Editorial Assistant: Courtney Martin
Development Editor: Kiran Kumar Panigrahi
Managing Editor: Sandra Schroeder
Senior Project Editor: Lori Lyons
Cover Designer: Chuti Prasertsith
Project Manager: Dhayanidhi Karunanidhi
Copy Editor: Krista Hansing
Editorial Proofreader: Jeanine Furino
Indexer: Erika Millen
Compositor: codemantra

© 2018 by Pearson Education, Inc.

For information about buying this title in bulk quantities, or for special sales opportunities (which may include electronic versions; custom cover designs; and content particular to your business, training goals, marketing focus, or branding interests), please contact our corporate sales department at corpsales@pearsoned.com or (800) 382-3419.

For government sales inquiries, please contact governmentsales@pearsoned.com.

For questions about sales outside the U.S., please contact intlcs@pearson.com.

Company and product names mentioned herein are the trademarks or registered trademarks of their respective owners.

1   18

ISBN-10: 0-13-428888-2
ISBN-13: 978-0-13-428888-8

Pearson Education LTD.
Pearson Education Australia PTY, Limited
Pearson Education Singapore, Pte. Ltd.
Pearson Education Asia, Ltd.
Pearson Education Canada, Ltd.
Pearson Educación de Mexico, S.A. de C.V.
Pearson Education—Japan
Pearson Education Malaysia, Pte. Ltd.

Library of Congress Control Number: 2018938453

We dedicate this book to Marjorie Snee and to the memory of Senecca Hoerl; spouses whose support and understanding went well beyond what was reasonable to expect.

Contents at a Glance

Register your copy of *Leading Holistic Improvement with Lean Six Sigma 2.0* at informit.com for convenient access to updates and corrections as they become available. To start the registration process, go to informit. com/register and log in or create an account. Enter the product ISBN (9780134288888) and click Submit.

Contents

Chapter 7   Managing the Effort 187

Chapter 8   Sustaining Momentum and Growing 219

Chapter 9   **The Way We Work** **261**

Chapter 10   **Final Thoughts for Leaders** **293**

Acknowledgments

We are pleased to acknowledge the numerous individuals who provided insights, suggestions, and constructive criticism in the development of our ideas on holistic improvement, eventually resulting in this book. The contributors are too numerous to name individually, but you know who you are!

Further, we also express our gratitude to Laura Norman, Lori Lyons, Kiran Kumar Panigrahi, Krista Hansing, and the rest of the team at Pearson, for their guidance and assistance in making this book a reality.

About the Authors

Ronald Snee, PhD, Founder and President of Snee Associates, LLC, has 25+ years of experience in process improvement, strategic planning, quality, management, training system design and delivery, and statistics. Prior to this role, he was employed by the DuPont Company for 24 years in a variety of assignments.

Roger Hoerl, PhD, Associate Professor of Statistics at Union College, formerly led the Applied Statistics Laboratory at GE Global Research. Co-authors of several books, Snee and Hoerl are each recipients of one of the American Society for Quality's highest honors, the Shewhart Medal.

Preface

Six Sigma has always been about radically improving the performance of an organization, a pursuit to which we have collectively dedicated more than 85 years of our careers. We first worked together at DuPont in the early 1980s. We continued our professional relationship over the years, and in 1995, we both independently began our work in Six Sigma. Having been involved in improvement efforts most of our careers, we were both amazed at the tremendous financial results produced by Six Sigma and, later, Lean Six Sigma, the integration of Six Sigma with Lean Enterprise. We continued our discussions of Lean Six Sigma over the next several years as we deployed the method in different organizations.

Although we began to see numerous books published on Lean Six Sigma, either they were narrowly focused on the technical tools of Lean Six Sigma (such as a statistics text) or they used hype and fanfare to sell the reader on implementation. Our colleagues and clients, on the other hand, were raising deeper issues about how to actually deploy Lean Six Sigma and avoid potholes along the way. These questions highlighted the paucity of practical guidance on the deployment of Lean Six Sigma. *Leading Six Sigma* (Snee and Hoerl, 2003) was our attempt to fill this void.

The Work Continues

Since we published *Leading Six Sigma* in 2003 we have pursued an active program of consulting, research, and publication on process and organizational improvement using Lean Six Sigma and other methodologies. We found that Lean Six Sigma was not the best methodology to attack every problem, so other approaches (in addition to Lean) needed to be brought into the mix. Properly integrated, this set of approaches produced even more significant improvements as measured by customer satisfaction, employee engagement, top-line growth, and bottom-line results. These efforts have included the following:

- We published *Six Sigma Beyond the Factory Floor* (Snee and Hoerl, 2005), focusing on using Lean Six Sigma to improve nonmanufacturing processes such as healthcare, finance, and human resources.

- We introduced the concept of holistic improvement, which expands improvement in a broad sense across the entire organization, and developed a more formal holistic improvement methodology needed to support the broader view of holistic improvement (Snee 2005, 2006, 2008).

- We researched how to best combine the concepts, methods, and tools of Lean Enterprise and Six Sigma (Snee and Hoerl, 2007). This research was motivated by a belief that the integration of Six Sigma and Lean in existing texts was simplistic and did not display a deep understanding of both methodologies. We pointed out the important fundamental that Lean focuses primarily on the flow of information and material from the supplier to product delivery—that is, what happens between steps in the process. Therefore, Lean is oriented primarily to productivity, not product quality. Six Sigma, on the other hand, focuses primarily on what happens within the process steps—that is, on the value-adding transform itself. Quality of the final product is typically a function of the value-adding transformations—that is, what happens within the process steps. Both flow and quality are important. Improvement is most successful when project selection and execution takes these differences into account instead of assuming that Six Sigma and Lean are fundamentally doing the same things.

- We continued our research on leadership and what is required to lead Lean Six Sigma and ultimately achieved holistic improvement.

- As we continued our work on improvement, we saw that many problems organizations faced were too large, complex, and unstructured to be adequately solved by Lean Six Sigma. We developed the statistical engineering discipline to handle such problems (Hoerl and Snee, 2010). It became clear that after a problem has been defined and structured, with project and analysis strategies developed, Lean Six Sigma (or perhaps other methodologies) becomes very useful in solving it.

We have presented these advances and debated them both in public sessions and in the published, peer-reviewed literature. The pinnacle of these concepts and approaches is the *holistic improvement system* discussed in this book.

How This Book Can Help You

If you are looking for an approach to start an improvement initiative, this book can help you start your Lean Six Sigma deployment. On the other hand, if you have been using Lean Six Sigma for a few years and are looking to take the initiative to the next level, this book can suggest ways to spread improvement across the organization. This evolves your approach to a holistic improvement system, or what we call Lean Six Sigma 2.0. In each case, you will be taking improvement to a new level in your organization.

Readers of this book will learn the following:

- How to initially deploy a Lean Six Sigma plan that reflects the unique organization, with key lessons learned from the world's best implementations to date

- How to avoid the common pitfalls that cause so many organizations to struggle with improvement initiatives

- Every facet of Lean Six Sigma leadership, including strategy, goal setting, metrics, training, roles/responsibilities, processes, reporting, rewards, and ongoing management review

- How to evolve a Lean Six Sigma deployment to true holistic improvement, the next level of improvement that involves the whole organization and uses a diverse array of improvement methodologies, including Big Data analytics

- How to use a focus on improvement as a leadership development tool

Six Sigma began at Motorola in the 1980s as a statistical measure of process performance and an overall approach to improve it. AlliedSignal and General Electric (GE) broadened and further popularized the approach in the 1990s. Their successes encouraged other companies (including DuPont, Dow Chemical, Bank of America, Ford, and American Express, as well as companies in Europe and the Pacific Rim) to undertake Six Sigma and, eventually, Lean Six Sigma initiatives. The methodology evolved significantly along the way. Today Lean Six Sigma 2.0 has grown into a holistic strategy for improving the performance of any organization.

Leading Holistic Improvement with Lean Six Sigma 2.0 integrates the improvement tools that have proven effective over the years into a comprehensive approach that improves customer satisfaction, employee engagement, top-line growth, and the bottom line. As a result, Lean Six Sigma 2.0 builds on what has been successful in the past and takes performance improvement to a new level of effectiveness.

Although the theory is simple, many who implement Lean Six Sigma struggle with the details of overall deployment. Being sold on Lean Six Sigma is of little value if it cannot be successfully implemented. Most companies have experienced tremendous success with Lean Six Sigma, but others have not. Our research indicates a lack of literature on why this is so. We have examined both very successful and minimally successful organizations to understand the root causes for success or failure. We have found that successful companies have important similarities in deployment, as do unsuccessful companies. Understanding these common success factors helps organizations significantly enhance the probability of success and enables them to avoid the potholes.

Of course, each organization is different. You cannot blindly adopt the Lean Six Sigma deployment models that other companies use and expect to be successful. It makes much more sense to understand what specifically led these companies to success and then *adapt* those approaches and methods to your own organization. Providing a roadmap to do just that is the focus of this book.

What Is Unique About This Book

This book is unique in several ways. It is the only book currently on the market that discusses recent research and learnings regarding the use of Lean Six Sigma to improve processes and organizations. Furthermore, it is the only available book that shows how to evolve Lean Six Sigma to an even more effective approach, holistic improvement.

This book documents the most important and useful recent advances in the theory and practice of Lean Six Sigma improvement—and improvement in general. The discussion includes case studies that illustrate critical aspects of holistic improvement. It should be useful to two important audiences: those just beginning to use Lean Six Sigma to improve organizational performance, and those that have mature deployment underway and are looking for new and better ways to move the initiative to the next level.

Next, this book introduces the concept, methods, and tools of holistic improvement, the paradigm shift that effectively makes improvement part of the management and operating culture of an organization. We refer to holistic improvement, combined with the infrastructure of Lean Six Sigma, as Lean Six Sigma 2.0. This is essentially the most recent evolution of Six Sigma that incorporates and integrates multiple improvement methodologies. With this approach, the specific improvement methodology to be applied is fit to the unique aspects of the problem being addressed—that is, the problem determines the solution method to use.

This book emphasizes the importance of management reviews for both projects and the overall deployment of holistic improvement. Experience has shown that improvement cannot be successfully sustained and grown over time without regular management review. No other Lean Six Sigma or improvement book currently on the market addresses this important consideration.

Finally, we emphasize and detail the use of holistic improvement as a leadership development tool. Many leading corporations, including GE, DuPont, and Allied-Signal/Honeywell, have used this approach. These and other organizations have required, or at least strongly recommended, Lean Six Sigma Green Belt or Black Belt certification for management positions.

These unique elements have been successfully applied in a variety of organizations and are worthy of consideration for any group seriously pursuing improvement.

What's in This Book

We present a deployment roadmap that has worked in many different types of organizations, large to small, manufacturing to financial services, in the United States and abroad. It shows how to get started, manage the important aspects of the initiative, maintain the momentum over time, and eventually evolve the initiative into a true holistic improvement system. Specific advice is given in such areas as these:

- Identifying your company's most promising improvement opportunities and leaders

- Providing leadership, talent, and infrastructure for a successful launch and sustainment of the deployment over time

- Incorporating additional improvement methodologies so that the initiative can effectively match the most relevant method to the specific problem at hand

- Implementing systems, processes, and budgets for ongoing improvement projects

- Measuring and maximizing the financial value of your improvement initiative

- Initiating and evolving Lean Six Sigma into holistic improvement, including creating an overall improvement organization and project selection system

- Clarifying roles of improvement leaders that help ensure project gains are sustained

This advice and the underlying experiences have been time-tested and will be useful in speeding up your improvement initiative and sustaining it over time.

Avoiding the Mistakes That Can Make Lean Six Sigma Fall Short

Our guidance is based on more than 44 years of experience deploying Lean Six Sigma and holistic improvement in large and small companies in many different areas, including manufacturing, research and development (R&D), healthcare, and financial services. Indeed, we have found that Lean Six Sigma can work everywhere, regardless of culture, country, industry, function, and process, if you follow the process. The chapters in this book cover the following critically important subjects.

A New Improvement Paradigm Is Needed

Clearly we live in a very different world—most would say a much more dangerous world—than when Six Sigma was invented in 1987 at Motorola. How should we think about continuous improvement in such a world? Is Lean Six Sigma the best approach to take for all problems, including large, complex, unstructured problems, such as climate change or the Millennial Development Goals? We argue that a different paradigm is needed to take continuous improvement to a new level in this world in which we now find ourselves.

In addition to developing a broader portfolio of improvement methodologies, organizations need to integrate process management and control systems (such as ISO 9000) with newer methodologies (including Big Data analytics and the increasingly important risk management methodologies). We refer to this paradigm as holistic improvement and recommend Lean Six Sigma 2.0 as the best methodology based on this paradigm. In Chapter 1, "A New Paradigm Is Needed," we briefly review the evolution of Six Sigma since 1987 and explain what we mean by Lean Six Sigma 2.0.

What Is Holistic Improvement?

As just noted, Lean Six Sigma is no longer adequate for the improvements that organizations need to survive and, better yet, prosper in the modern era. We call the needed new paradigm holistic improvement. In Chapter 2, "What Is Holistic Improvement?", we do the following:

- Define holistic improvement

- Show how holistic improvement is different from and more effective than previous approaches

- Provide a strategic structure for its use

It all begins with project selection: choosing the *right* projects. We then need to select the right methods for the specific project instead of relying on one method for all problems. It is critical to recognize that the Achilles' heel of any improvement approach is project selection (and, to some degree, method selection). This chapter looks at holistic approaches to both project identification and selection and method selection.

Critical Methodologies in a Holistic Improvement System

One obvious implication of a holistic improvement system is the need to have multiple methodologies at its disposal instead of relying on one "best" improvement method (or even two or three). The portfolio of methods needs to be dynamic and must evolve over time. In Chapter 3, "Key Methodologies in a Holistic Improvement System," we briefly review the improvement methods that we feel are logical for most organizations to consider. Obviously, we cannot cover every possible improvement method, so we focus on the ones we consider core methods. For readers who are not familiar with any of these methods, we recommend following up with the references given. Our purpose in this chapter is simply to provide a brief introduction to each method and place it in the context of holistic improvement.

Note that Chapters 1–3 are completely new to the second edition of this book.

Holistic Improvement Case Studies

Case studies are an excellent way to see how Lean Six Sigma and holistic improvement are deployed, including strategies utilized, plans developed, barriers encountered, and results achieved in terms of process performance and bottom-line results. In our earlier books on Lean Six Sigma (Snee and Hoerl, 2003, 2005), we examined several case studies that illustrated both successful and not-so-successful deployments. In the current Chapter 4, "Case Studies in Holistic Improvement," we discuss three more mature case studies: GE, DuPont, and Scott Paper. The DuPont and Scott Paper case studies have previously not appeared in the literature. These three cases demonstrate how the breadth of deployment grows over the years and how new improvement tools integrate into the growing holistic methodology. Of course, the goal remains to improve customer satisfaction, process performance, and financial results.

Successful Implementation of Holistic Improvement

In Chapter 5, "How to Successfully Implement Lean Six Sigma 2.0," we take another look at the case studies in Chapter 4 and those discussed by Snee and Hoerl (2003) to elaborate on the key factors that led to significant (or minimal) success in Lean Six Sigma, or a more holistic approach. We show how to analyze the keys to a successful deployment and integrate these key success factors into an overall, step-by-step process. Such an approach can also enhance a Lean Six Sigma system or move another improvement system currently in place toward a holistic system, which we refer to as Lean Six Sigma 2.0.

Getting Started

In Chapter 6, "Launching the Initiative," we define the launch phase of Lean Six Sigma to be roughly the period between making the decision to deploy and completing the initial wave of Black Belt training. At the end of this phase, you should have the following components in place:

- An overall deployment plan (strategy)
- The initial wave of projects
- Trained Black Belts and other key players

These are the key deliverables for the launch phase, and they should be considered in that order. Before developing the deployment plan, most organizations need to address the key preliminary question of which major deployment strategy to use. This decision affects virtually every aspect of the deployment plan, so it must be addressed first.

Managing the Effort

Chapter 7, "Managing the Effort," looks at how to manage the effort over time to realize its promised improvement in performance and how to also sustain it over time. This phase is of critical importance because, without it, your improvement initiative will dissipate over time, perhaps as soon as within two years. The elements of this phase are introduced and discussed in Chapter 7.

We refer to this next step in our deployment process as managing the effort. This phase goes roughly from completion of the initial wave of Black Belt training until the point at which the organization has trained everyone it originally intended to train and also completed projects in all the areas mentioned in the deployment plan. It typically lasts a minimum of 18 months, although organizations must continue to manage Lean Six Sigma deployment in subsequent phases. During this phase, it is important to begin adding more elements of a holistic improvement system so that organizations expand beyond Lean Six Sigma to Lean Six Sigma 2.0, holistic improvement.

Sustaining Momentum and Growing

Chapter 8, "Sustaining Momentum and Growing," focuses on both the defensive effort needed to sustain impetus and the offensive effort needed to expand the Lean Six Sigma initiative toward a true holistic improvement system. This phase of sustaining and growing is defined as the time between when the organization completes the training and projects in the original deployment plan and when the organization transforms Lean Six Sigma from an initiative to the normal way it works, or Lean Six Sigma 2.0.

This phase can last several years. The portfolio of improvement methodologies and improvement to the whole organization is expanded. This expansion across the organization might include introducing customers and suppliers to Lean Six Sigma and using Lean Six Sigma to increase revenue. Quality by design (QbD) projects that use different methodologies than Lean or Six Sigma can help drive new revenue. Lean Six Sigma can be applied to top-line growth as well, but QbD methodologies are better suited for new product and service development.

Transitioning to the Way We Work

In Chapter 9, "The Way We Work," we take Lean Six Sigma one step further and discuss how to integrate it into daily work processes. The changes an organization makes in its work as a result of Lean Six Sigma 2.0 comprise its control plan for the overall initiative and ensure that it maintains the gains it has achieved. The desired end game is that holistic improvement becomes such an integral part of the way the organization manages that there is no longer a need for a formal improvement initiative. Instead, a holistic improvement organization is now a stable and integral part of the company, analogous to finance, human resources, marketing, and so on. Bringing improvement to the level of day-to-day work includes integrating Lean Six Sigma (and other improvement methodologies) with operational and managerial processes, as well as developing an overall organizational improvement system. This chapter also discusses the use of holistic improvement as a leadership development tool.

Final Thoughts for Leaders

In Chapter 10, "Final Thoughts for Leaders," we provide additional guidance for leaders, to encourage a deepening understanding of holistic improvement and ensure the success of both individual improvement projects and the overall initiative. Particular attention is placed on helping managers understand what actually goes on in improvement projects, without burying them in the details of the technical tools.

How to Use This Book

Using this book as a guide, you can get your Lean Six Sigma deployment off to a solid start and help ensure its continuing success. We provide a body of knowledge on how to properly deploy Lean Six Sigma, as well as the pitfalls to avoid. You can speed up the deployment and success of Lean Six Sigma if you make use of what those who have gone before you have learned; you don't have to reinvent the wheel.

At the 2- to 3-year point in your deployment, you can use this book to begin the evolution of your improvement initiative to holistic improvement. Achieving each element of holistic improvement is relatively simple. However, putting it all together is the hard part. This book not only provides a roadmap for deploying Lean Six Sigma, but it also highlights the keys to successful deployment and provides a way to maintain the gains. You get everything in a single document.

By reading this book, you will learn what works and what doesn't, gain effective deployment strategies, and become fluent in the language of Lean Six Sigma and holistic improvement. Of course, a roadmap is not a cookbook; each organization stills need to customize its approach, based on its own unique situation.

Everyone involved in Lean Six Sigma can benefit from this book. Executives will learn how to design and lead the deployment process and how to focus on critical improvement areas. Champions will learn how to select and charter projects, as well as how to select and guide Black Belts and Green Belts. Master Black Belts will learn the deployment process, which is needed to work effectively with management, Champions and the Black Belts and Green Belts. Black and Green Belts will learn more about the Lean Six Sigma deployment process, which will deepen their understanding of their role.

Lean Six Sigma is becoming increasingly recognized not only as an effective process improvement methodology, but also as an effective strategy for culture change and leadership development. Lean Six Sigma obviously emphasizes the use of facts and data to guide the decision-making process. But the improvement project selection and review, recognition and reward, and communication processes used to support Lean Six Sigma are also effective culture change vehicles. Increasingly, companies are seeing Lean Six Sigma and other improvement methodologies as effective leadership development tools. Companies such as GE, Honeywell, and DuPont have required Lean Six Sigma Black Belt and Green Belt experience for managerial advancement.

Other Useful Resources

We believe that this book will get our two target audiences off to a good start: organizations that are just starting an improvement initiative and organizations that are looking to move their improvement initiative to the next level. It is important to recognize that other resources fit very nicely with this book as well and could be of use to these two audiences.

Improvement outside of manufacturing is a big opportunity for improvement. It is generally agreed upon that there is as much improvement opportunity outside of manufacturing as there is inside manufacturing.

Our book *Six Sigma Beyond the Factory Floor* (Snee and Hoerl, 2005) addresses this subject and provides time-tested concepts, methods, and tools that are useful in this environment. Also included are four case studies documenting improvement initiatives in Bank of America, Commonwealth Health Corporation, Motorola Finance, and GE Research and Development.

As an organization initiates a Lean Six Sigma deployment process, a variety of questions typically arise, including what can happen, good and bad, and what pitfalls to be on the lookout for. Snee and Hoerl (2003) address 31 commonly encountered deployment questions and issues and provide answers and guidance on how to respond.

Leading Six Sigma (Snee and Hoerl, 2003) also includes a Lean Six Sigma deployment roadmap that organizations can use to develop a tailored deployment plan. Ron Snee has helped more than 50 organizations customize this deployment framework to launch their improvement initiatives.

References

Hoerl, R. W. and R. D. Snee (2010) "Statistical Thinking and Methods in Quality Improvement: A Look to the Future," *Quality Engineering*, (with discussion) Vol. 22, no. 3, July-September 2010, 119–139.

Snee, R. D. (2005) "Utilizing a Holistic Approach to Performance Improvement," Presented at the FDA Quality and Six Sigma for Pharma and Biotech Conference, Philadelphia, PA, November 2005.

Snee, R. D. (2006) "Making Another World: W. Edwards Deming and a Holistic Approach to Performance Improvement," Deming Lecture presented at the Joint Statistical Meetings, Seattle, WA, August 7, 2006.

Snee, R. D. (2008) "W. Edwards Deming's 'Making a New World': A Holistic Approach to Performance Improvement and the Role of Statistics," *The American Statistician*, August 2008, Vol. 62, no. 3, 251–255.

Snee, R.D., and R. W. Hoerl. (2003) *Leading Six Sigma: A Step-by-Step Guide Based on Experience with GE and Other Six Sigma Companies*. Upper Saddle River, NJ: Financial Times/Prentice Hall.

Snee, R.D., and R. W. Hoerl. (2005) *Six Sigma Beyond the Factory Floor: Deployment Strategies for Financial Services, Health Care, and the Rest of the Real Economy*. Upper Saddle River, NJ: Financial Times/ Prentice Hall.

Snee, R. D. and R. W. Hoerl. (2007) "Integrating Lean and Six Sigma – A Holistic Approach," *Six Sigma Forum Magazine*, May 2007, 15–21.

—**Ronald D. Snee,** Newark, Delaware

—**Roger W. Hoerl,** Niskayuna, New York

1

A New Paradigm Is Needed

"The significant problems we face cannot be solved at the same level of thinking we were at when we created them."
—Albert Einstein

The history of Six Sigma goes back to Motorola in about the year 1987 (Harry and Schroeder, 2000). Motorola was facing stiff foreign competition in the pager market and desperately needed to both improve quality and lower costs to stay in business. By applying Six Sigma, the company was able to do both. Other electronics manufacturing companies, including Honeywell and AlliedSignal, saw Motorola's success and soon launched their own initiatives. In late 1995, GE CEO Jack Welch publicly announced that Six Sigma would be the biggest initiative in GE's history—and would be his own personal number one priority for the next five years (Snee and Hoerl, 2003). GE reported billions of dollars of savings in its annual reports over the next several years, resulting in a significant increase in GE stock price and prompting many more organizations to adopt Six Sigma.

Honeywell, GE, and others realized that a different approach was needed for designing new products and services. That is, when designing a new process, there's nothing to improve because the process itself doesn't exist yet. Based on earlier design work by Honeywell, GE developed the Define, Measure, Analyze, Design, Verify (DMADV) approach to design for Six Sigma (Snee and Hoerl, 2003). The GE LightSpeed CT scanner was the first new product GE developed using the DMADV process. The product, introduced in 1998, used multislice technology to reduce typical scanning time from about 3 minutes to 30 seconds. This was a big win for patients as well as hospitals because it significantly enhanced throughput in CT scanning. GE gained $60 million in sales during the first 90 days (GE, 1999).

Several major health networks launched Six Sigma initiatives during this time frame. Commonwealth Health Corporation reported $1.6 million in savings in the radiology department alone during the first year (Snee and Hoerl, 2005). Among other innovations to the Six Sigma methodology, GE developed an approach to applying Six Sigma outside of manufacturing, including to financial processes at GE Capital. Partly because of the success GE Capital demonstrated with Six Sigma, Bank of America became the first major bank to launch a Six Sigma initiative in 2001 (Snee and Hoerl, 2005). By the end of 2003, its cumulative financial benefits exceeded $2 billion (Jones, 2004). This development was important in demonstrating the universal application of Six Sigma: It is not simply a manufacturing initiative, but instead is a generic improvement methodology.

The Expansion to Lean Six Sigma

As early as 2003, practitioners were noticing limitations of Six Sigma (we return to this shortly). For example, Toyota had developed generally accepted principles of manufacturing excellence over several decades of intense improvement efforts on the assembly line. These principles, referred to as **Lean Manufacturing,** were often overlooked in Six Sigma projects because they were simply not well known. George (2002) suggested integrating Lean principles with Six Sigma to create the broader improvement initiative **Lean Six Sigma.** GE and others quickly transitioned their Six Sigma initiatives to Lean Six Sigma. Results continued to roll in.

Through deployments across diverse organizations, Six Sigma practitioners and researchers have deepened the body of knowledge driving continuous improvement in both theory and practice. For example, several journals have emerged to focus specifically on extending research on Six Sigma and continuous improvements; these include the *International Journal of Six Sigma and Competitive Advantage* (http://www.inderscience.com/jhome.php?jcode=ijssca), *Six Sigma Forum* Magazine (http://asq.org/pub/sixsigma/), and the *International Journal of Lean Six Sigma* (http://www.emeraldinsight.com/journal/ijlss).

Extending the theory and practice of continuous improvement is important, but the most easily quantifiable impact of Lean Six Sigma is financial. A diverse array of organizations spanning the globe have added billions of dollars to their bottom lines. Of course, financial results are perhaps more easily quantified than others; the impact on the quality of healthcare, safety of products and food supply, and even protection of the environment should not be overlooked. We argue that Lean Six Sigma applications have saved countless lives.

In short, based on the documented results in healthcare, finance, manufacturing, and other organizational areas, Lean Six Sigma clearly is the single most impactful improvement methodology in history. Therefore, we might logically ask, why change anything? As the old saying goes, "If it ain't broke, don't fix it." We answer this question in the next section.

Macro Societal Shifts Since 1987

Lean Six Sigma definitely has been a tremendous success, but the world has changed considerably since Six Sigma was originally developed in 1987. For that matter, the world has changed considerably since 2003, when we published the first edition of this book (Snee and Hoerl, 2003). Six Sigma has morphed and evolved along with the world, but in our opinion, this evolution has not been to the extent needed to move the discipline of continuous improvement to a new level. Before discussing the evolution of Six Sigma and its ongoing limitations, we briefly review a few of these macro societal shifts, discussed in the subsequent sections:

- Accelerated globalization

- Massive immigration into North America and Europe

- Growth of IT and Big Data analytics

- Recognition of the uniqueness of large, complex unstructured problems

- Modern security concerns such as terrorism and computer hacking

Accelerated Globalization

Obviously, massive shifts have occurred in the global economy since 1987. Motorola was already facing stiff global competition at that time, primarily from Japan, and globalization has accelerated even more dramatically since then. For example, India has become globally recognized for its vast resources in information technology, China has become a dominant player in global manufacturing, and large numbers of call centers supporting customers in Europe and North America have sprung up in developing countries such as the Philippines.

In fact, although globalization is not the focus of this book, it has become a critical issue in recent national elections, as with the "Brexit" vote in 2016 leading Great Britain to leave the European Union, the U.S. presidential election in the same year, and subsequent referendums in Italy and other European countries. There's no denying that we live in a truly global economy today. This was not the case in 1987, and it has obvious implications for the need to improve to meet global standards of excellence.

Massive Immigration into North America and Europe

Similarly, the matter of immigration has been a hot button issue in many elections and referendums. In addition to immigration concerns in the United States, large waves of immigrants have come into Europe from war-torn countries in the Middle East. Our point here is not political: We are simply noting that these waves of immigration have created more diverse workforces in many countries. Having staff with different cultural backgrounds and viewpoints impacts how teams go about problem solving in improvement projects. Unquestionably, employees in Western countries have a more diverse approach toward improvement than in the past. In our view, this can have a positive effect on teamwork, but it needs to be effectively managed.

Growth of IT and Big Data Analytics

In 1987, the Internet was in an embryonic stage of development. Today, of course, the Internet is ubiquitous in society, including healthcare, education, and business. Google and Amazon have become major players in the business world, despite having minimal brick-and-mortar facilities. Similarly, the state of information technology (IT) in 1987 is considered antiquated by today's standards. These developments in IT have led to a rapid expansion of data acquisition, storage, and analysis, a phenomenon commonly referred to as Big Data or data science (Davenport and Patil, 2012). We discuss Big Data analytics in more detail later in this chapter. Do these developments in IT, the Internet, and Big Data have implications for how we should go about continuous improvement? We feel that they clearly do.

Recognition of Uniqueness of Large, Complex, Unstructured Problems

The world has also recognized the need to collectively address large, complex, and unstructured problems. For example, the issue of global climate change cannot be addressed by any one organization or even one country; it is simply too big of an issue. Likewise, addressing emerging pandemics such as Zika, Ebola, or drug-resistant tuberculosis requires a global effort.

In the year 2000, the United Nations announced a set of ambitious development goals, referred to as the Millennium Development Goals (http://www.un.org/millenniumgoals/), which require global cooperation to achieve. These goals included such large, complex, unstructured issues as addressing extreme poverty, providing universal access to education, reducing instances of HIV/AIDS, and enhancing the status of girls and women. We further discuss the issue of large, complex, unstructured problems later in this chapter.

Modern Security Concerns

Security has always been a concern for both societies and businesses. However, the origins of Six Sigma predate the terrorist attacks on the United States on September 11, 2001. Before 2001, many people in the United States and some western European counties believed that terrorism occurred only elsewhere, not in their own countries. Since 2001, we have learned that terrorism is a serious concern everywhere; it's a global problem. Those of us who travel by air realize that we will never go back to the days of casually walking onto airplanes with minimal security delays.

Beyond terrorism, individuals and businesses both have serious security concerns over computer hacking. Providing protection from identity theft has become a billion-dollar industry in the United States alone.

Businesses across the globe received a wake-up call on December 18, 2013, in the heart of the Christmas shopping season, when someone hacked into the computer records of the retail giant Target and downloaded more than 40 million credit card numbers (http://money.cnn.com/2013/12/18/news/companies/target-credit-card/). Target spent vast amounts of money doing damage control, including providing free identity theft protection to customers whose numbers were stolen. Of course, the damage to Target's reputation was even worse. We discuss the issue of security and risk management in greater detail shortly.

Clearly, we live in a very different world—and, most people would say, also a much more dangerous world—than in 1987. How should we think about continuous improvement in such a world? Is Lean Six Sigma the best approach to take for all problems, including large, complex, unstructured problems, such as climate change or the Millennial Development Goals? We argue that a different paradigm is needed to take continuous improvement to a new level in today's world. We refer to this paradigm as holistic improvement, and we recommend **Lean Six Sigma 2.0** as the best methodology based on this paradigm.

Before describing what we mean by holistic improvement in the next chapter, we briefly review the evolution of Six Sigma here and explain what we mean by Lean Six Sigma 2.0.

Current State of the Art

What exactly do we mean by Lean Six Sigma 2.0? We borrow the numbering system of information technology and its numbering approach to software revisions. The first version of a software system is usually Version 1.0, for obvious reasons. Next, when minor updates are made, such as fixing bugs or providing incremental enhancements, the new version typically is listed as 1.1, or perhaps even 1.0.1, to indicate an even smaller change than 1.1 (https://en.wikipedia.org/wiki/Software_versioning). The version is not listed as 2.0 until it has a major enhancement, which often involves a total rewrite of the code.

In our view, Six Sigma has undergone considerable evolution during its lifetime. However, these enhancements have been primarily incremental in nature and have not rethought the fundamental paradigm of Six Sigma. We therefore refer to these enhancements as Six Sigma 1.1, 1.2,

1.3, and so on, as shown in Table 1.1. We feel that because of the radical changes in the world since 1987, a rethinking of the fundamental paradigm of Six Sigma is now required. We refer to this approach as **Lean Six Sigma 2.0**, and we discuss this in more detail in Chapter 2, "What Is Holistic Improvement?".

Let's take another look at how Six Sigma has evolved since 1987.

Table 1.1 Versions of Six Sigma to Date

Version	Description
1.0	Original rollout at Motorola: 1987
1.1	GE enhancements: circa 2000
1.2	Lean Six Sigma: circa 2005
1.3	Lean Six Sigma and Innovation (ambidextrous organizations): circa 2010

Versions 1.0 and 1.1

As noted in the previous section, we refer to the original development of Six Sigma at Motorola as Six Sigma 1.0. Recall that this methodology focused on manufacturing and ways to improve existing processes. GE made several enhancements to Six Sigma, as discussed previously. These included adding a Define stage, developing the DMADV approach to designing projects, and broadening the effort beyond manufacturing to also include finance, healthcare, and administrative processes. GE referred to applications outside of manufacturing as Commercial Quality (Hahn et al., 2000). Each of these enhancements was noteworthy and important in its own right. However, we could also argue that each enhancement was a logical extension of what came previously. Therefore, the GE version of Six Sigma around the turn of the millennium might accurately be referred to as Six Sigma 1.1. Version 1.1 was a significant improvement over Version 1.0, but it was based on the same fundamental paradigm.

Version 1.2: Lean Six Sigma

The first major integration effort occurred when Lean Manufacturing principles were integrated with Six Sigma, creating Lean Six Sigma (George, 2002). Before this integration, proponents of one of these methodologies commonly viewed the other methodology as the enemy. Six Sigma proponents tended to disparage Lean as simplistic and unscientific, and Lean proponents disparaged Six Sigma as expensive and academic, essentially trying to use dynamite to kill an ant. This competition confused management at many organizations, who tried to filter through the smoke to determine what approaches to use. A major advantage of Lean Six Sigma (which took several years to become popular enough to replace Six Sigma) is that it minimized this competition and put both sets of proponents on the same team. Of course, it also broadened the scope of problems that could be tackled effectively by offering a more diverse toolkit. We therefore refer to Lean Six Sigma as Version 1.2, a significant enhancement over Version 1.1.

Version 1.3: Lean Six Sigma and Innovation

More recently, both researchers and practitioners have investigated the relationship between Lean Six Sigma and innovation. Hindo (2007) evaluated issues in Six Sigma deployment at 3M and suggested that Six Sigma and innovation are antagonistic. That is, Hindo contended that although deploying Six Sigma offered important incremental improvements, it would damage creative, innovative cultures, such as the one at 3M, because it was too rigorous and disciplined.

We did not take this contention seriously because, throughout our careers, we have seen that virtually all Six Sigma projects require creative thought to be completed successfully. However, we understand that this claim needs to be answered via research. Hoerl and Gardner (2010) demonstrated that Lean Six Sigma can actually enhance the innovation of an organization. They pointed out that the scientific method, upon which Lean Six Sigma is based, has sparked creativity and accelerated innovation for centuries. More specifically, they suggested that a proper relationship exists between the development of business strategy and idea generation based on this strategy, and Six Sigma projects. This relationship incorporates both Design for Six Sigma and more traditional Lean Six Sigma projects.

Birkinshaw and Gibson (2004) noted that, to be successful in the long term, organizations need to be operationally efficient (that is, continuously improve existing operations) and also able to innovate to develop new products and services. Doing only one of these well is not sufficient over time. Birkinshaw and Gibson refer to organizations that can both optimize operations ("exploitation") and innovate ("exploration") as **ambidextrous.** Significant research has shown that when Six Sigma is properly implemented (for example, with a good balance of design projects and improvement projects), it does help organizations achieve ambidexterity. In addition, Six Sigma can enhance rather than stifle creativity and innovation (He et al., 2015; Gutierrez et al., 2012; Gutierrez et al., 2016).

We view the effective integration of Lean Six Sigma with creative efforts to innovate new products and services to be a significant step forward in the overall evolution of Lean Six Sigma. Therefore, we refer to this integration that produces ambidextrous organizations as **Lean Six Sigma 1.3.** Of course, additional skills and tools are needed to effectively innovate. This includes the theory of inventive problem solving, which is often referred to in the literature as TRIZ, the transliteration of its original Russian acronym (Altshuller, 1992).

We now consider the limitations of Lean Six Sigma 1.3 and look at a potential new paradigm for overcoming these limitations using a fundamentally new approach to improvement that is suitable for modern times.

The Limitations of Lean Six Sigma 1.3

Lean Six Sigma 1.3 offers many commendable improvements. For example, it covers a diverse array of application areas, from Internet commerce and other high-tech industries to healthcare, finance, and, of course, manufacturing. It has incorporated key Lean principles from the Toyota Production System, such as line of sight and 5S, to drive improvement even before data is collected. Furthermore, research has documented a clearer, more synergistic relationship between Lean Six Sigma and disruptive innovation, and also demonstrated how to use Design for Six Sigma projects to take innovative concepts to market. Despite these advantages, we feel that Lean Six Sigma 1.3 still needs to overcome the following limitations:

- Still not appropriate for all problems

- Does not incorporate routine problem solving

- Does not provide a complete quality management system

- Cannot efficiently handle large, complex, and unstructured problems

- Does not take advantage of Big Data analytics

- Does not address modern risk management issues

In this section, we highlight the importance of each limitation in greater detail. In our view, minor adjustments to Lean Six Sigma 1.3 will not address these limitations. Instead, a new paradigm is needed. Kuhn (1962) noted that the need for a new paradigm becomes apparent when the list of problems that existing paradigms cannot solve becomes too large to ignore. We feel that Lean Six Sigma 1.3 is now at this place.

Still Not Appropriate for All Problems

Six Sigma, not even in the form of Lean Six Sigma 1.3, is the most appropriate approach for all projects. For example, the second author of this book (Hoerl) was asked years ago to help a computer scientist with his Six Sigma project at GE. When Hoerl asked him about the project, he stated that it involved installing an Oracle database. Hoerl asked if he knew how to install an Oracle database, and he replied yes. Hoerl asked if he had already done this successfully, and the computer scientist again replied yes. Now with a puzzled look on his face, Hoerl asked what problem required a solution. The computer scientist replied that there was no problem to be solved, but his boss had told him to use Six Sigma on this installation, so this is what he was going to do.

This is a classic case of a "solution known" problem (Hoerl and Snee, 2013). We have a problem, but the solution is already known. This does not necessarily mean that the solution is easy to implement—properly installing databases is not trivial. However, there is no need to analyze data to search for a solution. We just need to ensure that the people doing the work have the right skills and experience, and perhaps procedures, to properly implement the known solution. The question of whether the solution is known or unknown is a key consideration in choosing a methodology, as we see in the next chapter.

The key point, we hope, is clear. Six Sigma was not needed, and perhaps not even helpful, for that installation. Of course, some type of formal project management system, and possibly database protocols, were needed to ensure success. But Six Sigma was not needed. Over the years, we authors have both had numerous similar conversations with people who were trying to force-fit Six Sigma where it was not needed—and sometimes where it was not appropriate. For example, as in this case, Six Sigma is helpful only for "solution unknown" problems. Simpler methods can address more straightforward problems. These include Work-Out, a team problem-solving method developed at GE (Hoerl, 2008), so-called "Nike projects" (Just Do It!), and "Is–Is Not" analysis (Kepner and Tregoe, 2013), to name just a few. We discuss each of these techniques within the context of a holistic approach to improvement in subsequent chapters.

Of course, integrating Lean into Six Sigma helps avoid force-fitting Six Sigma because Lean might be an appropriate methodology for a given problem when Six Sigma is not. For example, Lean has proven principles that provide excellent guidance on "solution known" problems (Hoerl and Snee, 2013). However, just as Six Sigma is not appropriate for all problems, Lean also is not appropriate for all problems. In short, any time we select the problem-solving methodology before we have clearly documented the problem, we are prone to force-fitting. Shouldn't we learn about the problem first and only then determine the best approach to find a solution? After all, no one would continue to see a physician who recommends treatment before learning about the patient's condition.

Does Not Incorporate Routine Problem Solving

Lean Six Sigma 1.3 does not incorporate routine problem solving. Suppose that a manufacturing line begins leaking oil at 3:30 AM. Clearly, this is not the time to put together a Six Sigma team to gather data and study the problem for a few months; someone needs to promptly stop the leak! Similarly, if someone notices mislabeled medication in a pharmacy, we wouldn't want the pharmacy to put together a Six Sigma team; it needs to identify and remove the mislabeled medication immediately, before anyone receives it.

By "routine problem solving," we mean the normal, day-to-day problem solving that occurs in all organizations, typically in real time. Of course, some people and some organizations are particularly good at it, and others aren't. The ideal is to have each employee well trained in how to approach routine problems, diagnose root causes, and identify and test solutions. Employees should also understand when to call for help. Most of the problems faced in the workplace, and even in our private lives, can be solved in a short amount of time with no data or minimal data. In the case of the leaking oil, you would just follow the oil to find the source of the leak.

Of course, some problems are not easily solved on a routine basis. For example, suppose that this is the fifth time this year that one of the machines in the plant has begun leaking oil. Why is this problem reoccurring? Is the fundamental root cause the oil itself, the equipment, the way we are operating the equipment, the way we are maintaining the equipment, or something else? To solve this higher-level problem, a team and some formal methodology (perhaps Six Sigma) is likely needed. The key point we are making is that routine problem solving is an important aspect of continuous improvement; however, we typically do not need Lean Six Sigma, nor is there time to conduct a lengthy project. Immediate solutions are needed.

Not a Complete Quality Management System

Fundamentally, Lean Six Sigma 1.3 is a project-based methodology for driving improvement, but it is not a complete quality management system. That is, it does not replace ISO 9000 quality systems or provide the same breadth as national quality awards, such as the Malcolm Baldrige National Quality Award (MBNQA) in the United States. For example, individual Six Sigma projects might lead to calibrating measurement equipment in a lab during the Measure phase, but they would not provide an overall laboratory calibration system. Similarly, one element of the MBNQA addresses strategic planning; however, we do not advise organizations to develop their strategic plan through Six Sigma projects. Of course, we hope that continuous improvement and enabling methods such as Lean Six Sigma are key elements of the strategic plan.

We could give many other examples here. Our point is simply that an organization's overall quality system should be developed in a top-down manner, based on its philosophy and strategic plan, to help meet business objectives. Six Sigma projects, on the other hand, are narrowly focused on specific problems that have been identified and that typically can be solved in roughly three to six months. Conversely, an overall quality management system should not be developed from the bottom up, based on a set of individual projects that were chosen for other purposes. If this is the case, then, by definition, the quality management system is not strategic in nature.

Before describing a recommended paradigm to address the limitations of Lean Six Sigma 1.3, we elaborate further on a few related phenomenon that we mentioned briefly previously: the issue of large, complex, unstructured problems; the emergence of Big Data analytics; and the increased importance of risk management in today's world.

Inefficient at Handling Large, Complex, and Unstructured Problems

We noted earlier that, since 1987, there has been a growing awareness that some problems are too large, complex, and unstructured to be solved with traditional problem-solving methods (including Lean Six Sigma). As noted by Hoerl and Snee (2017), applications in such areas as genomics, public policy, and national security often present significant challenges, even in terms of precisely defining the specific problem to be solved. For example, in obtaining and utilizing data to protect national security, we could perhaps develop an excellent system relative to surveillance and threat identification, but it would essentially result in a police state limiting privacy and individual rights. Few people would consider this a successful or desirable system.

Similarly, the system currently in place for approving new pharmaceuticals in the United States involves a series of clinical trials and analyses guided by significant subject matter knowledge, such as identifying likely drug interactions. No single experimental design or statistical analysis results in a new approved pharmaceutical. Furthermore, the system must balance the need for public safety with the urgent need for new medications to combat emerging diseases such as Ebola or Zika. This problem is complex.

Such problems are unique from most others that can be solved through routine problem solving, or even through Lean Six Sigma. In the following subsections, we briefly discuss some of the important attributes of these types of problems:

Too Large to Tackle with One Method

In terms of size, the problem is simply too large to be solved with any one methodology. Several tools, and perhaps several different disciplines, are required to address the full scope. The problem cannot be resolved in the usual three to six months needed for a Lean Six Sigma project. Hoerl and Snee (2017) gave the example of developing a default prediction methodology to protect a $500 billion portfolio at GE Capital. Several disciplines, including quantitative finance, statistics, operations research, and computer science, were needed to find an effective solution to this problem.

Complex and Challenging

The problem has significant complexity; it is not only technically difficult, but it has many facets (for example, political, legal, or organizational challenges in addition to technical challenges). Kandel et al. (2012) noted the dearth of research on how analytics are actually utilized within an organizational context and pointed out that this is critical to results. Typically, the technical problem cannot be addressed without understanding and addressing the nontechnical challenges. In the case of the default predictor, GE Capital insisted that, no matter how complex the predictor technology was, it had to provide clear and relatively simple advice to portfolio managers, without technical jargon.

Lack of Structure

The problem itself is not well defined, at least not initially. Many of GE's original Six Sigma projects faced this issue, which led to the addition of the Define step in the DMAIC process. However, large, complex, unstructured problems often have an even greater lack of structure initially, requiring more up-front effort to structure the problem. In the case of the default prediction system, the word *default* does not have a generally accepted definition within financial circles. For example, Standard and Poor's (S&P) uses a different definition of *default* than Dunn and Bradstreet (D&B). Therefore the team was asked to predict something that was not even defined.

Data Challenges

Most textbook problems in virtually all quantitative disciplines, from statistics to mechanical engineering, to econometrics, come with "canned" data sets. These might, of course, involve real data, but they are typically freely given with no effort required to obtain them. Generally, the data is of unquestionable quality, often presented in statistics texts as a "random sample." Naturally, researchers and practitioners who have to collect their own data understand how challenging it is to obtain high-quality data. Random sampling is an ideal that is rarely accomplished in practice. For many significant problems, the existing data either is wholly inadequate or comes from disparate data sources of different quality and quantity. In the default prediction case study, minimal data existed because GE Capital was largely built by acquisition; there was no "master" set of data.

Lack of a Single "Correct" Solution

Most textbook problems also have a single correct answer, often given in the appendix. Many real problems also have a single correct answer. Even in online data competitions, such as those on kaggle.com, an objective metric, such as residual standard error when predicting a holdout data set, typically is used to define the "best" model. However, complex problems do not have a "correct" solution that we can look up in the appendix or even a reference text. They are too big, too complicated, and too constrained because of the issues discussed previously. Certainly, some solutions might be better than others, but the problem also could be solved in multiple ways; saying that one particular solution was "correct" or "best" would be virtually impossible.

The Need for a Strategy

Given the issues noted earlier, it is not possible to theoretically derive the correct solution for large, complex, and unstructured problems. Readers with a theoretical mind-set might be frustrated with the inability to find an optimal solution. Conversely, however, working solely by experience (trying to replicate previous solutions, for example) is generally hit-or-miss because each problem has specific complexities that make it different. A unique strategy needs to be developed to attack this specific problem, based on its unique circumstances. Both theory and experience help quite a bit, but an overall strategy that involves multiple tools applied in some logical sequence (and perhaps one that integrates multiple disciplines, especially computer science) is required.

In this sense, we argue that a solution needs to be engineered using known science, and often including statistics, as the components. In our opinion, textbooks and academic courses across quantitative disciplines do not discuss strategy enough, if at all. Engineering solutions to large, complex, unstructured problems requires a problem solving mind-set, but it must be guided by both theory and experience. A problem-solving mind-set typically looks for an *effective* solution, realizing that an *optimal* solution does not exist for such problems. As we discuss shortly, this typically requires an engineering paradigm versus a pure science paradigm.

Statistical engineering (Hoerl and Snee 2017) has been proposed as an overall approach to developing a strategy to attack such problems. Statistical engineering is defined as "the study of how to best utilize statistical concepts, methods and tools, and integrate them with information technology and other relevant disciplines, to achieve enhanced results" (Hoerl and Snee, 2010, p.12). Note that statistical engineering is not a problem solving methodology, per se, as Lean Six Sigma is, but rather is a discipline. However, a generic statistical engineering framework to attack large, complex, unstructured problems was given by DiBenedetto et al. (2014). Figure 1.1 shows this framework.

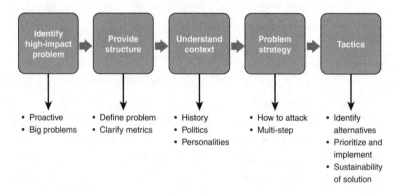

Figure 1.1   Framework for attacking large, complex, unstructured problems

In Figure 1.1, note that once the high-impact problem has been identified, it needs to be properly structured. Significant time and effort are typically required to understand the context of the problem. Large, complex problems have defied solution for a reason; a thorough understanding of the context of the problem is critical to finding a solution. By *context*, we mean such aspects as these:

- The full scope of the problem, including technical, political, legal, and social aspects, to name just a few

- How the problem came into existence in the first place

- What solutions have been attempted previously

- Why these solutions have been inadequate

Clearly, fixing a leak in an oil line does not require understanding this depth of context. However, addressing problems such as the Millennium Development Goals, discussed previously, certainly does. This is another illustration of why the solution needs to be tailored to the problem. Once the context is properly understood, the team is in a position to develop a strategy to attack this particular problem. The unique strategy typically entails several tactics or elements of the overall strategy. We discuss this framework in greater detail in Chapter 3, "Key Methodologies in a Holistic Improvement System." See DiBenedetto et al. (2014) or Hoerl and Snee (2017) for further details on this framework.

Does Not Take Advantage of Big Data Analytics

Recent advances in information technology (IT) have led to a revolution in the capability to acquire, store, and process data. Data is being collected at an ever-increasing pace through social media, online transactions, and scientific research. According to IBM, 1.6 zetabytes (10^{21} bytes) of digital data are now available. That's a lot of data—enough to watch high-definition TV for 47,000 years straight (Ebbers, 2013)! Hardware, software, and statistical technologies to process, store, and analyze this data deluge have also advanced, creating new opportunities for analytics.

At the beginning of the new millennium, the book *Competing on Analytics* (Davenport and Harris, 2007) foretold the potential impact data analytics might have in the business world. Shortly thereafter, Netflix announced a $1,000,000 prize for anyone who could develop a model to predict its movie ratings at least 10 percent better than its current model (Amartriain and Basilico, 2012). Picking up on the popularity of this challenge, the website **kaggle.com** emerged as a host to online data analysis competitions and became what might be called the "eBay of analytics." Through kaggle, organizations that lack high-powered analytics teams can still benefit from sophisticated analytics by sponsoring data analysis competitions involving their data.

Further demonstrating the power of data and analytics, in 2011, the IBM computer Watson defeated human champions in the televised game show *Jeopardy!*. Data science has emerged and grown rapidly as a discipline to help address the technical challenges of Big Data (Hardin et al., 2015). In fact, Davenport and Patil (2012) have described data scientists as having the "sexiest job of the 21st century." Programming languages such as R and Python have grown in popularity, and new methods have been developed to handle the massive data sets that are becoming more common. We're referring here to computer-intensive methods such as neural networks, support vector machines, and random forests, to name just a few (James et al., 2013).

There is a "dark side" to Big Data analytics, however. As noted by Hoerl et al. (2014), the initial success and growth of Big Data led many to believe that combining large data sets and sophisticated analytics guarantees success. This naïve approach has proven false, with several highly publicized failures of Big Data. For example, Google developed a model to rapidly predict outbreaks of the flu based on people googling words related to the flu, such as *flu, fever, sneezing*, and so on (Lazar et al., 2014). This model, which appeared to detect flu outbreaks faster than hospitals detected them, was an early poster child for the power of Big Data analytics. However, Lazar et al. went on to point out that the predictive capabilities of the Google model have deteriorated significantly since its original development, to the point at which now a simple weighted moving average performs better.

Our point is not to disparage the potential of Big Data analytics, but rather to point out that coding and sophisticated analytics have not replaced the need for critical thinking and fundamentals. Studying coding and algorithm development is important and quite useful in practice.

However, such study does not replace study of the problem solving process, statistical engineering, or continuous improvement principles. For example, as we said during our previous discussion of large, complex, unstructured problems, such problems have no optimal solutions. Therefore, we cannot develop an optimal algorithm to solve them; an overall, sequential approach involving several disciplines is typically required. To be sure, computer science is a key discipline that needs to be involved, but it is not the only needed discipline.

Cathy O'Neil, a self-described data scientist with a Ph.D. in mathematics from Harvard, wrote in more detail about the dark side of Big Data analytics in her uniquely named book *Weapons of Math Destruction: How Big Data Increases Inequality and Threatens Democracy* (O'Neil, 2016). Her fundamental point is not that data analytics or large data sets are inherently bad, but rather that programmers who are not properly trained in the fundamentals of modeling (including the limitations and caveats of models) are rapidly producing "opaque, unregulated, and uncontestable" models that are often blindly accepted as valid. Such invalid models are often applied to such important decisions as approving loans, granting parole, and evaluating employees or candidates.

Big Data and data science are frequently discussed in the context of analytics, statistics, machine learning, or computer science. In our experience, however, **Big Data is rarely discussed in the context of continuous improvement.** The reasons for this omission are not clear to us. Certainly, massive data sets provide unique opportunities to make improvements—assuming, of course, that they contain the right data to solve the problem at hand and that subsequent models go through appropriate vetting. Furthermore, newer, more sophisticated analytics, such as those mentioned earlier, provide additional options to consider when attacking problems, particularly the large, complex, and unstructured problems that cannot be easily solved with traditional methods. We feel strongly the Big Data analytics provide a significant opportunity for expanding both the scope and impact of continuous improvement initiatives.

Does Not Address Modern Risk Management Issues

As noted previously, the world certainly seems to be a more dangerous place than in the past, especially for business. Clearly, concerns over terrorism are not restricted to military or government institutions. For example, could Walt Disney have ever imagined the need for families coming to see Mickey Mouse to go through metal detectors and security checks? Yet they do, and for good reason. Financial institutions, energy companies, and businesses performing medical research on animals are frequent targets of threats of violence.

Of course, terrorism is not the only cause for concern from a risk management point of view. Identity theft is now a billion-dollar criminal enterprise in the United States alone. In many cases, the cost of illegal transactions, whether they are purchases with fake credit cards, fraudulent loans, or some other means, is borne not by the individual whose identity was stolen, but instead by the business that provided the loan or guaranteed the credit card purchase.

A more modern phenomenon is computer systems being hacked to obtain confidential information. As noted previously, the hack of Target's credit card database not only allowed 40 million credit card numbers to be stolen, but also did irreparable harm to Target's image. Beyond credit card numbers, organizations such as WikiLeaks (wikileaks.org) are more than eager to obtain and make public damaging information about businesses, including email exchanges, financial reports, and confidential legal documents. WikiLeaks generally obtains its material from other sources. Edward Snowden's top-secret information (https://en.wikipedia.org/wiki/Edward_Snowden) concerning the National Security Agency (NSA) is perhaps the most obvious example.

Along the same lines, confidential emails among members of the Democratic National Committee (DNC) were hacked in 2016 and published on WikiLeaks. This caused significant embarrassment for the DNC, including the revelation of efforts by Chair Debbie Wasserman Schultz to favor Hillary Rodham Clinton's campaign at the expense of Bernie Schultz's. On July 25, 2016, Wasserman Schultz resigned her position because of the revelation on WikiLeaks. Considerable drama surrounded the original DNC hack, including accusations that the Russian government orchestrated the hack in an effort to enhance Donald Trump's chances in the U.S. election (Sanger and Savage, 2016).

Clearly, businesses in the twenty-first century face unique security challenges, in addition to traditional business risks such as major lawsuits, environmental disasters, and catastrophic product failures. Therefore, risk management has become an even more critical business priority. What methods and approaches should be used for managing these types of risks, both the traditional ones and also the newer risks? We argue that the answer to this question is not obvious. However, it must be answered because the cost of failure in risk management is too high. Therefore, we consider risk management to be an integral element within a holistic improvement system.

A New Paradigm Is Needed

The proceeding discussion shows that Lean Six Sigma, even in its more modern form of Version 1.3, is not sufficient to address today's business improvement needs. We have reached the point noted by Kuhn (1962): Too many problems remain unaddressed by Lean Six Sigma 1.3 to ignore. For example, Lean Six Sigma was never intended as a means of managing modern business risks, integrating the power of Big Data analytics, or addressing large, complex, unstructured problems that cannot be solved in three to six months.

- Lean Six Sigma does not incorporate simpler methods, such as Work-Out or Nike projects.

- Lean Six Sigma does not guide routine process control efforts or provide an overall quality management system.

- A new paradigm, or way of thinking about improvement, is required to make significant progress going forward.

Fortunately, Six Sigma is excellent at what it was designed to do: solve medium-size "solution unknown" problems. Version 1.3 also incorporates innovation efforts, new product and process design, and Lean concepts and methods. Furthermore, the supportive infrastructure developed for Six Sigma is, in our view, the best and most complete continuous improvement infrastructure developed to date (Snee and Hoerl, 2003). Therefore, if this same infrastructure can be applied to a holistic version of Lean Six Sigma that addresses the limitations noted earlier, the resulting improvement system would be the most complete to date.

As already noted, addressing all these limitations would not be a minor upgrade, but rather would require a fundamental redesign based on a much broader paradigm. In other words, it would be Version 2.0, not simply Version 1.4. What paradigm would be required to develop Lean Six Sigma 2.0? In our view, the answer is clear: We need a *holistic paradigm of improvement.* By *holistic,* we mean a system that is not based on a particular method, whether it is Six Sigma, Lean, Work-Out, or some other method. Development would need to start with the totality of improvement work needed and then create a suite of methods and approaches that would enable the organization to address all the improvement work identified.

Note that a holistic paradigm would reverse the typical way of thinking about improvement. Traditionally, books, articles, and conference presentations on improvement focus on a particular method and promote that method over others, at least for specific types of problems. For example, it is easy to find books on Six Sigma, Lean, or TRIZ. However, very few, if any, books focus on general improvement. With a holistic paradigm, on the other hand, the focus is not on methods, but on the improvement work—that is, on the problems to be solved. Only after the problems have been identified and diagnosed are methods brought into discussion. The individual methods can then be applied to the specific problems for which they are most appropriate. Holistic improvement is essentially tool agnostic: The tools are *hows*, not *whats.* Improvement is our *what*, the focus of our efforts.

References

Altshuller, G. (1992) *And Suddenly the Inventor Appeared.* Worcester, MA: Technical Innovation Center.

Amartriain, X., and J. Basilico. (2012) "Netflix Recommendations: Beyond the 5 Stars, Part I" Netflix Tech Blog, April 6. Available at http://techblog.netflix.com/2012/ 04/netflix-recommendations-beyond-5-stars.html.

Birkinshaw, J., and C. Gibson. (2004) "Building Ambidexterity into an Organization." *MIT Sloan Management Review* 45, no. 4: 47–55.

Davenport, T. H., and J. G. Harris. (2007) *Competing on Analytics: The New Science of Winning.* Cambridge, MA: Harvard Business Review Press.

Davenport, T. H., and D. J. Patil. (2012) "Data Scientist: The Sexiest Job of the 21st Century." *Harvard Business Review* (October): 70–76.

DiBenedetto, A., R. W. Hoerl, and R. D. Snee. (2014) "Solving Jigsaw Puzzles," *Quality Progress* (June): 50–53.

Ebbers, M. (2013) "5 Things to Know About Big Data in Motion," IBM Developer Works blog. Available at: www.ibm.com/developerworks/community/blogs/5things/entry/5_things_to_know_about_big_data_in_motion?lang=en.

General Electric Company (1999), 1998 Annual Report, available at: http://www.annualreports.com/HostedData/AnnualReportArchive/g/NYSE_GE_1998.pdf

George, M. L. (2002) *Lean Six Sigma: Combining Six Sigma Quality with Lean Production Speed.* New York: McGraw-Hill.

Gutierrez, G., L. J. Bustinza, and V. Barales. (2012) "Six Sigma, Absorptive Capacity and Organization Learning Orientation." *International Journal of Production Research* 50, no. 3: 661–675.

Gutierrez, G., J. Leopoldo, V. Barrales Molina, and J. Tamayo Torres. (2016) "The Knowledge Transfer Process in Six Sigma Subsidiary Firms." *Total Quality Management & Business Excellence* 27, no. 6: 613–627.

Hahn, G. J., N. Doganaksoy, and R. W. Hoerl. (2000) "The Evolution of Six Sigma." *Quality Engineering* 12, no. 3: 317–326.

Hardin, J., R. Hoerl, N. J. Horton, D. Nolan, B. Baumer, O. Hall-Holt, P. Murrell, R. Peng, D. Roback, D. Temple Land, and M. D. Ward. (2015) "Data Science in Statistics Curricula: Preparing Students to 'Think with Data.'" *The American Statistician* 69, no. 4: 343–353.

Harry, M., and R. Schroeder. (2000) *Six Sigma: The Breakthrough Management Strategy Revolutionizing the World's Top Corporations.* New York: Currency Doubleday.

He, Z., Y. Deng, M. Zhang, X. Zu, and J. Antony. (2015) "An Empirical Investigation of the Relationship Between Six Sigma Practices and Organizational Innovation." *Total Quality Management and Business Excellence* (October): 1–22.

Hindo, B. (2007) "3M's Innovation Crisis: How Six Sigma Almost Smothered an Idea Culture." *Business Week* (June 11): 8–14.

Hoerl, R. (2008) "Work Out." In *Encyclopedia of Statistics in Quality and Reliability* , edited by F. Ruggeri, R. Kenett, and F. W. Faltin, 2103–2105. Chichester, UK: John Wiley & Sons.

Hoerl, R. W., and M. M. Gardner. (2010) "Lean Six Sigma, Creativity, and Innovation," *International Journal of Lean Six Sigma* 1, no. 1: 30–38.

Hoerl, R. W., and R. D. Snee. (2010) "Moving the Statistics Profession Forward to the Next Level." *The American Statistician* 64, no. 1: 10–14.

Hoerl, R. W., and R. D. Snee. (2013) "One Size Does Not Fit All: Identifying the Right Improvement Methodology." *Quality Progress* (May 2013): 48–50.

Hoerl, R. W., and R. D. Snee. (2017) "Statistical Engineering: An Idea Whose Time Has Come," *The American Statistician* , Vol. 71, no. 3, 209–219.

Hoerl, R. W., R. D. Snee, and R. D. De Veaux. (2014) "Applying Statistical Thinking to 'Big Data' Problems." *Wiley Interdisciplinary Reviews: Computational Statistics* (July/August): 22–232. (doi: 10.1002/wics.1306)

James, G., D. Witten, T. Hastie, and R. Tibshirani. (2013) *An Introduction to Statistical Learning*. New York: Springer.

Jones, M. H. (2004) "Six Sigma…at a Bank?" *Six Sigma Forum Magazine* (February): 13–17.

Kandel, S., A. Paepcke, J. M. Hellerstein, and J. Heer. (2012) "Enterprise Data Analysis and Visualization: An Interview Study." *IEEE Transactions Visualization and Computer Graphics* 18, no. 12: 2917–2926.

Kepnar, C. H., and B. B. Tregoe. (2013) *The New Rational Manager*. New York: McGraw-Hill.

Kuhn, T. S. (1962) *The Structure of Scientific Revolutions*. Chicago: University of Chicago Press.

Lazar, D., R. Kennedy, G. King, and A. Vespignani. (2014) "The Parable of Google Flu: Traps in Big Data Analysis." *Science* 343: 1203–1205.

O'Neil, C. (2016) *Weapons of Math Destruction: How Big Data Increases Inequality and Threatens Democracy*. New York: Crown Publishing Group.

Sanger, C., and D. E. Savage. (2016) "U.S. Accuses Russia of Directing Hacks to Influence the Election." *New York Times*, October 6: A1.

Snee, R. D., and R. W. Hoerl. (2003) *Leading Six Sigma: A Step-by-Step Guide Based on Experience with GE and Other Six Sigma Companies*. Upper Saddle River, NJ: Financial Times/Prentice Hall.

Snee, R. D., and R. W. Hoerl. (2005) *Six Sigma Beyond the Factory Floor; Deployment Strategies for Financial Services, Health Care, and the Rest of the Real Economy*. Upper Saddle River, NJ: Financial Times/Prentice Hall.

2

What Is Holistic Improvement?

"Only the over-all review of the entire business as an economic system can give real knowledge."

—Drucker

C hapter 1, "A New Improvement Paradigm Is Needed," reviewed the numerous changes that have occurred in the world since the first edition of this book was published (Snee and Hoerl, 2003). These changes have occurred in all aspects of society, as well as the business world. We concluded in that chapter that a new paradigm for improvement was needed. Lean Six Sigma is no longer adequate for the improvements that organizations need to survive and, better yet, prosper. We call this new paradigm **holistic improvement.** This chapter sets out to accomplish the following:

- Define holistic improvement

- Show how holistic improvement is different from and more effective than previous approaches

- Provide a strategic structure for the use of holistic improvement

It all begins with selecting the *right* projects. Next, we need to select the right methods for the specific project, not rely on one method for all problems. Project selection (and, to some degree, method selection) is the Achilles' heel of any improvement approach. We look at holistic approaches to project identification and selection, as well as method selection, in this chapter.

The Ultimate Objective: Comprehensive Improvement

The warning is wearyingly familiar, but it bears repeating: The leveling effects of globalization and information technology have enabled organizations and individuals around the world to compete successfully. All organizations need to improve continuously or face extinction. Improvement must come on all fronts—quality, cost, delivery, customer satisfaction, risk management, and more. It is in this brutally unforgiving context that attempts to integrate Lean and Six Sigma are taking place. If they are to succeed, and expand to Lean Six Sigma 2.0, they must first define the problem in terms of the ultimate objective. That objective is not to integrate Lean and Six Sigma, or perhaps other methods, but rather to improve performance as comprehensively and sustainably as possible.

Based on our more than 60 years of collective experience with improvement methodologies and improvement programs with leading companies, we believe that organizations that successfully pursue Lean Six Sigma 2.0 will do so by adopting these approaches:

- Taking a holistic view of the business and of business improvement

- Adopting a common improvement system

- Establishing an integrated project management system

Guided by those three simple but powerful principles, ambitious organizations can begin to achieve the full potential of Lean Six Sigma 2.0.

A Holistic View of Improving the Business

Reducing waste and cycle time is necessary but not sufficient. Reducing variation alone will not make you a winner. A holistic approach to improvement is needed, with a broader view of how to improve business performance and a deeper understanding of the various approaches to improvement.

The characteristics of holistic improvement show that a holistic approach is more than just a methodology for conducting improvement projects. The type of culture (business, country, or ethnic), function, leadership, management systems, and other key elements of the business must be taken into account as well. The bulleted list that follows shows the characteristics of holistic improvement:

- Works in all areas of the business—all functions, all processes
- Works in all cultures, providing a common language and tool set
- Can address all measures of performance (quality, cost, delivery, and customer satisfaction)
- Addresses all aspects of process management (process design/redesign, improvement, and control)
- Addresses all types of improvement (streamlining, waste and cycle time reduction, quality improvement, and process robustness)
- Includes management systems for improvement, based on Lean Six Sigma (plans, goals, budgets, and management reviews)
- Focuses on developing an improvement culture and uses improvement as a leadership development tool

No existing approach can perfectly satisfy all these characteristics, but this is the overall goal. Ultimately, a holistic approach helps develop a culture of improvement throughout the organization, including using improvement approaches as a tool for leadership development.

We define holistic improvement as follows:

> An improvement system that can successfully create and sustain significant improvements of any type, in any culture, for any business (Snee, 2009).

A discussion of the key words in this definition is helpful in understanding the breadth and depth of the approach.

First, to **create** and **sustain** improvement, certain components are needed. These include an infrastructure of management systems and resources, a continuous improvement culture, and leadership development (Snee and Hoerl, 2003). Also important are long-term solutions that stick and methods that actually work and have a track record of creating improvement.

Significant improvements refers to improvements that enhance all measures of organizational performance: quality, cost, delivery, customer satisfaction, risk management, and the bottom line. The improvements must be noteworthy, as breakthrough levels of improvement instead of ones restricted to routine problem solving.

Any type refers to the specific improvement needed, such as any of the process performance measures noted earlier (for example, to speed up the process flow, reduce variation, enhance process design, improve process performance, create better process control, and optimize process output.). This also encompasses design efforts and the improvement of existing processes. It involves addressing political, legal, or people issues, not just technical issues. A holistic improvement methodology is needed to address this broad array of improvement needs.

Improvement is needed is many places, in **any culture,** including in any function in the business and any region or culture in the world. In our experience, individual functions within an organization often develop their own cultures, leading to silos. In this situation, an organization is split up into multiple suborganizations, each with its own culture. Cooperation is difficult in these cases.

Organizations run many different types of businesses and processes: **any business** refers to manufacturing, finance, high-tech organizations, and services. Holistic improvement also works in nonprofit organizations such as healthcare, humanitarian, and government organizations. Obviously, the cultures in nonprofits, Wall Street financial firms, hospitals, and manufacturing plants tend to be quite different. Holistic improvement must be effective in each.

The suggested holistic improvement approach incorporates two major elements, producing what we call Lean Six Sigma 2.0:

1. Integration of a wide set of improvement methodologies so that the most appropriate method can be used to attack a given problem. In other words, no single methodology can solve the full breadth of the problems noted; therefore, multiple methodologies must be integrated. The problem should determine the methodology, not vice versa.

2. A deployment system that provides the needed infrastructure is required to create and sustain improvement across the spectrum of the problems. In our experience, the Lean Six Sigma deployment methodology is the most comprehensive and best-developed improvement deployment system. Therefore, we borrow this deployment methodology and apply it to a much broader set of improvement methods than just Lean Six Sigma.

What would such a holistic improvement system look like? To answer this question, we first consider one real-world example that illustrates some (but certainly not all) of the attributes of Lean Six Sigma 2.0.

An Example of Holistic Improvement

In this scenario, we look at the need to improve the manufacturing organization of a biopharmaceutical product (McGurk, 2004). The organization developed a new blockbuster drug and was creating a manufacturing organization to produce the drug. It soon became clear, however, that the manufacturing process would not be able to meet the market demand. An assessment of the entire organization was performed and found that organizational development was needed in addition to process improvement. A holistic approach was required to address this broad range of issues.

Using Lean techniques, batch release cycle times were reduced by 35–55 percent, depending on the product (Snee and Hoerl, 2005), which resulted in faster product release and reduced inventory and manufacturing costs. Six Sigma techniques were used to further process understanding and increase yield by 20 percent. Within the organization, many who had developed the product had an R&D mind-set, and this needed to evolve into a manufacturing mind-set. The company hosted leadership development workshops to accomplish this. Process operator training helped improve process reliability. Overall, the holistic approach delivered a 50 percent increase in capacity, enabling the process to meet market demand.

As this brief example makes clear, Lean Six Sigma cannot sufficiently address today's business improvement needs, even in its more modern form of Version 1.3 (Snee and Hoerl, 2017). We have reached the point at which too many problems remain unaddressed by Lean Six Sigma 1.3 for us to ignore (Kuhn, 1962). A new paradigm, or way of thinking about improvement is required to make significant progress going forward.

Six Sigma is excellent at what it was designed to do: solve medium-sized "solution unknown" problems. Version 1.3 also incorporates innovation efforts, new product and process design, and Lean concepts and methods. The supportive infrastructure developed for Six Sigma is the best and most complete continuous improvement infrastructure developed to date (Snee and Hoerl, 2003). If this same infrastructure can be applied to a holistic version of Lean Six Sigma that addresses the limitations discussed earlier, the resulting improvement system would be the most complete so far.

Addressing all the limitations previously noted would not be a minor upgrade; instead, it would be a fundamental redesign based on a much broader paradigm. It would be Version 2.0, not simply Version 1.4. What paradigm would be required to develop lean Six Sigma 2.0? The answer is clear: We need a holistic paradigm of improvement. We need a system that is not based on a particular method (whether that is Six Sigma, Lean, Work-Out, or something else); instead, the system must start with the totality of improvement work needed and develop a suite of methods and approaches with which the organization can address all the improvement work identified.

A holistic paradigm reverses the typical way of thinking about improvement. Traditionally, books, articles, and conference presentations on improvement focus on a particular method and promote that method over others, at least for specific types of problems. It's easy to find books on Six Sigma, Lean or TRIZ, for example.

But few, if any, books focus on general improvement. Within a holistic paradigm, the focus is not on methods, but on the improvement work and the problems to be solved. Only after the problems have been identified and diagnosed are methods discussed. The individual methods can be applied to the specific problems for which they are most appropriate. In other words, holistic improvement is tool agnostic—the tools are *hows*, not *whats*. Comprehensive improvement is the fosus of our efforts.

A Strategic Structure for the Holistic Improvement System

Figure 2.1 shows the high-level framework for a holistic improvement system. All improvement begins with the business and organizational context, which defines overall improvement needs and opportunities. These needs and opportunities also greatly depend on leadership, provided by the organization's management as defined in the organization's strategy. Clearly, holistic improvement is a strategic approach.

The holistic improvement system has three critical building blocks:

1. **Quality by design,** which focuses on innovation and the development of new businesses, products, and processes

2. **Breakthrough improvement,** which encompasses most of what traditionally is considered to be continuous quality improvement

3. **Quality and process management systems,** which is the defensive aspect of quality—managing processes with excellence to avoid errors and mistakes, as well as maintaining process control

These building blocks are linked and sequenced, as shown in Figure 2.1. The outputs of the building blocks are impactful and sustainable results, which then enhance the business and organizational context. The cycle continues. Clearly, breakthrough improvement assumes that we have something in place to improve. First, of course, we must identify the market opportunity and design new products and services to meet these opportunities. In addition, as noted in Chapter 1, although design and breakthrough improvements are "sexy" and exciting approaches, these is no substitute for problem prevention. Excellence in quality and process management is still critical to prevent problems and rapidly address routine problems before they become crises.

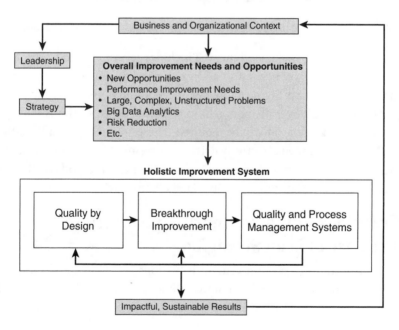

Figure 2.1   Strategic structure for the holistic improvement system

Figure 2.2 shows sample methods and approaches used within the building blocks. Addressing improvement from a holistic perspective puts the focus where it must be: on the problem and the improvement need. The methods are also important but are a secondary consideration. As a result, the impact and bottom-line results of an improvement system are increased and sustained over time.

Quality by Design	Breakthrough Improvement	Quality and Process Management Systems
Needs	**Needs**	**Needs**
• Business innovation	• Meet annual and strategic plans	• Quality & process management system
• Process design/redesign	• Better product/process performance	• Risk management system
• Product design/redesign	• Better organizational performance	• IT system
• Organizational design/redesign	• Mission critical problems	• Measurement system
		• Training system
Approaches	**Approaches**	**Approaches**
• Innovation/Creativity	• Six Sigma	• ISO/Baldrige
• DFSS	• Lean Enterprise	• Total Productive Maintenance
• TRIZ	• Statistical Engineering	• "Internet of Things"
	• Big Data Analytics	• Kepner-Tregoe
	• Work-Out	

Figure 2.2   Holistic improvement system needs and sample approaches

Note that each category in Figure 2.2 includes several methods; some or all of these might be needed to address a given issue. Of course, some methods, such as Six Sigma and Lean, incorporate numerous individual tools within their overall approach. In addition, other methods that are not listed in Figure 2.2 might be required. These are simply sample methods that we have seen effectively drive improvement and that we recommend for consideration. We discuss these individual methods further in Chapter 3, "Key Methodologies in a Holistic Improvement System."

Creating a Common Improvement System: The Case of Lean Six Sigma

The move to holistic improvement is obviously not easy, and requires careful planning, leadership commitment, and time. There are good reasons why jumping from one "bandwagon" to another—based on the latest fads in business journals—is more common than a systematic, long term approach to improvement. We would like to point out, however, that what we propose is certainly not the first attempt at creation of a common improvement system encompassing multiple methodologies. In particular, we would like to consider the case of Lean Six Sigma, which was essentially an integration of Lean Enterprise with Six Sigma. This integration is what we referred to as Lean Six Sigma 1.2 in Chapter 1. We believe this integration provides important lessons that can be applied to the development of a holistic improvement system.

As Figure 2.3 shows, many companies traditionally have focused on Lean or Six Sigma as their overall improvement approach (Snee and Hoerl, 2007). Beginning around the turn of the millennium, some organizations began working to integrate the two under the common name Lean Six Sigma (George, 2002). This integration produced significant results at numerous organizations, including GE, as discussed in Chapter 1. The integration of Lean and Six Sigma provides a positive example, but it does not go far enough for today's improvement challenges.

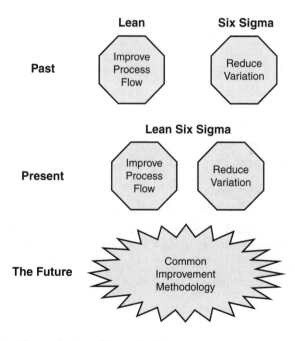

Figure 2.3   The evolution of Lean Six Sigma

Practitioners have found that Lean principles and tools can be used to deal with issues of waste, cycle time, process flow, and non-value-added work. Six Sigma tools have effectively shifted the process average, reduced the variation around the process average, identified the operating "sweet spot," and helped create robust products and processes while also reducing waste and cycle time.

A key development in Lean Six Sigma was the creation of a common improvement system. In GE, for example, we witnessed unhealthy competition between Six Sigma proponents and Lean proponents before the two methodologies were integrated into one system. It is a generally accepted policy that the players on a football team should not compete with each other, but should rather cooperate and work together to ensure the success of the team. The same is true within an organization: The competition is the other team, not one's own teammates! The individual improvement methods are not competitors, but rather diverse tools in a complete toolkit.

To truly integrate Lean and Six Sigma, one infrastructure for deployment was required. That is, the Lean specialists and Six Sigma specialists needed to be in the same organization, with the same leadership direction, funding, goals, and so on. We look at the Lean Six Sigma infrastructure here because we think it is the most complete. For example, the execution of projects in this common improvement system can be guided using the familiar DMAIC approach (Define, Measure, Analyze, Improve, Control). DMAIC originated in Six Sigma, but the project management framework of DMAIC can be sharply distinguished from the Six Sigma tools with which it is typically associated and generalized to a higher level as an overall framework for process improvement. Lean projects can be effectively deployed using a DMAIC project framework.

The lesson learned for holistic improvement is that the methods that are the most appropriate to a particular problem (whether Six Sigma, Lean, or something else) can be applied through the highly structured and sequenced approach of DMAIC. A common infrastructure and project framework helps ensure true integration.

As an important aside, we think there is no such thing as **Six Sigma tools** or **Lean tools**—after all, neither methodology invented the tools. In actuality, we have only **improvement tools**; we use the phrases

Six Sigma tools and Lean tools simply as a convenience to indicate tools typically associated with each initiative.

An Integrated Project Management System

Creating a common improvement system requires developing an integrated system for managing projects instead of using separate systems for Lean projects, Six Sigma projects, Nike projects, and so on. As Juran admonished, "Improvement happens project-by-project and in no other way" (1989). As noted earlier, improvement begins with selecting the right projects—not the right people, not the right methods, but the right high-priority projects to make the organization successful. The project management system should therefore employ a project-by-project selection and management approach.

In addition, a key element of the project management system is to identify the most appropriate method for each project. As with any effective project management system, processes should guide and sustain improvement: for example, project tracking and review, communications, recognition and reward, and training. In this chapter, we focus on selecting a project and assigning the improvement method. Chapter 7, "Managing the Effort," covers the other elements of the project management system.

In our experience, project selection is often where the battle is won or lost. When debriefing after unsuccessful projects, it frequently becomes clear that the project was a poor choice from the start. Maybe it had a vague objective, was disconnected from management objectives, or could not significantly impact the problem due to issues beyond the team's control. The importance of selecting a good project cannot be overemphasized.

Before the selected project starts, the selection team must identify the right improvement approach and assign the right personnel for that approach. Obviously, not every employee is an expert in every improvement methodology. Therefore, putting together a team with the right skills depends on the methodology selected. This principle not only takes project selection to a new level, but also puts the selection of both project and improvement approach ahead of personnel selection. Many organizations mistakenly begin with personnel selection.

This enhanced project selection process should identify the *right* projects that will deliver the following:

- Produce the highest value in relation to business goals

- Improve performance of processes

- Improve the flow of materials and information while reducing waste and cycle time

Figure 2.4 schematically shows our recommended approach to selecting the right projects (Snee and Hoerl, 2007). It includes elements of both Six Sigma and Lean, with the ultimate goal of achieving maximum sustainable process improvements.

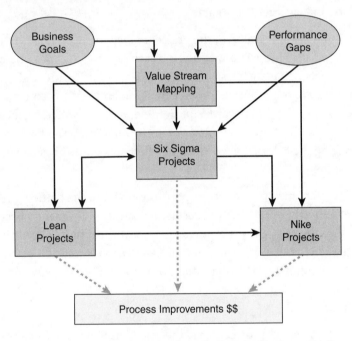

Figure 2.4   A novel approach to project selection within Lean Six Sigma

Within a Lean Six Sigma approach, process improvements typically result from three major types of projects, which require varying amounts of time for completion:

- **Nike projects:** Can be accomplished almost immediately. If they fail, they cost little in lost time and resources.

- **Lean projects:** Often referred to as rapid improvement projects. These projects are typically completed in 30 days or less.

- **Six Sigma projects:** Typically are completed in three to six months, but can be completed even more quickly.

Even within a Lean Six Sigma approach, numerous projects do not require the rigor of Six Sigma or Lean. These become quick hits, or Nike projects (Just Do It!). As Figure 2.4 suggests, all these types of projects are generated directly or indirectly from business goals or performance gaps. A top-down approach generates projects from business goals; a bottom-up approach addresses performance gaps that arise from within the operations of the organization. Business goals and performance gaps can directly generate Six Sigma projects, which is the customary approach for project selection in pure Six Sigma improvement systems. Note that this project selection process was specific to Lean Six Sigma. As we explain in subsequent chapters, this process needs to become much broader within a holistic improvement system. The principles stay the same, but obviously, there are many more options for types of projects.

Even in a holistic improvement system, goals and gaps can provide inputs for value stream mapping (VSM), a technique that is often employed in Lean but that can also be used to generate other types of projects (Martin and Osterling, 2013). For example, Six Sigma is typically used to address complex problems that have an unknown solution. If a VSM within a Lean project uncovers a complex problem with no known solution, a Six Sigma project might result. In the course of its execution, a Six Sigma project may uncover quick hits or generate Lean projects.

If VSM uncovers non-value-added activity for which Lean tools might be appropriate, then a Kaizen event might be convened to brainstorm solutions. (A Kaizen event is a focused project that takes place over one to three days, with improvements that are not only planned, but actually implemented.) That Kaizen event might then initiate a longer Lean project; alternatively, it might uncover a quick fix or might even find that there is no known solution, which would then generate a Six Sigma project.

Note that the category of Lean Six Sigma projects is conspicuously absent from the framework. This is because a Lean Six Sigma approach is essentially the integration of two methodologies, Lean Enterprise and Six Sigma. Individual projects are either more suited to a Lean approach, more suited to a Six Sigma approach, or perhaps quick hits (see Figure 2.4). They draw on a common toolbox that previously was separated according to methodology. Depending on the nature of the problem, of course, tools traditionally regarded as Lean tools or those associated with Six Sigma might dominate. Consider, for example, the types of commonly encountered improvement needs:

- Streamline process flow to reduce complexity, downtime, and cycle time, and to reduce waste

- Improve product quality

- Achieve consistency in product delivery

- Reduce process and product costs

- Reduce process variation to reduce waste (such as the waste of defective products)

- Improve process control to maintain stable and predictable processes

- Find the "sweet spot" in the process operating window

- Achieve process and product robustness

In all of these cases, as well as others, the nature of the improvement to be pursued and the root causes standing in the way of improvement help define the appropriate approach and tools to be used. When shifting the process average or reducing process variation is appropriate for the problem at hand, Six Sigma dominates. When improving process flow or reducing process complexity is appropriate, Lean tools dominate. Contrary to popular belief, however, both Lean and Six Sigma approaches can deal effectively with reduction of waste, cycle time, and non-value-added work (see Figure 2.5). This is additional proof that truly integrating Lean and Six Sigma can make available the best possible tools, regardless of their methodological origins. Hoerl and Snee (2013) provide more detail on selecting the most appropriate improvement methodology based on attributes of the problem.

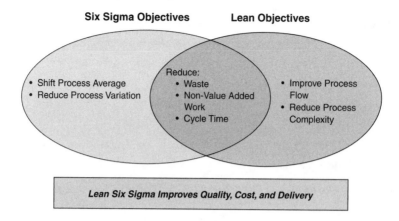

Figure 2.5 Convergence of Six Sigma and Lean

Summary and Looking Forward

In this chapter, we discussed the critical principles of holistic improvement and examined how the approach works. This discussion included the following areas:

- Characteristics of holistic improvement

- An overall strategic structure for holistic improvement

- Typical methodologies within each major building block of the overall strategic structure

- The case study in methodology integration provided by Lean Six Sigma

- Integrated project management systems

In the next chapter, we discuss the key methodologies in Figure 2.1. Subsequent chapters look at the details of the infrastructure required for holistic improvement, such as systems for training, budgeting, tracking progress, and providing rewards and recognition.

References

George, M. L. (2002) *Lean Six Sigma: Combining Six Sigma Quality with Lean Speed.* New York: McGraw-Hill.

Hoerl, R. W., and Snee, R.D. (2013) "One Size Does Not Fit All: Identifying the Right Improvement Methodology." *Quality Progress* (May 2013): 48–50.

Juran, J. (1989) *Leadership for Quality: An Executive Handbook.* New York: Free Press.

Kuhn, T. (1962) *The Structure of Scientific Revolutions.* Chicago: University of Chicago Press.

Martin, K., and M. Osterling. (2013) *Value Stream Mapping: How to Visualize Work and Align Leadership for Organizational Transformation.* New York: McGraw-Hill.

McGurk, T.L., (2014), "Ramping Up and Ensuring Supply Capability for Biopharmaceuticals", *Biopharm International*, 17, 1, 38-44.

Snee, R. D. (2009) "Digging the Holistic Approach: Rethinking Business Improvement to Improve the Bottom Line." *Quality Progress* (October 2009): 52–54.

Snee, R. D., and R. W. Hoerl. (2003) *Leading Six Sigma: A Step-by-Step Guide Based on Experience with GE and Other Six Sigma Companies.* New York: Financial Times/Prentice Hall.

Snee, R. D., and R. W. Hoerl. (2005) *Six Sigma Beyond the Factory Floor: Deployment Strategies for Financial Services, Health Care, and the Rest of the Real Economy.* New York: Financial Times/Prentice Hall.

Snee, R. D., and R. W. Hoerl. (2007) "Integrating Lean and Six Sigma: A Holistic Approach." *Six Sigma Forum Magazine* (May): 15–21.

Snee, R. D., and R. W. Hoerl. (2017) "Time for Lean Six Sigma 2.0?" *Quality Progress* (May 2017): 50–53.

Welch, Jack. (2001) *Jack Straight from the Gut.* New York: Warner Books.

3

Key Methodologies in a Holistic Improvement System

"If all you have is a hammer, every problem looks like a nail."
—Anonymous

As discussed in Chapter 1, "A New Improvement Paradigm Is Needed," and Chapter 2, "What Is Holistic Improvement?", Lean Six Sigma 2.0 is based on a holistic approach that incorporates and integrates multiple improvement methodologies. The specific improvement approach to be taken fits the unique aspects of the problem to be addressed. One obvious implication is that such a holistic system needs to have multiple methodologies at its disposal instead of relying on one "best" improvement method—or even two or three. The portfolio of methods needs to be dynamic; new methods are developed over time, and some older methods might no longer be appropriate at a certain point. For these reasons, we do not recommend one "optimal" portfolio of improvement methods. Instead, we advocate including certain logical methods in most organizations' portfolios, but we think the final set of methods should be unique to the organization.

In this chapter, we briefly review the improvement methods that we feel are logical for most organizations to consider. Obviously, we cannot cover every possible improvement method; we focus instead on the ones we consider core methods. We organize them into the categories explained in Chapter 2: quality by design, breakthrough improvement, and quality and process management systems. Whole books have been written on each of these improvement methods, so we obviously cannot fully do them all justice in a single chapter. If you are not familiar with any of these methods, we recommend following up with the references given at the end of this chapter. Our purpose here is simply to briefly introduce each method and place it in the context of holistic improvement.

We begin with Six Sigma for the following reasons:

- It was the focus of the first edition of this book.

- It is arguably the most successful improvement method developed to date. Thus, it deserves consideration by any organization that is serious about continuous improvement.

- It is both an overall improvement initiative, with a rigorous set of management systems and procedures (infrastructure), and a type of improvement project.

As Chapter 2 explained, it is important to consider both the overall Six Sigma framework for managing an improvement system and also Six Sigma projects. This is because Six Sigma projects represent only one of several options within the overall improvement system. In our experience, the overall management framework utilized for Six Sigma initiatives is the best system yet seen. Therefore, even though we are expanding the project types, we recommend continuing to use the same Six Sigma management framework for holistic improvement. We explain this more in the next section.

Six Sigma: An Overall Framework and One Option for Improvement Projects

Snee and Hoerl (2003) explained that Six Sigma can be viewed as both an overall management initiative and also a set of methods and tools. In our experience, most readers tend to focus on the latter, a set of tools and project structure. However, the primary reason for the tremendous success of Six Sigma has been its overall management infrastructure, which involves developing formal roles, including Six Sigma in budgets, using project selection systems, conducting formal project reviews, implementing financial tracking systems, and so on. Many earlier improvement approaches, such as Total Quality Management, lacked these management fundamentals (Snee and Hoerl, 2003).

We said in Chapter 2 that we think the overall management infrastructure developed for Six Sigma at major deployments such as Honeywell,

GE, and Bank of America, among others, is the best organizational system developed to date for leading and managing improvement. Therefore, although we acknowledge that several other improvement methods are needed within the holistic system, we recommend using the Six Sigma infrastructure for the overall improvement system. Of course, it can be modified and improved. However, beginning with this infrastructure provides a solid starting point for any organization embarking on a holistic improvement initiative. In the remaining chapters, we provide specific guidance on how to do just that.

We now want to turn our focus to Six Sigma as an option for an improvement project. Faced with a defined problem, how can an organization know whether Six Sigma is a good choice for attacking this problem or whether to use Lean, Work-Out, or some other method? As should be clear by now, Six Sigma is not the best approach for all problems. For which is it a likely choice?

First of all, Six Sigma projects are generally of the breakthrough improvement type. They are intended to take a process to a level of performance that it has not seen before. Conversely, Six Sigma is not the best approach for fixing things that are broken; that is problem solving, which fits best under quality and process management systems. We consider Design for Six Sigma (DFSS) projects separately, under quality by design. Additionally, Six Sigma projects can be further classified according to the number of required participants. Green Belt projects typically can be completed by one person; Black Belt projects, on the other hand, generally require a cross-functional team. In this section, we focus on the more common Black Belt projects.

The main structure for a Six Sigma project is Define, Measure, Analyze, Improve, Control (DMAIC). This overall approach gives practitioners a plan of attack for virtually any Six Sigma project, including ones involving finance, healthcare, or other nonmanufacturing projects. Figure 3.1, from Snee and Hoerl (2003), shows the purpose of each step, the main deliverables (what each step is attempting to produce), and some sample tools used. Of course, every project is unique; no "cookie cutter" approach will always be appropriate. Therefore, the tools in Figure 3.1 should be viewed as typical but not always the most appropriate.

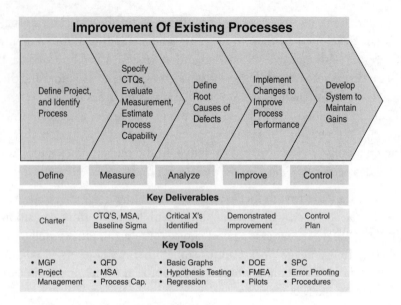

Figure 3.1 The DMAIC methodology and key tools

A closer examination of these steps and tools reveals some attributes of projects that are well suited to a Six Sigma approach:

- A process already exists.

- The problem has no known solution; we need to obtain data to identify and address root causes.

- The project is complex enough that it requires significant time to generate breakthrough improvement. In our experience, typical Six Sigma projects take roughly three to six months to complete.

- A multidisciplined team is required to successfully complete the project.

Conversely, many projects do not possess these attributes and thus are not suitable for a Six Sigma approach. For example, design projects do not have an existing process. In many Lean projects, we already know what to do (provide line of sight to the process, for example); we just have to figure out exactly how to do that. Additionally, for routine problem solving, we are rarely willing to wait three to six months for a solution.

Much more can and has been written about Six Sigma projects; see, for example, Harry and Schroeder (2000), Snee and Hoerl (2003), Jones (2004), and Snee and Hoerl (2005). Our assumption is that readers are generally familiar with Six Sigma, so we have provided only a brief overview. These references deliver more detail if desired.

Quality by Design Approaches

As we noted in Chapter 2, quality by design is the element of the holistic improvement system in which new products, processes, and initiatives are identified and implemented. The importance of designing quality into products and services instead of trying to fix issues later has been well known for some time (Juran and DeFeo, 2010). The U.S. pharmaceutical industry, in particular, has made quality by design a major emphasis within the process of rolling out new drugs (Snee, 2016).

Use of Six Sigma projects is not as appropriate here because there is no existing process to study and improve. However, when we have an identified business, product, or process opportunity, Design for Six Sigma (DFSS) projects can be deployed to bring them to market. Before getting to DFSS, of course, we must identify the opportunity. As Hoerl and Gardner (2010) explain, methods quite different from DFSS are required to identify and prioritize such opportunities. In Chapter 2, we classified them under the general category of innovation and creativity. All improvement methods require some amount of these attributes, but they clearly merit a front-and-center focus when identifying new opportunities. Snee (2016) provides a more detailed discussion of quality by design, the methodologies typically applied, and how it fits into an overall quality system.

Innovation and Creativity

As explained by Xu et al. (2006), before designing a new product or process, organizations must go through an idea generation process to identify opportunities, come up with potential ideas for capturing them, and prioritize those ideas. This process is typically based on business strategy, as well as customer and competitive intelligence. Drucker (2006) provides significant practical guidance on driving innovation and fostering entrepreneurship within an organization. However, aside from formal marketing research methods and knowledge-based tools for prioritization, such as interrelationship digraphs and multivoting (Brassard, 1996), few formal, analytical tools exist for conducting such work. This is one reason innovation is so challenging and not done well by many organizations.

Despite the limited number of formal tools, we incorporate innovation and creativity in the holistic improvement system because this is a critically needed element. As we stated in Chapter 1, Birkinshaw and Gibson (2004) have noted that organizations that want to succeed in the long term must become ambidextrous—that is, they must be able to both innovate and optimize the efficiency of existing operations. Doing one or the other well is no longer sufficient to ensure organizational success. Fortunately, after identifying and prioritizing ideas, formal approaches such as DFSS and TRIZ can be applied to produce conceptual and, eventually, detailed designs.

Design for Six Sigma (DFSS)

At this point, we are ready to consider how to actually bring to fruition a new opportunity. DFSS can be very effective at this point in the innovation cycle. Early in its Six Sigma journey, GE noticed that applying the DMAIC process to new product, service, or process design efforts was usually a forced fit. For example, when attempting to measure the process, there was no existing process on which to take measurements. After struggling with this issue for some time, GE finally developed a Design for Six Sigma process using the DMADV approach. This approach borrowed heavily from ongoing design efforts at Honeywell and other organizations (Hahn et al., 2000).

Figure 3.2, analogous to Figure 3.1 for DMAIC projects, highlights the purpose, objectives, and sample tools in each phase of DMADV projects. Note that the Define phase is similar in both approaches: It is intended to develop an overall project charter to provide structure and guide the project. The Measure phase in DMADV is quite different: In this case, the team needs to determine *what* to measure and rigorously define the critical to quality variables (CTQs). In the case of DMADV, typically several CTQs will exist. During design, we do not have the luxury of focusing on only one CTQ; we must identify all of them.

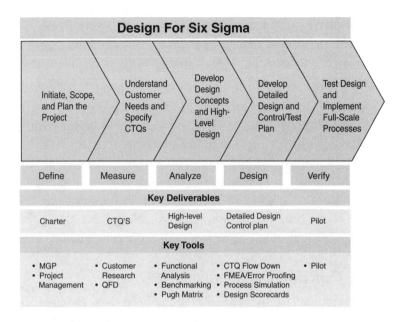

Figure 3.2   The DMADV methodology and key tools

The **Analyze phase** is perhaps the most different from DMAIC because there is no data on the process to analyze. At this point, the team analyzes the CTQs and considers how to best achieve them, ideally with a novel approach. This leads to a focus on conceptual design that is significantly better than current options. This focus is called **conceptual design** because no hardware or physical process might yet exist—it could be just a concept. Assuming that the concept appears to deliver a significant advantage, perhaps through developing and evaluating a prototype, the team can move on to the Design phase. In the Design phase, the details are added to the concept to create a detailed design. As the old saying goes, "The devil is in the details." This tends to be the most time-consuming phase of DMADV projects.

Once a detailed design has been developed, it needs to be verified before commercial release. The intent is to rigorously evaluate the design under realistic (as opposed to ideal) conditions. Even if a prototype performed very well in a laboratory environment, a more stressful test is needed. For example, a design involving a new IT system would not be verified by professional computer scientists at night with a quiet network. Instead, it would be verified by typical end users during peak hours for network traffic. Only if the system performed well under these realistic conditions could the organization be confident that it would ultimately be successful in practice.

Clearly, typical DFSS projects require more time than DMAIC projects. The team needs to develop an entire product and process from scratch while considering all CTQs. However, if the charter indicates that this is likely to take more than a year to complete, a helpful strategy is to break the overall design project into several subprojects, using an approach called multigenerational planning (MGP). Note that MGP is listed as a key tool in the Define stage in Figure 3.2. For further details on DFSS, Creveling et al. (2002) is a classic reference; Neagu and Hoerl (2005) provide a novel application of the DMADV process to finance.

Quality Function Deployment (QFD)

Quality Function Deployment (QFD) has been used for decades to design new products and services based on customer needs (King, 1989). In fact, it has been integrated into DMAIC and DMADV Six Sigma projects, as shown in Figures 3.1 and 3.2. However, Six Sigma projects that have used QFD have typically borrowed only parts of the overall process. Many practitioners thus do not realize that QFD is an extensive, multistep methodology in its own right.

Many versions of QFD are used in practice, but its standard four-step approach is useful. This approach creates a series of matrices that map customer needs, often in raw and unstructured form (for example, "I want a knowledgeable sales rep") first to rigorous metrics and eventually to process parameters to help manage the process (Hoerl, 2008). The four matrices, called houses of quality, sequentially translate higher-level information to lower-level information:

- From fuzzy customer needs to measureable quality metrics

- From quality metrics to process functional requirements

- From functional requirements to process steps

- From process steps to process control measures

Each of these translations uses a matrix with a house structure, hence the term *house of quality*. Figure 3.3 shows House 1, which translates customer needs for small bank loans into measureable quality metrics (Hoerl, 2008). Note that the customer needs are written on the left side of the matrix. Potential tangible measures are written across the top. The team then fills in the interior of the matrix using its subject matter knowledge, indicating how strongly the team believes each metric is related to each customer need. For example, in this case, the team felt that measuring the actual loan amount divided by the requested loan amount would show a strong relationship to the customers' perception of easy access to capital. The bull's-eye indicates a strong relationship, the open circle represents a moderate relationship, and the triangle represents a weak relationship. A blank indicates a minimal relationship or no relationship.

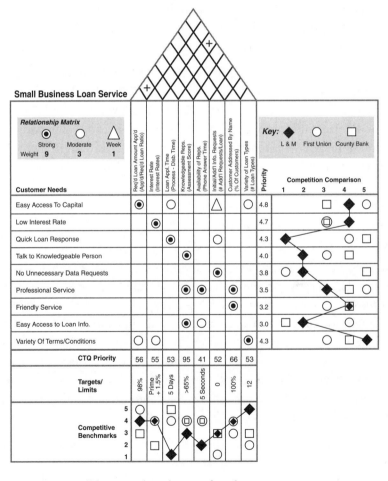

Figure 3.3   Small business loan house of quality

The matrix can be quantified by assigning a numerical priority score to each customer need (on the right side of the matrix) and then assigning a numerical value to each symbol (typically 9, 3, 1 for strong, moderate, and weak, respectively). To see the importance of the metric actual loan/requested loan, we go down the matrix, multiply each symbol's value by the need priority score, and then add the numbers to obtain a total. In this case, that would be: $9 \times 4.8 + 3 \times 4.3 = 56$. Doing the same for all metrics, we obtain a relative importance for each metric.

The far-right "room" of the house shows a potential comparison of how customers rate their current satisfaction of these needs from our bank relative to the competition. The bottom room shows targets that the team has set for the metrics, relative to how competition is performing. The "roof" of the house shows how the metrics might correlate with one another, to determine which targets are reasonable and achievable.

As Figure 3.3 shows, a house of quality from a QFD contains valuable information that is useful in design projects. Typically, this first house is included in Six Sigma projects. As noted, however, completing the second, third, and fourth houses in a formal QFD exercise provides an overall integrated approach to product and process design, including process control measures. See Akao (2004) for a more complete reference on QFD.

Theory of Inventive Problem Solving (TRIZ)

TRIZ, also known as the theory of inventive problem solving, is a rigorous methodology for resolving contradictions, primarily in conceptual design. The acronym comes from a transliteration of the Russian letters for *theory of inventive problem solving*. As explained by Altshuller (1996), the method has Russian origins. The underpinnings of the method involve a couple critical assumptions. The first is that design will always involve contradictions or trade-offs. However, true innovation occurs when we seek to "have our cake and eat it, too"—that is, to creatively identify a novel solution that resolves the contradiction and allows us to obtain all attributes desired in the design.

As a trivial example, consider the design of a new commercial aircraft. Airlines want a plane to have excellent fuel economy, to minimize costs. At the same time, however, they want a large interior, to make room for more passengers. Of course, large interiors and fuel economy present a contradiction: A large plane generally has poor fuel economy, whereas a plane with great fuel economy tends to be small. At first glance, most designers would pick one attribute or the other, depending on which was considered the most important. However, suppose that we designed the plane with a novel metal alloy that had outstanding strength and also was extremely light? Might we be able to design an aircraft with both a large interior and also excellent fuel economy? In this simple case, refusing to accept the contradiction might lead to true innovation.

The second major assumption is that someone, somewhere in the world, has probably struggled with the same type of contradiction we are currently struggling with. The specific application might differ, but someone might have also struggled with size versus fuel economy—perhaps with a car, for example. Therefore, if we can identify and catalog the major contradictions seen in the design world and determine how they have been resolved, we would have an excellent resource for resolving our own contradiction. Various catalogs have been developed, in both matrix and schematic form. See, for example, Hua et al. (2006), and the references at the end of this chapter.

Additional Breakthrough Improvement Methods

As discussed previously, quality by design is the point at which we identify, evaluate, develop, and refine new business opportunities, new products, and new processes. This phase is critical because it is difficult to improve a poorly designed process to the point of true excellence. Six Sigma uses the term *entitlement* to refer to the maximum level of performance designed into a process (Harry and Schroeder, 2000). It is *entitlement* in the sense that management is *entitled* to this level of performance; management has paid for this quality level in the original design.

Unfortunately, the vast majority of processes perform well below their entitlement (Snee and Hoerl, 2003). In many cases, the designed performance is never achieved; in others, the process performs well initially but settles for suboptimal performance over time because of wear and tear, misuse, operator error, and so on. At that point, improvement methods for achieving new levels of performance are needed. As noted, this might mean finding new levels of performance that have never been achieved or making a dramatic improvement back to performance levels that have not been seen in some time.

The key point is that breakthrough improvement is not problem solving; it is not fixing something that is broken. We are not simply returning a broken system to normal; we are taking it to new levels. This is not to imply that problem solving is bad. If oil starts leaking on the floor at 3:00 AM, we need to fix the leak immediately, not launch a Six Sigma project. However, doing so just returns things to normal—it does not take us to a higher level of performance. We cover managing processes with excellence to avoid or quickly solve problems in our discussion of quality and process management systems.

Note that we have already discussed Six Sigma as an improvement method, as well as an overall framework for our holistic improvement system. Therefore, we do not discuss Six Sigma further here. Additionally, the quick-hit projects often referred to as Nike projects (Just Do It!) do not follow a formal methodology, so we do not examine Nike project methodology.

Lean Enterprise

Lean Enterprise, originally known as Lean Manufacturing, has its roots in the Toyota Production System (Monden, 2012). Lean Enterprise can be defined in many ways, although Womack and Jones (2003), who wrote one of the classic texts on Lean, emphasize Lean as an approach to eliminate waste of any type, such as excess floor space, excess inventory, excess work in progress, wasted capital, wasted effort, and wasted time. The overall approach to eliminating waste seeks to clearly identify the value that is being created, line up all activities that produce this value along a value stream, and then make the flow of the value stream a pull system instead of a push system. A pull system is one in which production is pulled, or initiated by customer orders; conversely, in a push system, products are produced as rapidly as possible and the organization attempts to push the product now in inventory to potential customers.

Womack and Jones (2003) identify five key principles of Lean:

- Specify *value* by specific product
- Identify the *value stream* for each product

- Make value *flow* without interruptions
- Let the customer *pull* value from the producer
- Pursue perfection

Although its roots are in manufacturing, Lean principles have been applied to such diverse areas as banking, healthcare, and education, producing Lean Enterprise. As noted earlier, George (2002) was an early proponent of the integration of Lean and Six Sigma, to create Lean Six Sigma.

In our experience, the greatest successes of Lean have typically involved improving the flow of materials and information. This includes push versus pull systems, a reduction in inventory and work in progress through Just in Time instead of Just in Case approaches, and so on. In other words, this is Lean's sweet spot (Hoerl and Snee, 2013). Specifically, we have found that Lean projects are particularly useful in these applications:

- Factory and production line layout
- Work station design
- Waste reduction
- Cycle time reduction
- Work in progress (WIP) and inventory reduction

Another key Lean approach is the Kaizen event or rapid improvement project, often used to accomplish the tasks just noted. In a Kaizen event, a process is torn apart and reassembled with a more efficient flow, typically over three days or less (George, 2002).

Table 3.1 includes some of the most common tools used in Lean Enterprise projects (Womack and Jones, 2003). It should be clear that most of these tools are not statistical in nature. In particular, Lean tends to focus on a broad application of proven principles of efficiency and waste reduction instead of data analytics or cause/effect to identify root causes. Therefore, Lean tends to work best for "solution known" problems (Hoerl and Snee, 2013).

Table 3.1 Common Tools Applied on Lean Enterprise Projects

Common Tools	Description
Process mapping (value stream maps)	Depicts the creation of value
5S method (sort, set in order, shine, standardize, sustain)	Creates a clean, structured work space
Work standardization	Reduces variation in how work is done
Line balancing	Reduces variation in production lines
U-shaped work cell	Minimizes the need for human movement
Single-minute exchange of dies (SMED)	Reduces time required to switch products
Poka-yoke (mistake proofing)	Avoids mistakes before they occur
Kanban (Just in Time)	Minimizes in-process inventory

Statistical Engineering

In Chapter 1, we described growing awareness of the importance of addressing large, complex, unstructured problems, such as the Millennium Development Goals. Typically, problem-solving methodologies are oriented toward well-defined problems that are medium to small in size. Therefore, a unique approach is needed when facing complex problems, especially those that are not well structured. The challenge in developing a model to predict corporate defaults in finance (discussed in Chapter 1), is one such example. As noted in Hoerl and Snee (2017), there was no generally accepted definition of the word *default*, no agreed-upon metrics to measure success, and, in fact, no data available on which to build the model. Furthermore, economic theory suggested that developing such a model was not feasible. Clearly, this problem was large, complex, and unstructured.

Obviously, no "7-step" method can easily resolve such problems. Even more rigorous methods such as Six Sigma are not well suited to complex problems that require more time and the integration of novel methods. Statistical engineering (Hoerl and Snee, 2010) has been proposed as an overall approach to developing a strategy to attack such problems. Statistical engineering is defined as "the study of how to best utilize statistical concepts, methods and tools, and integrate them with information technology and other relevant disciplines, to achieve enhanced results"

(Hoerl and Snee, 2010, p. 12). Note that statistical engineering is not an improvement methodology, per se, such as Lean or Six Sigma, but rather a discipline. This is why it is defined as "the study of" something rather than the use of specific tools in a specific way.

This definition also emphasizes integration: the integration of multiple tools and also multiple disciplines, especially information technology. As we discuss shortly, the availability of large data sets has grown exponentially in the past few decades. The capability to acquire, store, retrieve, and analyze this data for improvement purposes has become critical to the competitive position of most organizations. Therefore, information technology is often a key element of statistical engineering applications. Other disciplines, such as various branches of engineering, economics, and operations research, might also be key, depending on the nature of the particular problem being addressed.

The underlying theory of statistical engineering incorporates an overall framework for attacking large, complex, unstructured problems (DiBenedetto et al., 2014). This framework was shown in Chapter 1 and is repeated here as Figure 3.4. Note that this framework illustrates the phases that statistical engineering projects typically go through; these are not well-defined steps with specific methods applied, as in DMAIC or DMADV projects. Recall that statistical engineering is a discipline instead of a methodology; although this framework provides a generic approach to attacking large, complex, unstructured problems, it is not a step-by-step approach.

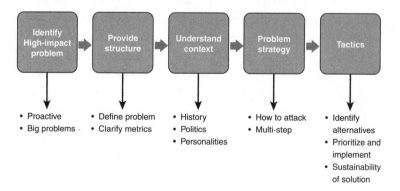

Figure 3.4 Statistical engineering framework for attacking large, complex, unstructured problems

Note that these types of complex problems are often not recognized as problems that quantitative methods can address. Issues such as poverty, gender-based violence, and corporate culture are too often accepted as "just the way things are," without recognizing that even such large and complex problems can often be addressed to some degree with the right approach. Therefore, significant effort typically is required to identify such opportunities and incorporate them into a project selection system. Without proactive effort to identify and "tee up" the problem, it will likely continue from year to year, with no organized attempt to address it.

After the problem is identified, it needs to be structured. By definition, these types of problems come unstructured. In other words, the specific problem to be solved, as well as its measures of success, is not obvious. Consider the case of an attempt to modify the culture at a research institute from a pure R&D mind-set to more of an industrial research lab culture—that is, one focused on solving the specific problems the organization faces instead of conducting research for the sake of advancing science. What is the specific objective of the project? How would we know if we succeeded? What are the measures of success? These questions have no obvious answers here, unlike in other areas, such as when attempting to reduce waste in a factory.

After the problem is structured, a thorough evaluation of the background of the problem and its history is generally required to develop a viable solution. We refer to this background as the context of the problem. Such large problems have defied solution over the years, for a reason: Simple solutions have not proven effective. Having a thorough understanding of where the problem came from, the factors reinforcing its continuation (such as politics and personalities), why it has defied solution, and what has been tried before is critical to success. Only when we thoroughly understand the context can we develop a plan of attack. Obviously, all problems require some degree of knowledge of root causes and context. However, for large, complex, unstructured problems, the roots are deeper and more complicated.

A tailored strategy then can be developed to address a given problem. This strategy typically involves multiple steps and multiple methodologies because of the complexities of these types of problems. No "cookie cutter" strategy or textbook solution works here; creative thought needs to help identify the best approach. A multistep strategy generally incorporates numerous tactics or specific elements.

In the default prediction case study, some of the individual tactics involved in the overall strategy were identifying an effective data smoothing algorithm, developing a mapping from default probability and its slope to tangible actions to be taken (buy, sell, and so on), and deriving a monitoring scheme that uses censored data techniques to detect when the system needs to be retuned (Neagu and Hoerl, 2005). This last tactic helped ensure the sustainability of the solution, which is a critical element of any improvement approach.

For further examples of statistical engineering applications, see Anderson-Cook and Lu (2012). This reference is a special edition of the journal *Quality Engineering* that is devoted to statistical engineering; it includes several case studies and applications.

Big Data Analytics

Data is being collected at an ever-increasing pace, through social media, online transactions, and scientific research. According to IBM, 1.6 zetabytes (10^{21} bytes) of digital data are now available. That's a lot of data—enough to watch high-definition TV for 47,000 years (Ebbers, 2013). Hardware, software, and statistical technologies to process, store, and analyze this data deluge have also advanced, creating new opportunities for analytics. Although many definitions of the word *analytics* could be used, we define analytics as quantitative methods used to discover meaningful information in data. This somewhat generic definition avoids debate over what is statistics versus applied math, machine learning, data science, and so on, which is not our focus.

Many new modeling methods (spanning statistics, machine learning, and computer science) have been developed in the past 30 or so years to take advantage of these large amounts of data. Methods such as neural networks, classification and regression trees (CART), and support vector machines (SVM) are now commonly used. Recently, ensemble methods that resample the data and integrate multiple models into an overall grand model have become more popular (James et al., 2013). These approaches include random forests and boosting methods, among others. Because they resample the data, take multiple paths, and include highly nonlinear fitting, these methods are computationally intensive. However, such computing is practical with recent advances in computing power. Note that such tools are much more sophisticated than those typically utilized in Six Sigma projects.

Many businesses, academic institutions, and even the U.S. government have made major investments in Big Data analytics (National Research Council, 2009). FICO (Fiar, Isaac, and Company) is perhaps the earliest example of an analytics-based business model; it was founded in 1956 to provide analytics for credit scoring. A more recent example is Google, whose search engine is perhaps the greatest success story of analytics today: Google has a market capitalization of more than half a trillion dollars as of this writing.

Interestingly, most Big Data analytics organizations tend to operate as standalone silos, without any connection to other groups that are working on improvement (Snee and Hoerl, 2017). This obviously inhibits their involvement in the major improvement efforts of the company, to the detriment of all. In our view, a much more logical approach is to assimilate groups performing Big Data analytics into the improvement organization, thereby integrating this important new methodology with other important improvement approaches. Such a synergistic relationship is likely to produce greater benefit than having each group work in isolation. Too often, such isolation results in unhealthy internal competition, as discussed in Chapter 1.

In addition, the emphasis on massive data sets by Amazon, Google, and similar organizations often masks the importance of smaller but more carefully selected data sets, such as those obtained through designed experiments. In our experience, large data sets that are retrospective in nature, not designed, can suggest hypotheses through abnormal patterns in the data. However, randomized experiments are needed to test these hypotheses and evaluate causation versus correlation (De Veaux et al., 2016). In essence, we obtain the best results when we consider all data (big, small, and intermediate) to solve the problem. See Hoerl et al. (2014) for further discussion of the impact of Big Data analytics, and see James et al. (2013) for rigorous elaboration of the methods themselves.

Work-Out Approach

GE CEO Jack Welch developed Work-Out in the late 1980s as a unique approach to improvement in the workplace (Elrich et al., 2002). He had recently built the Crotonville leadership development center and was delighted with the open atmosphere there that encouraged business leaders to share both their ideas and their concerns about issues facing GE. However, Welch remained frustrated that he didn't sense a similar environment elsewhere in the GE businesses. In too many places, he saw a bureaucracy filled with controlling leaders who pretended to have all the answers and stifled workers who were afraid to open up and share their true feelings.

Realizing that he couldn't bring all GE employees to Crotonville, Welch decided to take Crotonville to all the employees. He created a process that mimicked what he experienced in Crotonville and could be replicated around the world. Perhaps due to his Massachusetts roots, Welch decided to model the process after a New England town meeting. This consisted of a group of typically 40 to 60 people, facilitated by someone outside of GE (originally, local college professors) to ensure that people felt free to speak openly. The fact that the participants' managers were not invited to the Work-Out was critical. The facilitator defined the scope of the issue being addressed and then got people to share their ideas and frustrations about it. Welch (2001) notes that, at some of these meetings, people shared such passionate feelings that they began to swear at each other. However, they also moved past the bureaucracy to the core issues, which often involved unnecessary reports and meetings that got in the way of serving customers. Much of the focus was, and still is, on eliminating non-value-adding work.

The Work-Out sessions were a big success and eventually grew to involve hundreds of thousands of GE employees. Not only did they produce tangible results, but they also helped people feel empowered after some difficult years of downsizing in the company. They created an atmosphere in which employees worked across global and organizational boundaries for the benefit of GE as a whole, with good ideas respected regardless of the rank, gender, age, or ethnicity of the person submitting the idea.

So what are the essential elements of Work-Out that make it a unique aspect of a holistic improvement system? It was founded on the following core principles:

- An open environment in which people are free to speak their mind without fear of retribution by management

- Enlistment of the front-line workers, who are most familiar with the issue at hand, instead of a panel of experts

- Use of impartial facilitators instead of management leaders to conduct the meetings

- Short interactions (two to three days) and immediate decisions by management for at least 75 percent of the team suggestions—no burying the proposals by sending them to committees for "further study"

- An emphasis on busting bureaucracy, eliminating unnecessary meetings, reports, approvals, and so on

Clearly, the Work-Out approach is not the best method for solving every problem that can occur within an organization. Complex technical problems will require more sophisticated data-based approaches, such as Six Sigma. Based on our experience, Work-Out is best suited to problems with the following attributes (Hoerl, 2008):

- We believe that a relatively simple solution exists that will not require extensive data collection and analysis to find.

- We believe that the people working within the process have knowledge of potential solutions (a "solution known" problem).

- We believe that the wisdom of good solutions will be readily apparent to those working within the process, minimizing the need for a test period to evaluate the solution.

As of this writing, Work-Out is still utilized at GE and other companies. See Elrich et al. (2002) or Welch (2001) for more details on the background, objectives, and process of Work-Out.

Quality and Process Management Systems

Innovation and breakthrough improvement might be considered the offensive aspects of improvement: We score points and move the ball down the field. However, an old saying in sports holds true here as well: Offense sells tickets, but defense wins championships. The point, of course, is that although identifying new opportunities and making significant improvements to existing processes is critical, so is maintaining excellence in the ongoing management of existing operations. It is far better to avoid issues rather than have to launch project teams to resolve issues after they occur. Most organizations with long-standing reputations for excellence have outstanding systems for quality and process management. The Toyota Production System, which has institutionalized many of the principles of Lean Enterprise, is one obvious example.

Just as specific methods must be used for innovation and breakthrough improvement, we need specific methods to manage the overall quality of products and services, as well as the processes that produce them. Different methods are more appropriate for specific organizations facing specific challenges; no single approach is universally superior. In this section, we briefly discuss several proven approaches that we feel organizations should seriously consider.

ISO 9000

ISO 9000 is a series of standards for quality and process management that are widely utilized on a global basis. Many organizations in the European Union require certification to ISO 9001, the main standard of the series, as a condition of doing business. The most recent version as of this writing is ISO 9001-2015, which is the 2015 update. The standard itself is produced and updated by the International Organization for Standardization (www.iso.org), but approved third parties generally perform the actual certification to 9001.

ISO 9001 provides some guidance on effective quality management, but at its core, it requires organizations to carefully document their quality and process management procedures and then verify that they actually follow them. For this reason, some critics consider ISO 9001 as "minimally adequate." The more recent updates, such as 9001-2015, place greater emphasis on documentation of results. According to the ISO website, more than a million organizations in 170 countries are certified to ISO 9001 as of this writing.

Figure 3.5 provides an overall model for quality management systems, based on the 2015 version of the standard itself. Numbers 4–10 refer to the sections of the standard in which these topics are discussed.

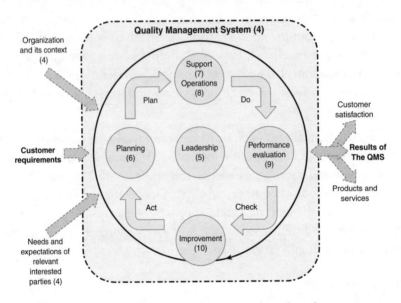

Figure 3.5   ISO 9000 2015 model of a process-based quality management system

Although ISO 9001 is not prescriptive in terms of the specific methods to deploy, it highlights the critical areas organizations must incorporate into their quality systems. Table 3.2 lists the key principles of ISO 9001. It should be obvious that ISO 9001 is a much more holistic approach to quality and process management than Six Sigma, which is project based. However, as shown by Snee and Hoerl (2003), Six Sigma in consistent with and reinforces the key principles of ISO 9000.

Table 3.2 Key Principles of ISO 9001

Principle	Description
Customer focus	Customers ultimately determine our success or failure.
Involvement of people	All employees should help drive improvement.
Process orientation	All work occurs through processes that can be improved.
System approach to management	We must ensure that we are improving the overall system.
Continual improvement	Improvement is an assignment we will never complete.
Factual approach to decision making	Data and the scientific method trump "gut feel."
Mutually beneficial supplier relationships	We work with suppliers to improve the system for everyone.

Malcolm Baldrige National Quality Award

The Malcolm Baldrige National Quality Award (MBNQA) is a competitive quality award established by the U.S. Congress in 1987 and overseen by the National Institute of Standards and Technology (NIST). It is also the basis for several state quality awards. MBNQA winners receive their awards annually from the President of the United States. Multiple winners are named each year because there are separate awards for different types of organizations. The award categories follow:

- Manufacturing

- Service companies

- Small businesses

- Education

- Healthcare

- Nonprofit

The Baldrige criteria for performance excellence are broken down into seven categories, shown in Table 3.3 (http://asq.org/learn-about-quality/malcolm-baldrige-award/overview/overview.html). A comparison of Tables 3.2 and 3.3 clearly reveals overlap between ISO 9001 and MBNQA. However, it should be noted that although ISO 9001 is a standard to which any number of organizations might be certified, MBNQA is competitive and typically names only one winner in each category per year. Furthermore, MBNQA places greater emphasis on results.

It should also be pointed out that organizations often use the MBNQA criteria as a template for developing a holistic quality and process management system without ever actually applying for the award. That is, the benefit of MBNQA is not limited to winning an award. In fact, the criteria listed in Table 3.3 can be used simply to identify opportunities for improvement. In this way, MBNQA ties directly into breakthrough improvement. As we have noted, the three major components of the holistic improvement system should be well integrated instead of acting as three independent silos.

Table 3.3 Baldrige Criteria for Performance Excellence

Criteria	Description
Leadership	How upper management leads the organization, and how the organization leads within the community.
Strategy	How the organization establishes and plans to implement strategic directions.
Customers	How the organization builds and maintains strong, lasting relationships with customers.
Measurement, Analysis & Knowledge Management	How the organization uses data to support key processes and manage performance.
Workforce	How the organization empowers and involves its workforce.
Operations	How the organization designs, manages, and improves key processes.
Results	How the organization performs in terms of customer satisfaction, finances, human resources, supplier and partner performance, operations, governance, and social responsibility; and how the organization compares to its competitors.

We believe that, depending on the nature of the organization in question, either ISO 9001 or the MBNQA criteria can be considered a guide to develop and evaluate an overall quality and process management system. No individual tool or method will sufficiently address quality and process management excellence; therefore, organizations need to think strategically about how to approach the development and evaluation of their overall system. In our opinion, ISO 9001 and MBNQA can provide invaluable help in doing so.

Kepner—Tregoe Approach

Problem solving has been recognized as a critical skill in numerous disciplines for decades, if not centuries. However, formal research on the best approaches to problem solving is limited (DiBenedetto et al., 2014). In this context, we use the term *problem solving* to refer to the identification and correction of the root causes of issues that have occurred. This differs from process improvement, which is intended to move to new levels of performance. Instead, problem solving fixes things that are broken, returning performance to the normal level. Both process improvement and problem solving are needed in a holistic improvement system.

One of the most formal approaches to problem solving that we have seen produce significant results comes from Kepner and Tregoe (2013). The Kepner–Tregoe approach, often referred to as "Is–Is Not analysis," is a rigorous approach to carefully documenting an issue so that root causes, rather than symptoms, can be addressed. Specifically, it notes when, where, and how an issue has been observed, as well as when, where, and how it has *not* been observed but could have been. By comparing where the problem is and where it is not, we can obtain clues to the root causes of the problem. For example, if a manufacturing problem occurred on line 3 but not on lines 1 and 2, we know that the root cause must be related to uniqueness of line 3 relative to lines 1 and 2.

As a preliminary step, we must carefully describe the problem under study; this defines the *what*. Next, we ask about the *where*. Where, specifically, have we observed the problem? And what about the *when*? Depending on the nature of the problem, we might also ask about the *who*, the people involved. We may also need to know the *how* (that is, the mode of failure) or the *why* (if potential root causes are known). Once we have established these parameters for where the problem *is,* we can ask these same questions about where the problem *is not*. For example, if the problem involved some type of contaminated product, what other issues would we have expected to occur with a contaminated product that *did not* occur? Did it not occur in certain regions, with certain versions of the product, or at other times? Collectively, that information would give us clues to the root causes of the problem.

A case study in Hoerl and Snee (2012) applied Is–Is Not analysis to late deliveries in a distribution process. Figure 3.6 shows the information that resulted from that analysis. In this case, careful consideration of exactly when the problem occurred and where it did and did not occur provided important clues to root causes. These led to potential explanations or theories on the root cause of the problem. The potential explanations lead to specific actions that can be taken to follow up and verify the potential causes. This approach and the specific questions involved might seem simplistic, but our experience is that carefully documenting the answers facilitates a quick evaluation of theories on potential root causes. No matter how passionately someone champions a theory, if it is not consistent with the facts, we need to move on to other theories.

Analysis

Questions	Is	Is Not	Potential Explanation	Actions
Where?	Northeast U.S.	South, Midwest, or West	Different Warehouses	Review Data on Individual Warehouses
What?	Out of Stock on Variety of Parts	Late Delivery on Stocked Parts	Delivery Process OK, but Inventory Management Is Not	Check Inventory Management System
When?	Problem Started Around Beginning of October	Prior to That Time	New Computer System Installed End of September, Efforts to Reduce Inventory Levels Began in October	Check for Differences in Inventory Management Algorithms Between Computer Systems; Document any Change in Targeted Inventory Levels
Who?	Involves All Order Takers	NA	NA	NA

Figure 3.6 Is–Is Not analysis of late deliveries

This approach is obviously intended for "solution unknown" problems because it searches for root causes. Also, our experience has shown that it is not an effective approach to process improvement because no specific problem might have occurred. We might have always had this level of performance, for example, but it is no longer acceptable and now needs to be improved. For problem solving, on the other hand, something clearly has gone wrong. This approach then can be very effective in identifying root causes for the problem. See Kepner and Tregoe (2013) for further details on this methodology.

Total Productive Maintenance (TPM)

Total Productive Maintenance (TPM) is a formal approach to optimizing maintenance of plant and equipment, to achieve the maximum possible productivity at the lowest possible cost (https://en.wikipedia.org/wiki/Total_productive_maintenance). Historically, maintenance in manufacturing organizations was performed only after equipment failed, as so-called breakdown maintenance. Gradually, organizations realized that this was an expensive approach. Not only does it permit severe damage to the equipment, but it also can involve hours or days of lost productivity while trying to repair the broken equipment.

Organizations gradually learned that preventative maintenance was a preferable approach. Replacement of parts or materials at fixed intervals, such as replacing motor oil in a car after 5,000 miles, is one approach to planned maintenance. Fixed-time replacement was often much less expensive in the long run and reduced unplanned outages. However, it still results in money left on the table, in the sense that some parts or materials are thrown out at a specific interval and not necessarily when they actually need to be replaced.

The next advance was a more sophisticated approach of predictive maintenance. In this approach, measurements on the equipment are tracked regularly to determine how close the equipment is to failure (assuming that this can be predicted). For example, most automobile manufacturers today do not recommend replacing the oil at fixed intervals; instead, they use sensors to take internal measurements of the oil itself and then use analytics to predict when the oil needs to be replaced to avoid problems. Depending on how and where the car is driven, the oil might need to be replaced before 5,000 miles, or perhaps not until 6,000 or 7,000 miles.

A unique aspect of the TPM approach is to analytically evaluate both the ability to predict failure and the consequences, to determine an optimal overall maintenance strategy. For example, breakdown maintenance might still be the best strategy for replacing light bulbs in an office. Fixed-time replacement, or installing sensors to evaluate the status of the bulb in real time, is not likely cost-effective. However, for major mechanical systems, a predictive approach is better. See Borris (2006) or Prabhuswamy et al. (2013) for further details on TPM.

The Internet of Things

The so-called Internet of Things (IoT) is not a methodology, but rather a building block of effective quality and process management. IoT refers to connecting physical devices via the Internet. For example, most modern aircraft currently have thousands of sensors monitoring various aspects of the engine and airplane in general, such as exhaust gas temperatures, emissions and cabin air quality. Furthermore, the computers on these planes are connected in real time via satellite with tracking stations of the airline or a service organization. Therefore, someone (or computers) in the United States or Europe can be tracking flights between Johannesburg and Singapore, and perhaps notifying the ground crews in Singapore of specific maintenance that will be needed when the plane arrives.

The connection of physical devices via the Internet, often without direct human intervention, has significant implications. The concept of "smart cities" that can direct traffic from congested roads to open roads, manage water and electrical resources in real time, and reduce carbon footprints is based on IoT (Marr, 2015). Its potential is virtually limitless. Some people fear that IoT could usher in a science fiction scenario of robots taking over the world, but the truth is, to a significant degree IoT is already here.

For our purposes, IoT is not a *what*, but rather a *how*. That is, we are focused not on IoT, per se, but rather on how the connection of physical devices might enable more efficient quality and process management systems. For example, we would view smart cities as a case in which IoT enables more efficient and effective process management than has ever been seen in government. We believe the same opportunities exist in the private sector. In the case of TPM, discussed previously, IoT is largely enabled by the physical plant and equipment in which sensors take data in real time and are connected to other computers and devices.

Our main point is that organizations seeking world-class quality and process management need to make sure their physical assets are connected and communicating in real time. Big Data Analytics also ties directly into IoT because analytics are necessary to make effective use of the data being transmitted. A holistic approach to improvement encourages the integration of multiple methodologies on given initiatives and projects. See Chui et al. (2010) for further details on IoT.

Summary and Looking Forward

Chapter 2 showed what a holistic improvement system might look like, using diverse methodologies from three major categories:

- **Quality by design:** The identification and development of new business opportunities, products, and process

- **Breakthrough improvement:** Performance taken to new levels not previously seen

- **Quality and process management systems:** The proactive work done to ensure process excellence

This chapter dug a little more deeply into these categories and identified some of the individual methodologies that organizations might consider as part of their holistic improvement system. We want to again emphasize that these are only some of the methods that fit into each category; this is not a complete list. Other methods are available, and might need to be considered for specific problems. Furthermore, the list of methods should be dynamic; additional methods will surely be developed in the future.

A question that begs asking is, can any organization actually successfully implement each of these methods? Probably not! However, some organizations have implemented several of them, resulting in a more holistic improvement system than is typically seen. These organizations have made significant progress toward Lean Six Sigma 2.0. In Chapter 4, "Case Studies in Holistic Improvement," we share the stories of a few of these organizations. In subsequent chapters, we explain how organizations can go about putting the necessary systems in place to create a successful holistic improvement system tailored to the organization.

References

Akao, Y. (2004) *Quality Function Deployment: Integrating Customer Requirements into Product Design*. New York: Taylor and Francis.

Altshuller, G. (1996) *And Suddenly the Inventor Appeared*, 2nd ed. Worcester, MA: Technical Innovation Center.

Anderson-Cook, C. M., and L. Lu., guest editors. (2012) Special Issue on Statistical Engineering. *Quality Engineering* 24, no. 2.

Birkinshaw, J. and C. Gibson. (2004) "Building Ambidexterity into an Organization." *MIT Sloan Management Review* 45, no. 4: 47–55.

Borris, S. (2006) *Total Productive Maintenance*. New York: McGraw-Hill.

Brassard, M. (1996) *The Memory Jogger Plus+*. Salem, NH: GOAL/QPC.

Chui, M., M. Loffler, and R. Roberts. (2010) "The Internet of Things." *The McKinsey Quarterly* (March). Available at http://www.mckinsey.com/industries/high-tech/our-insights/the-internet-of-things.

Creveling, C. M., J. L. Slutsky, and D. Antis. (2002) *Design for Six Sigma in Technology and Product Development*. Upper Saddle River, NJ: Prentice Hall.

De Veaux, R. D., R. W. Hoerl, and R. D. Snee. (2016) "Big Data and the Missing Links." *Statistical Analysis and Data Mining* 9, no. 6: 411–416.

DiBenedetto, A., R. W. Hoerl, and R. D. Snee. (2014) "Solving Jigsaw Puzzles." *Quality Progress* (June): 50–53.

Drucker, P. F. (2006) *Innovation and Entrepreneurship*. New York: HarperBusiness.

Ebbers, M. (2013) "5 Things to Know About Big Data in Motion." IBM developerWorks blog. Available at www.ibm.com/developerworks/community/blogs/5things/entry/5_things_to_know_about_big_data_in_motion?lang=en.

Elrich, D., S. Kerr, and R. Ashkenas. (2002) *The GE Work-Out: How to Implement GE's Revolutionary Method for Busting Bureaucracy and Attacking Organizational Problems—Fast!*. New York: McGraw-Hill.

George, M. L. (2002) *Lean Six Sigma: Combining Six Sigma Quality with Lean Production Speed*. New York: McGraw-Hill.

Hahn, G. J., N. Doganaksoy, and R. W. Hoerl. (2000) "The Evolution of Six Sigma." *Quality Engineering* 12, no. 3: 317–326.

Harry, M., and R. Schroeder. (2000) *Six Sigma: The Breakthrough Management Strategy Revolutionizing the World's Top Corporations.* New York: Currency Doubleday.

Hoerl, R. (2008) "Work-out." In *Encyclopedia of Statistics in Quality and Reliability*, edited by F. Ruggeri, R. Kenett, and F. W. Faltin, 2103–2105. Chichester, UK: John Wiley & Sons.

Hoerl, R. W., and M. M. Gardner. (2010) "Lean Six Sigma, Creativity, and Innovation." *International Journal of Lean Six Sigma* 1, no. 1: 30–38.

Hoerl, R. W., and R. D. Snee. (2010) "Moving the Statistics Profession Forward to the Next Level." *The American Statistician* 64, no. 1: 10–14.

Hoerl, R. W., and R. D. Snee. (2012) *Statistical Thinking: Improving Business Performance*, 2nd ed. Hoboken, NJ: John Wiley and Sons.

Hoerl, R. W., and R. D. Snee. (2013) "One Size Does Not Fit All: Identifying the Right Improvement Methodology." *Quality Progress* (May 2013): 48–50.

Hoerl, R. W., and R. D. Snee. (2017) "Statistical Engineering: An Idea Whose Time Has Come." *The American Statistician*, To Be Published.

Hoerl, R. W., R. D. Snee, and R. D. De Veaux. (2014) "Applying Statistical Thinking to 'Big Data' Problems." *Wiley Interdisciplinary Reviews: Computational Statistics* (July/August): 221–232. (doi: 10.1002/wics.1306)

Hua, Z., J. Yang, S. Coulibaly, and B. Zhang. (2006) "Integration of TRIZ with Problem Solving Tools: A Literature Review from 1995 to 2006." *International Journal of Business Innovation and Research* 1, no. 2: 111–128.

James, G., D. Witten, T. Hastie, and R. Tibshirani. (2013) *An Introduction to Statistical Learning*. New York: Springer.

Jones, M. H. (2004) "Six Sigma … at a Bank?" *Six Sigma Forum Magazine* (February): 13–17.

Juran, J. M., and J. A. DeFeo. (2010) *Juran's Quality Handbook: The Complete Guide to Performance Excellence*, 6th ed. New York: McGraw-Hill.

Kepner, C. H., and B. B. Tregoe. (2013) *The New Rational Manager.* New York: McGraw-Hill.

King, B. (1989) *Better Designs in Half the Time*, 3rd ed. Salem, NH: GOAL/QPC.

Marr, B. (2015) "How Big Data and the Internet of Things Creates Smarter Cities." Forbes Online (May 19). Available at https://www.forbes.com/sites/bernardmarr/2015/05/19/how-big-data-and-the-internet-of-things-create-smarter-cities/#2f3da1e21767.

Monden, Y. (2012) *Toyota Production System: An Integrated Approach to Just-In-Time*, 4th ed. Boca Raton, FL: CRC Press.

National Research Council. (2009) *Frontiers in Massive Data Analysis*. Washington, DC: The National Academies Press.

Neagu, R., and R. W. Hoerl. (2005) "A Six Sigma Approach to Predicting Corporate Defaults." *Quality and Reliability Engineering International* 21: 293–309.

Prabhuswamy, M., P. Nagesh, and K. Ravikumar. (2013) "Statistical Analysis and Reliability Estimation of Total Productive Maintenance." *IUP Journal of Operations Management* XII 1 (February): 7–20.

Snee, R. D. (2016) "Adjust, Adapt, Advance: An Enhanced Version of Quality by Design—A Risk Based Dynamic Approach to Improving Products and Processes." *Quality Progress* (May): 34–41.

Snee, R. D., and R. W. Hoerl. (2003) *Leading Six Sigma: A Step-by-Step Guide Based on Experience with GE and Other Six Sigma Companies.* Upper Saddle River, NJ: Financial Times/Prentice Hall.

Snee, R. D., and R. W. Hoerl. (2005) *Six Sigma Beyond the Factory Floor; Deployment Strategies for Financial Services, Health Care, and the Rest of the Real Economy.* Upper Saddle River, NJ: Financial Times/Prentice Hall.

Snee, R., and R. W. Hoerl. (2017) "Time for Lean Six Sigma 2.0?" *Quality Progress* (May): 50–53.

Welch, J. (2001) *Jack: Straight from the Gut.* New York: Warner Books.

Womack, J. P., and D. T. Jones. (2003) *Lean Thinking.* New York: Free Press.

Xu, K., C. Sikdar, and M. M. Gardner. (2006) "Six Sigma Roles in Innovation." Paper presented at the IEEE International Conference on Management of Innovation and Technology, Singapore.

4

Case Studies in Holistic Improvement

"Those who are ignorant of history are doomed to repeat it."
—George Santayana

C ase studies are an excellent way to see how Six Sigma is deployed because they look at strategies utilized, plans developed, barriers encountered, and results achieved in terms of process performance and bottom-line results. In our earlier books on Six Sigma (Snee and Hoerl, 2003, 2005), we discussed several case studies that illustrated both successful and not-so-successful deployments.

By circumstance, all the case studies discussed Six Sigma in the early years of deployment. The Six Sigma approach to improvement was just starting to be used. In this chapter, we discuss case studies on three companies: GE, DuPont, and Scott Paper. The DuPont and Scott Paper case studies have not previously appeared in the literature. These three cases demonstrate how the breadth of deployment grows over the years and how new improvement tools are integrated into the growing holistic methodology. Of course, the goal throughout the process is to improve customer satisfaction, process performance and financial results.

Case Study: Inside the GE Deployment

In the first edition of this book, the story of GE's original Six Sigma implementation was presented from the personal viewpoint of Roger Hoerl. Here we cover this same material, somewhat abbreviated, and also update it with more recent developments since 2003. In particular, we discuss the expansion to Version 1.3 and the inclusion of additional methods in the direction of a holistic system. As with the 2003 version,

---

all views expressed are the personal opinions of this author and should not be construed as representing GE.

We present this case study for several reasons. First of all, it provides a useful historical perspective on the development of Lean Six Sigma—in particular, what works and what roadblocks are to be expected. These learnings can be helpful to other organizations deploying Lean Six Sigma. In addition, it hopefully illustrates the different versions in the evolution of Lean Six Sigma so that the uniqueness of Lean Six Sigma 2.0 (holistic improvement) can be better appreciated.

The Beginnings: Jack Never Bluffs!

Within two months of starting at GE's Research and Development Center in Schenectady, New York, I was informed one day in September 1995 that all employees at the Center were to come to the auditorium for an important video presentation. No one knew what to expect when we heard that Jack (CEO Jack Welch) had made a video that he wanted shared with every employee of the company. (Within GE, the CEO is commonly referred to by his or her first name—a symbol of informality, not disrespect.)

The video lasted only a few minutes. It consisted of a brief statement from Jack explaining that GE was about to embark on a major new initiative called Six Sigma. Jack noted that the company had a number of quality-related issues to address and that he felt Six Sigma was the solution. He made his famous statement that this initiative would be the most important priority of the company for the next five years and that we would be a totally different company at the end of that time because of it. He was particularly proud that GE had not invented Six Sigma but had been mature enough to overcome the NIH (Not Invented Here) Syndrome and adopt a proven methodology pioneered by others, such as Motorola and AlliedSignal. More details were to follow from our individual business leaders.

Being somewhat skeptical of grandiose managerial pronouncements, I commented to a colleague as we stepped outside the auditorium: "That sounds great, *if* he's really serious."

The colleague, aware that I was new to GE, shot back: "There's one thing you need to understand about GE. Jack never bluffs."

"What does that mean?" I asked.

"It means that if Jack says he's going to do something, he's going to do it. You can take it to the bank."

That pretty much summarized my experiences over the next five years with Six Sigma. Jack wasn't bluffing.

No Second Guessing

Within a few weeks, I was attending the first Master Black Belt (MBB) training session being held at GE's executive development center in Crotonville, New York. What struck me most as I sat with newly appointed MBBs from the various GE businesses was the degree of focus everyone had on what needed to be done. There was no debating the merits of Six Sigma: Were the reported results from AlliedSignal or Motorola real? Would it apply to GE? Was this just a repackaging of TQM? Instead of debating these questions, virtually all the MBBs were asking about how to implement Six Sigma as quickly and effectively as possible.

This was another unique aspect of GE culture. A lot of debate took place over important decisions, but once the decision was made, very little debate continued on whether this was the correct decision. This was definitely not the culture I was used to.

When my two colleagues and I got back to the R&D center, we were extremely excited about this initiative. We could see the tremendous potential of getting armies of talented people trained in a sound improvement methodology, with full management support and commitment, systematically attacking the company's biggest issues. An open debriefing meeting was held at which we reported what we had learned at this session.

The vast majority of people shared our enthusiasm, although there was some isolated skepticism. Unfortunately, both at the Research Center and across GE, such rare skepticism led some leaders to leave GE. Such reactions might seem extreme, but they go back to a statement Jack made that if executives could not support Six Sigma 100 percent, GE was not the right company for them. Debating the merits of Six Sigma while the issue was still being considered was acceptable, but once the decision had been made, there was no time to continue the debate: We had to focus totally on implementation. Leaders had to lead.

The First Year: 1996

This turned out to be a year of learning for both GE and me (see Table 4.1). The major focus was on improving manufacturing processes using the MAIC (Measure, Analyze, Improve, Control) process. GE Capital (the financial services business of GE) subsequently added the Define stage, to ensure that an appropriate project has been selected and that it is properly defined, scoped, and planned. This turned out to be one of several major enhancements GE made to Six Sigma, and it changed the standard acronym to DMAIC. Each business in GE began its own separate initiative, but with a lot of interaction and sharing of best practices, utilizing the Corporate Executive Council (CEC) and newly created councils for MBBs and Quality Leaders (Champions). The opportunity to learn from others' successes and failures within GE turned out to be a major advantage.

Table 4.1   Focus of GE's Six Sigma Efforts

Year	Focus Areas
1995	Official launch: getting started on right foot
1996	LSS 1.0: Year of learning, manufacturing, DMAIC
1997	Tangible benefits, commercial quality, DFSS, Green Belts
1998–2000	LSS 1.1: Customer needs, ACFC, e-commerce
2001–2005	LSS 1.2: Reinvigoration, integration (Lean, Work-Out, and so on)
2005–2010	LSS 1.3: Innovation, integration with TRIZ

We certainly made a number of mistakes along the way, each of which became a test of leadership's commitment. For example, some businesses named part-time MBBs and Black Belts. Leaders wanted people to be change agents and focus on breakthrough improvements while continuing to do their regular jobs. Of course, this is a recipe for disaster, at least at the start-up of the initiative. Fortunately, when businesses began reporting large numbers of assigned MBBs and Black Belts to corporate headquarters in Fairfield, Connecticut, senior management asked them to revise their numbers to include only dedicated, full-time Black Belts and MBBs. The numbers dropped dramatically, and these businesses realized that they were going to have to bite the bullet and dedicate their Six Sigma resources.

There was suspicion that some businesses were assigning people to the Six Sigma effort based on availability. One of the common problems with business improvement initiatives is that those who are available, or perhaps those who can't do anything else well, are often assigned to work on these initiatives, while the best people are off doing the "really important" stuff. When corporate began asking to see previous performance appraisals for those who were put into Black Belt and MBB roles, top performers started appearing in Six Sigma roles.

This ties to another important point: GE never viewed the MBB or Black Belt as a permanent role for technically oriented people. This was intended to be a temporary developmental role for future leaders of the company. If this critical work had been delegated to techies, there would never have been a fundamental shift in the company's "genetic code," as Jack referred to it.

We needed future leaders who had the experience of being dedicated to process improvement work. This important point was later reinforced in the 2000 Annual Report:

> It is a reasonable guess that the next CEO of this Company, decades down the road, is probably a Six Sigma Black Belt or Master Black Belt somewhere in GE right now, or on the verge of being offered—as all our early-career (3–5 years) top 20% performers will be—a two-to-three-year Black Belt assignment. The generic nature of a Black Belt assignment, in addition to its rigorous process discipline and relentless customer focus, makes Six Sigma the perfect training for growing 21st century GE leadership.

NOTE

Jeff Immelt had already been named Jack's successor as CEO, hence the "next CEO" mentioned will be Jeff's successor.

Using Six Sigma as a developmental role for future leaders does not appear to have been an approach that many other companies copied. The assumption in most companies is, "Leadership is okay—we just need to improve things in operations." Fortunately, despite its success, GE did not have an arrogant culture. Senior management realized that even its leaders had to continuously learn and improve.

Financially, businesses started reporting huge savings from their initial projects. Were people stretching the truth to make their business look better than it really was? Leadership's response was to require that someone in the finance department personally sign off on each project, verifying that the claimed savings were real and noting specifically where they would show up on the bottom line. Corporate auditors periodically audited these evaluations. The size of the reported savings from Six Sigma projects decreased dramatically once the audits were put into place. It also became impossible to get credit for intangible benefits, such as customer satisfaction, the impact of one process improvement on other processes in the same system, and so on.

Despite healthy skepticism from some people, I am confident that the publicly reported savings from Six Sigma at GE have been underestimated, as a result of these financial controls and audits. This conservative estimation of benefits has been even greater in Design for Six Sigma (DFSS) projects, which typically do not have a direct base of reference to which costs can be compared. Interestingly, the net payoff from Six Sigma that first year was negative: $200 million invested, $170 million saved. GE leadership accepted this, realizing that it would have significant start-up costs. In this first year, the businesses were pushed for activity, not necessarily for tangible results. This changed in 1997.

The Push for Tangible Benefits

Jack had given the businesses investment money to backfill MBBs and Black Belts, conduct training, and so on. By 1997, he was expecting a payoff. To reinforce the point, he announced that 40 percent of bonuses paid to managers would be tied to Six Sigma results. This certainly got people's attention, and the money began to roll in seriously in 1997. The official numbers for 1997 were $400 million invested, $700 million saved.

Recall that all of these numbers were rigorously audited—no creative accounting was involved. In 1997, GE also began to place heavier focus on three initiatives that had begun in 1996: commercial quality (CQ) applications, creation of Green Belts (GBs), and Design for Six Sigma (DFSS). As noted, the initial applications of Six Sigma had focused on improvements in manufacturing. However, GE Capital, a large financial services conglomerate in itself, accounted for approximately 40 percent of GE's profits at that time. Focusing on manufacturing would miss at least 40 percent of the potential benefits to the company.

Similarly, even in an engineering company such as GE Aircraft Engines or GE Power Systems, a very small percentage of the people or work processes are directly associated with manufacturing. For example, manufacturing businesses have accounts payable and accounts receivable processes, inventory management processes, pricing processes, and so on, each of which involve large sums of money. We gradually discovered that there is often more money to be found, and obtained more easily, in these processes than there is in manufacturing. We referred to these processes originally as transactional quality, although we later changed the terminology to commercial quality (CQ).

GE had to pretty much pioneer the field. We weren't able to find anyone who had done CQ deployment in a holistic, systematic way, or who knew a lot about it. This was also a learning experience for me, too, because most of my previous experience had been in manufacturing and engineering improvements. In 1997, I was asked to focus on CQ, and I took a leap of faith that Six Sigma would apply equally well here; admittedly, at the time, I had no idea how. One project in credit card collections that resulted in annual savings of $2.9 million (see Hahn, Doganaksoy, and Hoerl, 2000) solidified my convictions that Six Sigma would apply anywhere. Surprisingly, at that time, most other corporations focused on manufacturing in their Six Sigma efforts. A couple of showcase nonmanufacturing examples were identified, but based on the published literature, the vast majority of the effort appeared to be stuck in manufacturing.

DFSS and a Critical Mass of Green Belts

The second big push in 1997 was with DFSS. We were discovering that there were limits to the level of improvement we could obtain with existing processes. At some point, we needed a new design to reach a step-change level of improvement beyond the entitlement of the existing process. This was equally true for soft processes, such as handling manual account reconciliation, as with hard processes, such as running antiquated manufacturing equipment. As with CQ applications, there was no textbook solution. We enlisted the assistance of a consultant, who brought valuable additional tools and a framework in which to integrate them.

Combining these tools and this framework with what we already had, we developed an overall process for DFSS that was analogous to DMAIC: Define, Measure, Analyze, Design, Verify (DMADV). Rolling out this process across GE became a focal point for corporate R&D. It led to such success stories as the LightSpeed CT scanner from GE Medical Systems, which reduced full-body CT scans from about 3 minutes to less than 30 seconds and brought $60 million in orders in the first 90 days of release (see the 1998 GE Annual Report).

The third big push in 1997 was creating a critical mass of Green Belts to complement the MBBs and Black Belts. Businesses were putting their best people into MBB and Black Belt roles. Those chosen were receiving intangible rewards such as recognition and visibility, and they soon started receiving tangible rewards, including bonuses and stock option grants. Understandably, many of those not selected for MBB or Black Belt roles, especially those who wanted to be, began to feel left out. A we–they mind-set between those who were directly involved in Six Sigma and those who weren't began to develop. This could have caused serious problems if not addressed promptly. Obviously, nothing less than getting everyone in the game was required to completely transform the company. This is a lot easier said than done.

The creation of the Green Belt role had been announced previously, but now it was receiving major emphasis. These Green Belts would be people trained in the methodology of Six Sigma who applied it to their work part time. They would still be accountable for their regular duties, but they would also conduct Six Sigma projects. With dedicated MBBs and Black Belts maintaining momentum, this move turned out to be an excellent way of ensuring that everyone could get into the Six Sigma game. And just about everyone did.

A Refocus on Customers

The focus of Six Sigma changed again in 1998. Although senior management was ecstatic about the bottom-line impact Six Sigma was having on the company, leaders were disturbed with feedback from key customers. The quote that appeared in the 1998 Annual Report was: "When do I get the benefits of Six Sigma? When does my company get to experience the GE I read about in the GE Annual Report?"

Up to this point, most projects had focused on opportunities for GE to generate internal savings. While many of these process improvements ultimately affected customers positively, at that time, it was certainly fair to say that Six Sigma had done more for GE's stockholders than for its customers. In 1998, the direction was to focus more projects on direct customer issues, such as product delivery processes. In addition, primary emphasis was placed on reducing variation in such processes, not just fixing the average. The 1998 Annual Report is one of very few instances of a Fortune 500 CEO providing a detailed explanation of why focusing on the average is insufficient and why a company must reduce process variation as well.

Application to Finance

In November 1998, I became the Quality Leader of the corporate audit staff (CAS), a part of corporate finance. While maintaining a core competency in financial auditing, CAS devotes considerable effort to driving corporate initiatives (such as Six Sigma, globalization, services growth, and e-commerce), compliance issues, acquisitions, and other critical business issues. It obtains additional influence from the fact that it is a key leadership development program in GE, with a number of key business leaders being graduates of CAS.

The head of CAS wanted to accelerate the staff's Six Sigma efforts and make sure they were in a position to be true Six Sigma leaders, particularly in financial applications. I knew virtually nothing about finance, but I had a core belief that Six Sigma could (and should) be applied everywhere. Personally, it was somewhat of a challenge to prove my belief. Some auditors initially balked, but both the leader of CAS and his replacement made it clear that Six Sigma would be implemented in a way to ensure success. This leadership commitment won 80 percent of the battle. I was able to focus entirely on deployment, without wasting any time trying to win people over. This reinforced my belief that there is no substitute for leadership!

Details of CAS's Six Sigma efforts have been well documented (Hoerl, 2001). Six Sigma went from being added work to being a means of doing better finance. CAS (in partnership with GE businesses) pioneered the use of Six Sigma in a variety of application areas, such as digitization (e-commerce), cash flow, collections, product delivery, reserves, the auditing process, hedging of foreign currencies, compliance, acquisition integration, and many others. Snee and Hoerl (2003) have provided a list of 20 specific financial projects completed at CAS.

Digitization and Six Sigma

In 1999, dotcoms were all the rage and there was a general belief that small startups were in a much better position to succeed in e-commerce than large conglomerates. Blue-chip companies were seen as too slow to change and stuck in a traditional business paradigm. GE took the Internet seriously, however, and began pushing web-based business, as well as internal digitization. Many businesses started putting their Quality Leaders and MBBs into e-commerce roles. Part of the rationale was that these employees tended to be the top talent in the company, and part was a desire to put those with a Six Sigma mind-set into e-commerce.

At the Research Center, which I was to return to shortly, we took a DFSS approach to digitizing business processes, such as cash application, deal approval, and new product development. Six Sigma's rigor forced us to take a holistic approach and avoid the rush to get websites online without thinking through the overall business process. This enabled us to avoid the fulfillment trap that plagued many dotcoms: They were great at putting up websites and taking orders, but they had poorly designed fulfillment processes. Although I have only anecdotal evidence that Six Sigma significantly impacted our e-commerce efforts, it seems a strange coincidence that a huge conglomerate such as GE was subsequently named the e-commerce company of the year by business publications such as *Internetweek* (June 2000). More recently, GE has become a leading proponent of the Internet of Things (IoT).

At the Customer, for the Customer (ACFC)

The focus in 2000 was primarily on making Six Sigma work for customers and on institutionalizing it into the GE culture. The push to enable customers to feel the benefits of Six Sigma had begun some time ago, but we were now taking it to a new level. We progressed from doing projects that would benefit customers, to partnering with customers on joint projects, to having GE Black Belts go into customer operations and do projects solely for the benefit of the customer. This type of project was referred to as "at the customer, for the customer."

The vast majority of these projects done for customers were completed at GE expense, with no direct monetary reward for GE. The primary motivation is improved customer relationships and loyalty. The competition can always cut its prices to match ours and might be able to provide similar product features, in some cases, but none can offer the same level of Six Sigma expertise. This unique benefit gives GE a significant advantage in wooing major customers. More than 2,000 at the customer, for the customer (ACFC) projects were documented in the first year.

We refer to the application of Six Sigma to e-commerce, along with a clear focus on customer needs through such initiatives as ACFC, as Six Sigma Version 1.1.

An Expansion and Reinvigoration

In 2001, new CEO Jeff Immelt announced a reinvigoration of Six Sigma. This was an important step symbolically because there was some concern that the emphasis on Six Sigma might decline once Jack Welch retired. The reinvigoration included a push to further increase the percentage of senior executives with dedicated Six Sigma experience, acceleration of ACFC projects (more than 10,000 in 2002), and standardization of Black Belt course material and certification criteria across the company.

Soon thereafter, GE started incorporating additional methods into the improvement portfolio. Up to this point, the focus had been almost exclusively on Six Sigma. Gradually, Lean training and Lean projects started appearing. Within a few years, the initiative was formally relaunched as Lean Six Sigma, what we today call Lean Six Sigma 1.2. Lean approaches were incorporated into the training system, and more projects used primarily Lean tools, such as value-stream mapping, 5S, and Kaizen events to shift to line-of-sight production lines. Initially, some unhealthy competition temporarily cropped up between Six Sigma and Lean proponents, but as the initiatives were merged, this gradually faded.

Other methods were added to the mix as well. For example, Work-Out had been around for decades but, to some degree, got lost in the shuffle of Six Sigma. People began to realize that, for more straightforward problems, Work-Out was still a useful approach that could general results faster than Lean or Six Sigma. I was personally involved in some of these formal Work-Out sessions. Some businesses, such as GE Transportation, the locomotive business, utilized the Shainin methods for problem solving (Steiner et al., 2008). Some of these methods were also incorporated into Lean Six Sigma curricula, broadening them further.

Connection to Innovation and New Product Development

At the GE Global Research Center, the quality organization began to seriously study the science of innovation and how it might be integrated with Lean Six Sigma. Clearly, there was a need to incorporate additional methodologies beyond DFSS to what would be called quality by design today. This was particularly true in conceptual design. Xu et al. (2006) provided a map between idea generation, conceptual design, and product launch. TRIZ was identified as a key tool to be employed in developing conceptual designs that would address design contradictions, as discussed in Chapter 3, "Key Methodologies in a Holistic Improvement System." TRIZ was subsequently added to the training conducted by the quality organization at GE Global Research, particularly for scientists and engineering.

Externally, Birkinshaw and Gibson (2004) noted the importance of organizations becoming ambidextrous—that is, being able to both innovate and perform efficiently—in order to prosper over the long term. Hoerl and Gardner (2010) built upon this discussion, specifically looking at the integration of creativity, innovation, and Lean Six Sigma. In some sense, the combination of these streams of research can be viewed as the beginning of Lean Six Sigma 1.3.

Lessons Learned

This case study illustrates several important points relative to holistic improvement:

- GE was a leader in the development and application of Six Sigma and Lean Six Sigma; much can be learned from its experiences.

- Six Sigma can produce tremendous financial returns, measured in the billions of dollars.

- Despite this financial impact, Six Sigma was not able to solve all the issues in GE. Other approaches were added and integrated over time.

- Top leadership commitment is a critical success factor.

In summary, although GE was not the originator of Six Sigma, it clearly had a critical role in its development and evolution, not to mention its popularity. In particular, GE can be viewed as the primary developer of Version 1.1 and also played a key role in developing Versions 1.2 and 1.3 (refer back to Table 4.1).

Case Study: The DuPont Story

The DuPont Company was founded in 1802 to produce high quality black powder. At that time, the quality of black powder in the United States was very poor (DuPont Company, 1952). Guides at the Hagley Museum in Wilmington Delaware, the site of DuPont's original powder mill on the Brandywine River, explain that DuPont's advantages partly came from developing a device to measure the explosive charge of gunpowder in manufacturing, which then enabled the company to reduce variation below that of their competitors (Hoerl, 1990).

The DuPont Company has gone through many changes during its more than 200 years. Science and technology have been at its core, with DuPont's businesses focused on bringing innovative, high-quality products to market. In 2002, the company had annual revenues of $24 billion. Such a large and diverse company, often led by scientists and engineers, naturally produces many different approaches to improvement.

The DuPont Story is important to this book's theme of holistic improvement because it shows how a major global company can build on its improvement history, deploy improvement across the corporation to all its businesses, and expand and integrate improvement methodologies as it encounters new improvement challenges and opportunities.

Improvement at DuPont: 1950–1990s

Before we get to the story of Six Sigma at DuPont, we need to look at the various approaches the company used before the deployment of Six Sigma. We will see that DuPont continually focused on improving products and processes. We will also see that, as the discipline of continuous improvement advanced, DuPont utilized an evolution of approaches, retaining the useful aspects of the current approaches and adding newer approaches to overcome the limitations (Snee, 2004a).

Beginning in the 1950s, DuPont utilized formal approaches to design, control, and improvement of products and processes in various parts of the company. Statistical quality control (SQC), statistical process control (SPC), and design of experiments (DOE) were used in varying degrees in different parts of the company. These methods were applied and promoted by DuPont's Applied Statistics Group (ASG), which was part of the Engineering Department. Arthur E. Hoerl (Roger Hoerl's father) was the first member of this group and the first statistician DuPont hired in 1950. Ron Snee worked in the group from 1968 to 1991. Roger Hoerl served as a summer intern in the group in 1981 and 1982 while in graduate school.

Over the years, DuPont personnel broadly used formal techniques for improvement. During the 1960s and into the 1970s, ASG taught many workshops on Strategy of Experimentation (SOE) which relied heavily on DOE techniques. Courses and workshops were also offered on SQC and SPC and related statistical methods. Additionally, ASG developed and distributed software to implement these techniques, which was a novel contribution at that time.

Strategy of Experimentation

As noted previously, ASG promoted the use of design of experiments utilizing a strategic approach called Strategy of Experimentation (SOE). The SOE approach put business needs first and then provided a strategy to identify what experiments should be run to solve the stated problem, meet the objectives of the study, and so on. The SOE approach integrated a variety of DOE concepts, methods, and tools to accomplish this goal. SOE is itself an example of a holistic approach to experimentation. As of 2015, more than 40,000 DuPont employees had participated in the SOE workshop (Bailey, 2017b). Beginning in the mid-1970s, DuPont externally marketed SOE.

Product Quality Management

In the mid-1970s, DuPont's Dacron fiber business experienced a quality crisis that threatened the future of the business. Leadership felt that greater product consistency was needed across the eight global manufacturing sites. To accomplish these objectives, procedures were needed for the consistent application of improvement tools to meet business needs, and novel approaches were needed to manage the connections between technology and business functions. The global business systems concept and Product Quality Management (PQM) were born within DuPont. PQM had two components:

- A framework for managing the quality of a product or service

- An operational system that enabled marketing, R&D, production, and support personnel to work together to meet increasingly stringent customer requirements

The PQM system technology consisted of sampling and data collection strategies, production process control, measurement process control, product release, and product and process audits and reviews. Here we see another early instance of integration of diverse tools and approaches, a hallmark of holistic improvement.

Although statistical tools were used to address most of these needs, the paradigm was now reversed. DuPont was leading with the business need, not the technology. The business needs addressed follow:

- Setting specifications

- Handling product characterization and release

- Improving process and product performance

- Communicating with customers

- Managing and improving test methods

- Measuring and monitoring progress

- Keeping the system up-to-date

Within a year the quality crisis was resolved and a new era had begun. Richard E. Heckert, DuPont Chairman and CEO, commented: "Within two years product quality had improved to the point of commanding a marketplace advantage and more than $30 million had been gained in operating cost improvements. The data-based Product Quality Management system developed for Dacron was expanded to other products with further contributions in earnings" (Heckert, 1986).

Other Approaches

Several other quality initiatives were launched within DuPont in the same general time frame. In the early 1980s, for example, the "quality revolution" began in the United States in response to foreign competition. Much of this competition came from Japan and fueled the NBC whitepaper, *If Japan Can, Why Can't We?* Foreign competition was also affecting DuPont. Two of DuPont's biggest businesses, Polymers and Textile Fibers, were major leaders in this effort. Textiles had begun its own quality revolution in the 1970s with its development of and focus on PQM. Now DuPont's Project Engineering Division used a Quality in Engineering initiative to focus on improvement within engineering.

With the advent of the Malcolm Baldrige National Quality Award (MBNQA) in 1988, DuPont turned its focus to a Corporate Continuous Improvement System based on the Baldrige Criteria. Motorola had won the Baldrige Award in 1988 and was requiring its suppliers, one of which was DuPont Electronics, to apply for the award. Several DuPont businesses proceeded to develop improvement initiatives based on the Baldrige Criteria. The Textile Fibers and Polymer Products businesses subsequently applied for the MBNQA.

The ISO 9000 quality standard was released in the late 1980s and became important to DuPont in two ways. First, it provided a minimal system for establishing the quality of products and processes. More important, however, ISO certification was being required to do business in Europe. The DuPont Applied Statistics Group, which became known as the Quality Management and Technology Center (QMTC), led the way in this initiative, providing training and consultation on ISO certification. In the 2000s the ISO Quality work was transferred elsewhere in DuPont and the QMTC returned to its focus on applied statistics under the banner of The DuPont Applied Statistics Group.

Six Sigma Begins in 1998

The approaches discussed previously were in use in DuPont in the 1990s and served as a basis for the deployment of Six Sigma, which began in 1998. The deployment approach used at DuPont relied heavily on the experiences of GE and AlliedSignal, which had initiated their Six Sigma deployments earlier in the 1990s. Here we discuss the overall deployment of Six Sigma at DuPont, with a focus on the growth, breadth, and depth of the deployment as it grew into a holistic approach. Harry and Linsenmann (2006) provide further details of the deployment and some of the significant improvement projects conducted.

DuPont Specialty Chemicals was the first business unit to deploy Six Sigma in 1998. As discussed previously, DuPont had a strong foundation on which to build because many of the tools and approaches of Six Sigma were already in place. Six Sigma provided the integrating framework to lead improvement in an effective way.

This decision was followed by a corporate-wide deployment beginning in 1999, led by CEO Chad Holliday. Don Linsenmann was appointed Vice President of Six Sigma Deployment to lead the effort. The Six Sigma Academy was contracted to provide the initial Six Sigma training. The initial focus was on operations, first manufacturing in 1999 and then transactions in 2000.

Following GE's lead, DuPont moved Six Sigma into marketing and sales in 2002, focusing on top line growth (TLG) and providing a closer focus on the customer. The push for TLG, which also utilized Design for Six Sigma, involved more than 2,500 TLG projects producing more than $1.5 billion in revenue (Harry and Linsenmann, 2006).

As at GE, the program was called At the Customer, for the Customer. In this initiative, Six Sigma was used to help DuPont customers solve problems, enabling customers to have more effective businesses. This was a reinvigoration of what some DuPont businesses had been doing for a long time. For example, Ron Snee spent eight years of his tenure at DuPont providing statistical and data analytic services to customers of DuPont's Organic Chemicals business.

In 2004, DuPont started to utilize Six Sigma in the R&D function using the Design for Six Sigma (DFSS) approach. The specific project framework utilized was DMADV: Define, Measure, Analyze, Design, Verify. One major reason for the relative ease of internalization of Six Sigma methods in the R&D organizations could be that DuPont did not emphasize Six Sigma as a standalone initiative. Instead it was embedded within the larger, stage-gated new product commercialization framework, alongside strategic marketing methods. The emphasis was never on the methodology, but on the commercially viable end result for the customer.

Lean manufacturing was reintroduced in 2005, producing Lean Six Sigma. We say that Lean was *reintroduced* DuPont had utilized it in the 1980s under the name of continuous flow manufacturing (CFM). Lean Six Sigma integrated the two process objectives, managing the flow of information and materials, as well as improving quality and creating robust processes.

So during the 1999–2004 time frame, DuPont moved its improvement approach from Cost to Cost and Growth, to Cost, Growth, and Customer. The integration of the improvement initiative was accomplished on two main fronts: improvement methodologies and focus of the improvement work. Various improvement methodologies, including Lean and DMADV, were integrated during this time period. Diverse corporate functions became involved and cooperated on the effort—manufacturing, administration, marketing and sales, and R&D, for example.

Important to DuPont's success was the development of a supporting infrastructure for the Lean Six Sigma initiative (Bailey 2017a):

- Overall governance of Lean Six Sigma deployment from the corporate level into the businesses and to the operational units at the process level

- Human resource practices to support deployment, including recognition and reward, certification, and promotion plans

- Information technology tools such as statistical analysis systems, process mapping and modelling, project tracking, and metrics management scorecards

- Creation of database systems, including project management systems and project execution tools

- Finance practices related to project financial return validation rules and audits

In all instances, the supporting infrastructure was integrated with existing systems to eliminate any duplication of work.

Creating a Holistic System

The preceding discussion shows how DuPont Lean Six Sigma involved a number of businesses and management functions. Further evidence of this evolution toward a holistic improvement system is illustrated by the variety of improvement projects discussed by Harry and Linsenmann (2006) and summarized in Table 4.2.

Table 4.2 Examples of DuPont Improvement Projects

Function	Project	Financial Impact
Shipping and transportation	Reduce demurrage time	$750,000
Sales—customer retention	Reduce raw material cost by using DuPont as a single supplier	Customer savings $1.1 million; DuPont revenue increase $2.2 million
Nylon manufacturing cost reduction	Manufacturing, sales, and marketing improvement	$210 million in 2001, 43 percent over savings target; rail car maintenance schedule revision produced $400 million in savings
Quality control for paint	Fading paint colors	$1.8 million in increased sales
Global services	Improvements in HR, procurement, financial reporting, sourcing, and so on	$77 million in first two years of deployment
Production	Cyrel film raw material not meeting specifications	$200,000 due to increased efficiency and less waste; $250,000 in expanded capacity
Legal process streamlining and improvement	Reduce legal case cycle times	$1 million hard savings due to cycle time reduction

Deploying a large number of improvement approaches without integration could create dysfunctional islands of improvement. Fortunately, further integration toward a more holistic approach was possible and undertaken in the form of several subsequent initiatives, noted next.

DuPont Production System

In 2006, with Lean Six Sigma being widely deployed across DuPont businesses, Lean was being employed as an improvement methodology. DuPont took the next step toward integration and expansion of improvement by creating the DuPont Production System (DPS). The DPS covered process management and control, as well as improvement. Although DPS was based on Lean thinking and principles, it still included process management and control methodologies such as product and process sampling for product release, statistical process control, and process modeling.

Modeled after the Toyota Production System, DPS focused on speeding up the value chain by reducing and eliminating waste, redesigning the value chain, and installing pull instead of push manufacturing systems. DPS required some innovative thinking because chemical processes are much different from the "make parts and assemble products" production systems common at Toyota. Peter King (2009), who helped lead the use of Lean in DuPont, discusses some of the unique features of the process industries:

- Capital intensive versus labor intensive

- Throughput limited by equipment instead of labor

- Equipment that is large and difficult to relocate

- Processes that are difficult to start and restart

- Complex product changeover issues

- Finished product inventory versus work in process

- Hidden work in process

- Material flow patterns

This isn't to say that Lean doesn't work in the process industries; Lean just takes on a different form than in the assembly industries.

DuPont Integrated Business Management

Another approach to improvement DuPont used was to integrate the processes along the supply chain, creating an overall supply chain management system called DuPont Integrated Business Management (DIBM). The focus was on optimizing processes, policy, organization, and systems along the supply chain. Lean and Six Sigma were integral to DIBM: Lean focused on the flow of information and material, and Six Sigma focused on speed of improvement, variation reduction, the *how* of problem solution, and continuous improvement.

The infrastructure created in deploying Lean Six Sigma was easily revised to include the use of Lean principles and tools in both the DuPont Production System and the DuPont Integrated Business Management System.

Product Commercialization Framework

Shortly after the deployment of Six Sigma in R&D, DuPont saw the need to bring marketing, sales, and R&D together under the umbrella of the Product Commercialization Framework (PCF). DuPont was a market-driven science company and focused on moving useful, customer-valued ideas through its development pipeline. This was accomplished through the discipline of a stage-gate product development process supported by extensive use of Six Sigma projects and tools.

Training in various Six Sigma methodologies was heavily focused on innovation process champions. These were future innovation leaders drawn from both the marketing side and the technology side of the organization. The innovation process champions from marketing and R&D trained together and worked together. The focus was on high-level projects that enabled organizations to push improvement and innovation along the pipeline.

Lessons Learned

DuPont's Lean Six Sigma deployment was successful in part because it did a lot of the right things learned from the GE and AlliedSignal experiences:

- Leadership by top management

- Clear bottom-line focus

- Involvement of top talent

- Supporting infrastructure created, including recognition and reward systems

- Holistic focus, including deployment in all aspects of the business and integration of a wide variety of improvement concepts, methods, and tools

The deployment and impact grew in breadth and depth as experience developed and as the company encountered new opportunities and challenges. This growth led to a more holistic approach: As more aspects of

DuPont's business deployed Lean Six Sigma, improvement methodologies were integrated. Business systems then were developed that embedded Lean Six Sigma methodologies in the resulting approaches.

DuPont's Lean Six Sigma initiative was very successful, producing billions of dollars in bottom-line savings and additional revenue (top-line growth). Harry and Linsenmann (2006) report the following:

- Specialty Chemicals: $100 million in the first two years
- DuPont Corporate: $1 billion in first year and $2.3 billion in the first five years

It is instructive to express Lean Six Sigma savings as a percent of annual revenue yielding:

- Specialty Chemicals ($1.5 billion annual revenue)—3.3 percent per year, for $100 million savings in two years
- DuPont Corporate ($24 billion in 2002)—4.2 percent per year in first year, for $1 billion savings; 1.9 percent per year in first five years, for $2.3 billion savings in five years

These annualized returns compare favorably with experiences of other companies: 2 to 4 percent for companies with annual revenues of $1 billion to 4 billion , and 1 to 2 percent for larger companies (Snee, 2004b).

Case Study: The Scott Paper Experience with Holistic Improvement

Scott Paper Company is not a name people in the quality field typically think of when discussing world-class continuous improvement systems. After all, Kimberly-Clark bought out the company in 1995, after Scott Paper fell into severe financial difficulties. However, partially in response to its financial difficulties, Scott Paper was making serious efforts to improve the quality of its products and services in the late 1980s and 1990s. Tangible results from these efforts were only beginning to appear at the time of the buy-out, but some important lessons can be gleaned from Scott's efforts, both positive and negative.

We present this case study for several reasons. First of all, it illustrates how diverse improvement approaches are needed to drive significant improvement. As we will see, these approaches were originally not integrated well, causing serious deployment issues. However, later integration efforts led to considerable synergy. Integration of multiple methodologies rather than a focus on individual tools is a core principle of holistic improvement. One of the important lessons learned from the Scott Paper story is that tactical efforts to deploy improvement methodologies and powerful individual tools are not sufficient to achieve and sustain improvement. As discussed in this case study, there is no substitute for leadership or for sound business strategy and well-planned deployment.

Roger Hoerl worked for Scott Paper at its corporate headquarters in Philadelphia from 1987 until 1995, before he joined GE. This account is based on his Scott Paper experience. It provides an interesting contrast with the Six Sigma deployment at GE. For example, the deployment at Scott never had the same level of senior leadership commitment that Jack Welch provided at GE. The Scott deployment was primarily led by middle managers who saw that this was the right thing to do. For example, a Scott quality policy was developed and shared within the organization, but unfortunately, it was signed by business unit managers in the U.S. business, not the CEO. As discussed elsewhere, an effort led from the middle tends not to be the most successful approach.

Similarly, very little formal infrastructure was developed to support the initiative at Scott Paper. Aside from those within the existing quality organization, no formal roles were developed with specific accountabilities. Instead, people interested in pursuing this work joined in on an informal basis in addition to performing their regular duties. No formal budgets had line items to support improvement efforts, nor were expected tangible benefits incorporated into financial goals. Because of the informality of the effort, individuals tended to select their own projects, without guidance or approval from management. Not surprisingly, when project leaders ran into roadblocks on projects, they did not receive the level of support they hoped for from management because these projects simply were not high on the managers' priority lists.

Given these limitations, it is understandable that Scott Paper was not able to overcome its financial difficulties and survive. However, despite these serious limitations, a lot of valuable quality work was going on in the company in the late 1980s and early 1990s. If these efforts had been better supported by leadership and better managed through formal infrastructure, Scott Paper might still be in existence—and thriving— today. Let's take a look at some of these efforts.

Process Control Initiative

I was hired into the corporate headquarters of Scott Paper Company in Philadelphia in 1987. Scott hired me to plan, organize, and lead a process control initiative across the U.S. tissue business (that is, the business that made tissue products such as toilet paper, paper towels, facial tissue, and so on). There was growing awareness among middle management that poor process control resulted not only in inconsistent product, but also waste, rework, and other unnecessary expenses. The goal was to improve the product quality, particularly consistency, and also reduce manufacturing costs. The focus of the effort at that time was manufacturing.

A major component of the process control initiative was training engineers and hourly workers in statistical process control, particularly control charts. Of course, control charts are key tools in Six Sigma projects, especially in the control phase. Scott used these charts to diagnose problems and help the operators determine when they needed to intervene with the paper-making equipment. In this sense, the charting was part of what we would today call the quality and process management system more than breakthrough improvement.

As the control charting began to take hold, additional methods, such as experimental design, were added to the mix. Experimental design was particularly appealing to engineers, who were trained in the scientific method, and employees at Scott's R&D center, who conducted frequent trials. This method can be considered breakthrough improvement today, but Scott did not use these designations.

The subsidiary of Scott that made printing papers for magazines, S.D. Warren, was at that time deploying an improvement initiative based on the teachings of W. Edwards Deming (Deming, 1986). This approach provided an overall quality philosophy, not a specific set of tools.

Warren therefore began widespread training in Kepner–Tregoe (2013) problem-solving methods such as Is–Is Not analysis. Using benchmarking between the organizations, Scott began to add this training as well, to bolster its existing quality and process management efforts. Similarly, Warren added statistical process control training to its efforts.

Progress was made in enhancing overall process control in the paper and pulp mills, but it was limited by the issues just noted, such as lack of supporting infrastructure. Certainly, the initiative more than paid for itself, but money also was left on the table, in terms of lost opportunities due to limited deployment.

Parallel Efforts

At this same time, other improvement initiatives were ongoing at Scott Paper. Unfortunately, these efforts were not well coordinated initially, resulting in a disjointed approach and sometimes open competition. Organizations often had to choose which improvement approach to select among several alternatives. Two other major efforts at that time were a total productive maintenance initiative and a training initiative focused on hourly workers in the paper mills.

We discussed total productive maintenance (TPM) in Chapter 3 (also see Boris, 2006). Scott was actually an early adopter of TPM in the United States. Major investments were made in enhancing the overall approach to maintenance within the tissue mills. Paper making is a capital-intensive business, requiring very expensive manufacturing equipment. Therefore, making even minor improvements in maintenance can a have huge financial impact. Some of the major focus areas were improving overall uptime of the equipment, reducing maintenance costs, and improving safety. Evidence shows that when maintenance occurs on an emergency basis instead of being planned, accidents are much more likely because employees are rushing in their repair work.

The training initiative utilized the principles of competency-based training, and top-down training, and it radically changed the way hourly employees were trained. In competency-based training, specific competencies are determined as a first step; the employees are expected to master a certain set of tasks that are identified and documented. Then the training is organized to develop these specific skills, including demonstration of expertise. This might sound like common sense, but before this initiative, training hourly employees was typically based on what the engineers thought was important instead of carefully considering the tasks required of the workers. Furthermore, most of the Scott paper mills were unionized, so introducing demonstration tests of required skills was complicated and required negotiation with the unions.

In top-down training, the instruction flows from the big picture to the details. That is, instead of first discussing the specific piece of equipment that the employee would be operating, the instructions first gave an overview of the entire process, making it clear how this employee's work fits into the big picture of making paper. Again, there is evidence that instruction flows more smoothly if those being trained understand the broader context of their work—how what they do fits in with the steps before and after them (Hoerl and Snee, 1995).

These and other initiatives discussed shortly could be considered some of the building blocks of a holistic approach. The specific methodologies and initiatives typical of holistic improvement that were present at Scott Paper follow:

- Statistical process control (SPC)

- Design of experiments

- Kepner–Tregoe (Is–Is Not)

- Total productive maintenance (TPM)

- Competency-based training

- Lean manufacturing

- Quality Function Deployment (QFD)

- Quality system redesign

Most of these are considered part of quality and process management, although there are certainly elements of both breakthrough improvement and quality by design, as we see shortly.

Early Efforts Toward Lean Design

Lean manufacturing principles were well known at this time, as discussed in Chapter 3. However, the term *Lean* was not yet popular. Efforts

---

to eliminate waste, particularly in-process and in final product inventory, were often referred to then as just-in-time (JIT), in the sense that organizations moved to a pull versus a push system (Monden, 2012). Product was produced as needed in the marketplace, and processing steps were utilized only to the extent that they were needed to meet production demands—just in time.

Particularly in its new Italian paper mills, Scott Paper was making serious efforts toward JIT, as well as some other elements of what we would today call Lean. For example, it designed and built paper mills in Alanno (central Italy) and Romagnano Sesia (northern Italy) based on JIT, and it minimized the non-value-added movement of materials. Most paper mills require significant movement of raw materials, pulp, in-process product, and final product, much of which is wasteful because it doesn't add value. Moving large rolls of paper to the third floor for storage and then bringing them back to the first floor a month later for processing does not make the final product any more valuable, but it certainly adds cost.

The equipment in the new Italian mills was logically laid out so that the product naturally moved from one workstation to the next one, with no unnecessary transportation required. Most paper mills I'd visited had fleets of forklift trucks to move materials and a crew of forklift drivers. The mill in Alanno had only one forklift, used primarily for moving equipment. Furthermore, these mills were kept impeccably clean, another key Lean principle that today falls under the 5S approach. I was shocked to see clean floors with no puddles of water or oil when I visited these mills.

In discussions with the Alanno plant manager, we learned that he had also designed the mill. His leadership had told him that he would manage the plant for at least five years after it opened. Knowing that he would be responsible for the quality and cost of the facility for five years led him to think very differently about the design. In particular, he was motivated to design a mill to succeed long term, even if it required a little more upfront time and cost in construction. This strategy worked.

Scott subsequently utilized these same principles of minimal movement of materials, a clean work environment, and significant cross-training of hourly workers in the design and construction of a new paper mill in Owensboro, Kentucky. Today we would consider this mill to be based on the principles of Lean manufacturing. As with the Italian mills, the Owensboro mill proved to be considerably more efficient—and, ultimately, more profitable—than traditional Scott Paper mills. A major disappointment is that these same principles were not deployed across all mills within the corporation.

Reorganization of the Quality Organization

Around 1990, Scott began to experience financial difficulties, for a variety of reasons that are beyond the scope of this book. As a result, Scott soon began a series of major layoffs that impacted most of the U.S. businesses, including corporate headquarters. I survived the layoffs, but after one of them in 1992, I landed in a new position. Instead of leading the process control initiative, I was assigned to lead the corporate quality group. Management felt that the quality management system in place at the time was outdated and needed to be modernized. I agreed with them.

This quality management system had a number of limitations, but a major issue was that it was very much inspection based—that is, it was oriented toward finding bad product before it was shipped to customers instead of controlling processes tightly to ensure that bad product wasn't made. Furthermore, the quality organization owned most of the responsibility for ensuring quality in products and services. In other words, manufacturing was primarily responsible for handling productivity, and sales and marketing were primarily responsible for driving sales through the distribution channels. If there was a quality problem, the first phone to ring was within the quality organization.

The fundamentals of quality management (Juran, 1988) assert that inspection-based systems are inefficient and, in general, do not succeed. In the 1970s and 1980s, many U.S.-based companies had started moving to a more process control–oriented quality system. Those with good process control were moving to a quality by design approach. Similarly, it is generally well accepted (Juran, 1988; Deming, 1986) that the people making the product or providing the service should be primarily responsible for quality. The quality organization has an important role, but it should focus on managing the overall system, not trying to correct mistakes made in other departments. In short, everyone should be responsible for the quality of his or her own work.

We began a multiyear journey to move from the traditional system to one based on modern quality principles and methods. The concept of holistic improvement was not clear to us at the time, but it soon became obvious that, to control processes well, the right tools were needed—SPC, design of experiments, and so on. We therefore embedded the use of statistical and quality tools into the quality management system. For example, the new quality information system replaced tables of data with control charts of key parameters, as well as exception reports based on statistical signals that important product or process variables had changed over time. Such tools help managers focus on the most important information instead of asking them to wade through pages of numbers to find something noteworthy. Clearly, *data* is not synonymous with *information*, much less *insight*.

As a second example, the system for periodically evaluating the laboratory measurement of paper incorporated designed experiments to quantify accuracy, precision, and stability over time of the measurement system (Hoerl and Snee, 2012). As one example of early integration of methods, we realized that the top-down training principles being developed for machine operators would work well in quality training and drive consistency across the organization.

As might be imagined, the journey was not an easy one and met with significant resistance. My greatest surprise was discovering that many people did not want to accept responsibility for the quality of their own work. For example, people in marketing, who were responsible for product design to fulfill the brand strategy, often said to us: "Quality is not my responsibility—it's yours." I was amazed that people responsible for the financial success or failure of the brand would want to outsource the design of their product. Similarly, some managers in manufacturing did not want to be held accountable for the quality of the product they produced. They were happy to be measured on productivity, safety, or cost, but not quality. This was an excellent illustration of the importance of business strategy and values, and it showed why the quality system must be in alignment with the strategy to achieve success. A quality system cannot be installed in a vacuum.

Quality by Design

As part of the ongoing quality improvement and process control efforts, it became painfully clear that, for some of the products currently on the market, the fundamental problem was not a lack of process control, but rather products that were poorly designed in the first place. That is, even if manufacturing could perfectly match the product specifications in production, customers still wouldn't find the product attractive, at least not relative to competitive products on the market. With hindsight, this is another illustration of the importance of an integrated approach to improvement, linking quality management and process control with improvement methods and also incorporating quality by design.

Quality Function Deployment (QFD), discussed in Chapter 3, was chosen as a key methodology to guide the design efforts for three major brands, Scott Tissue, Scott Towels, and Scotties (table napkins). QFD was selected for several reasons: It was becoming very popular in the United States, primarily because of its broad usage in the automotive industry at that time; it is a knowledge-based tool, and management believed that the organization had the collective expertise to determine a redesign that would likely succeed in the marketplace; and it is a collaborative process, utilizing a transparent team approach.

This last point was considered important because, due to some of the leadership issues noted earlier, there was significant distrust between different parts of the organization. For example, manufacturing personnel were concerned that research and development folks would design a product that couldn't be effectively produced, the hourly workers were concerned that changes would cause production problems that would make their lives more difficult, and marketing leaders were concerned that manufacturing personnel would design a product that was easy to make but very hard to sell.

Although it took time, the QFD approach involving all relevant parts of the business and facilitated by the new quality organization proved to be a very effective process. Over a couple of years, all three products were substantially redesigned to better match customer needs and also ensure that the product could be efficiently manufactured. These redesigns resulted in better performance in the marketplace, as well as more consistent production.

Perhaps most important, the use of this process began to build trust within the organization. As an added bonus, having the quality organization facilitate the process—bringing in expertise in the methods themselves, but staying out of the business decisions on redesign—helped solidify the group's new role as being responsible for management of the quality system and quality methodologies, but not assuming responsibility for product quality. Marketing ultimately owned the design, and manufacturing ultimately owned conformance to the design in production.

Early Attempts at Integration

Fortunately, some people within the ranks of Scott Paper management realized there would be significant advantages to integrating the improvement efforts discussed earlier. Clearly, integrating multiple methodologies is at the heart of holistic improvement. As noted previously, most of the improvement efforts were originally led by different people with different objectives and were not well integrated.

The manufacturing organizations were therefore typically bombarded with requests to participate in the SPC rollout, competency-based training, TPM, quality by design efforts, quality system redesign, and so on. This was obviously overwhelming for folks whose primary responsibility was to get good product out the door each and every day. Manufacturing managers could pick and choose efforts to participate in, based on personal preference, or simply gave up and opted not to participate in any. Recall that these efforts were not led by senior management, so there was no coordinated vision or direction to lower-level managers.

One of the midlevel managers at Scott Paper had previous experience with another paper company that had utilized an early version of holistic improvement. According to him, management had developed an overall vision there for coordinated improvement efforts. The intent was, as it is today, to fit the solution to the problem instead of the other way around. This manager's experience turned out to be extremely helpful at Scott Paper.

As a first step, those leading the various improvement efforts were brought into the same organizational group. Obviously, it is very difficult to integrate efforts led by different organizations that might have different objectives. A quality laboratory within the R&D organization that was developing new paper-testing methodologies was also brought into this improvement group. This way, the group developing new test methods and the group responsible for overseeing usage of the test methods in the paper mills were within the same organization.

An even more important advantage of integration was the new way this organization would approach manufacturing units. Instead of having several individuals come from headquarters to promote their own methods and make a pitch for manufacturing to adopt their approach, there was now one team. This team would set up interactions with manufacturing to discuss their current situation, their issues, and where they felt they most needed help. This was, in essence, a holistic approach, that chose the methodology to fit the specific problem instead of choosing the method in advance.

Based on these interactions, overall priorities were set and roles were clarified. The manufacturing unit now had a major role to play, not only in clarifying its own problems, but also in determining its own priorities for improvement. Furthermore, the team was integrally involved in selecting its own solutions, with guidance and help from the improvement organization. The manufacturing unit might determine that SPC was most needed or, because of ongoing maintenance struggles, TPM was most important at this time. In some cases, a combination of methods, rolled out in a logical sequence, was chosen. In short, we found these interactions to be much more productive than series of individuals pushing their own methods.

Unfortunately, the broader issues at Scott Paper, discussed previously, began to overshadow these improvement efforts. As discussions of mergers and potential acquisitions became common, managers were less willing to launch major improvement efforts that might not be completed in an uncertain future. In 1995, Kimberly-Clark announced its intentions to purchase most of Scott Paper Company, and the acquisition was completed in December of that year. Products under the Scott brand are still sold by Kimberly-Clark, but the Scott Paper Company no longer exists.

Lessons Learned

Scott Paper's experience gives us some important lessons:

- There is no substitute for leadership.
- A key element of leadership is to provide a clear vision for improvement.
- Infrastructure is critical to support improvement efforts.
- No single methodology can address all the improvement needs of an organization.
- Integration of multiple methodologies, not competing approaches, is core to holistic improvement.

Scott Paper certainly did not invent these principles; they are more common sense ideas that intelligent people would eventually think of themselves. However, it is true that Scott Paper applied many of the principles and methods discussed in this book, despite its leadership issues.

Unfortunately, Scott Paper's experience provides another reminder that there is no substitute for leadership. Without a good business strategy and motivational vision provided to the organization based on this strategy, people within the organization can do little to ensure long-term success. Leading from the middle is not a winning strategy for holistic improvement. Scott Paper lacked the vision and leadership of Jack Welch at GE, and in my opinion (and others' as well), this is what ultimately made the company a relic of the past.

True leadership, as in the case of Jack Welch at GE, understands the importance of infrastructure, the organizational systems and structure that are needed to sustain improvement efforts. Infrastructure refers to such things as well-defined and -documented roles, inclusion into budgeting and planning systems, management-led project selection and review systems, and so on. We discuss each of these systems in more detail in later chapters. Without a solid infrastructure, driving improvement is like swimming upstream against the current: lots of resistance and limited progress. However, with infrastructure supporting the effort, it is more like swimming downstream with the current—making progress is much easier.

Scott realized early in its journey that no single methodology, whether it be SPC, TPM, design of experiments, JIT (Lean), or anything else, would address all the improvement needs within the organization. Multiple methods are required for different types of improvement needs. Of course, launching multiple methods that are not well integrated typically results in disjointed efforts and, eventually, competition for resources and management's attention. Scott began with disjointed improvement efforts, but it eventually saw the problems being caused by this approach and worked toward integration. The effort to integrate quality and process management with quality by design and breakthrough improvement methods under one umbrella was perhaps particularly advanced for that time. Unfortunately, it turned out to be too little, too late. On the positive side, we are in a great position to learn from Scott Paper's mistakes and avoid them ourselves.

Summary and Looking Forward

Much can be learned from studying the experience of companies using Lean Six Sigma over a long period of time. The deployment and impact grows in breadth and depth as experience develops and new opportunities and challenges are encountered. These three case studies illustrate the following critical success factors.

- A holistic focus includes deployment in all aspects of the business and integration of a wide variety of improvement concepts, methods, and tools.

- Top leadership commitment and involvement is a critical success factor. A key element of leadership is to provide a clear vision for improvement.

- There must be a clear bottom-line focus. Six Sigma can produce tremendous financial returns, measured in the billions of dollars.

- Involvement of top talent is critical. Improvement, or changing how we work, is too important and too difficult to be left to anyone who is not a recognized leader in the organization.

- Despite its impact, Six Sigma was not able to solve all the issues in these companies, so other approaches were added and integrated over time. No single methodology can address all the improvement needs of an organization.

- Integration of multiple methodologies, not competing approaches, is core to holistic improvement

- Supporting infrastructure is critical to support improvement efforts. The infrastructure created should also include recognition and reward systems.

In our experience, these success factors apply to all deployments, ensuring successful launches, steady growth of deployments, and, ultimately, a holistic approach to improvement. In the next chapter, we discuss how to successfully implement Lean Six Sigma with an eye toward evolving the long-term approach to holistic improvement.

References

Bailey, S. P. (2017a) "DuPont Six Sigma Deployment: Experiences and Recommended Practices." National Lean and Six Sigma Forum, Costa Rica, March 24.

Bailey, S. P. (2017b) "From Statistical Consultant to Effective Leader." Presented at Joint Statistical Meetings, Baltimore, MD, July 29.

Birkinshaw, J., and C. Gibson. (2004) "Building Ambidexterity into an Organization." *MIT Sloan Management Review* 45, no. 4: 47–55.

Borris, S. (2006) *Total Productive Maintenance.* New York: McGraw-Hill.

Deming, W. E. (1986) *Out of the Crises.* Cambridge, MA: MIT Press.

DuPont Company. (1952) *DuPont: An Autobiography of an American Enterprise.* Wilmington, DE: E. I. DuPont de Nemours and Company.

Hahn, G. J, N. Doganaksoy, and R. W. Hoerl. (2000) "The Evolution of Six Sigma." *Quality Engineering* 12, no. 3: 317–326.

Harry, M., and D. Linsenmann. (2006) *The Six Sigma Fieldbook: Based on DuPont's Successful World-Wide Six Sigma Deployment.* New York: Currency Doubleday.

Heckert, R. E. (1986) "President's Invited Address." American Statistical Association Annual Meeting, Chicago, August, 19.

Hoerl, R. W. (1990) Personal communication.

Hoerl, R.W. (2001) "Six Sigma Black Belts: What Do They Need to Know?" *Journal of Quality Technology* 33, no. 4: 391–435.

Hoerl, R. W., and M. M. Gardner. (2010) "Lean Six Sigma, Creativity, and Innovation." *International Journal of Lean Six Sigma* 1, no. 1: 30–38.

Hoerl, R. W., and R. D. Snee. (1995) *Redesigning the Introductory Statistics Course.* Technical Report #130, Center for Quality and Productivity Improvement, University of Wisconsin–Madison, July.

Hoerl, R. W., and R. D. Snee. (2012) *Statistical Thinking: Improving Business Performance*, 2nd ed. Chichester, UK: John Wiley & Sons.

Juran, J. M. (1988) *Juran on Planning for Quality.* New York: The Free Press.

Kepner, C. H., and B. B. Tregoe. (2013) *The New Rational Manager.* New York: McGraw-Hill.

King, P. L. (2009) *Lean for the Process Industries: Dealing with Complexity.* Boca Raton, FL: CRC Press.

Monden, Y. (2012) *Toyota Production System: An Integrated Approach to Just-In-Time*, 4th ed. Boca Raton, FL: CRC Press.

Pfeiffer, C. G. (1988) "Planning Efficient and Effective Experiments." *Materials Engineering* (May): 35–39.

Snee, R. D. (2004a) "Six Sigma: The Evolution of 100 Years of Business Improvement Methodology." *International Journal of Six Sigma and Competitive Advantage* 1, no. 1: 4–20.

Snee, R. D. (2004b) "Can Six Sigma Boost Your Company's Growth?" *Harvard Management Update* (June): 2–4.

Snee, R. D. (2005) *Six Sigma Beyond the Factory Floor: Deployment Strategies for Financial Services, Health Care and the Rest of the Real Economy.* Upper Saddle River, NJ: Financial Times/Prentice Hall.

Snee, R. D., and R. W. Hoerl. (2003) *Leading Six Sigma: A Step-by-Step Guide Based on Experience with GE and Other Six Sigma Companies.* Upper Saddle River, NJ: Financial Times/Prentice Hall.

Steiner, S. H., R. J. Mackay, and J. S. Ramberg. (2008) "An Overview of the Shainin System for Quality Improvement." *Quality Engineering* 20: 6–19.

Xu, K., C. Sikdar, and M. M. Gardner. (2006) "Six Sigma Roles in Innovation." Presented at the IEEE International Conference on Management of Innovation and Technology, Singapore, June 23.

5

How to Successfully Implement Lean Six Sigma 2.0

"If you don't know where you are going any road will get you there."

—Alice in Wonderland

In previous chapters, we introduced holistic improvement and looked at integrating Lean and Six Sigma as an example of building an improvement system that uses various improvement methodologies. An important point to remember from previous chapters and the cases studies discussed in Snee and Hoerl (2003) is that jumping on the "improvement bandwagon", by any name, is no guarantee of success.

We take another look at those previous case studies in Chapter 4, "Case Studies in Holistic Improvement," and also explore those discussed by Snee and Hoerl (2003) to elaborate on the key factors that have led to significant (or minimal) success in Lean Six Sigma or an overall holistic approach. We show how to analyze the keys to a successful Lean Six Sigma deployment and how to integrate them into a step-by-step process. Such an approach can also be applied to enhance a Lean Six Sigma system or other improvement system currently in place; we refer to this more holistic system as Lean Six Sigma 2.0. In subsequent chapters, we provide more detail on how to effectively move through each deployment phase.

Why Are Organizations Successful in Implementing Lean Six Sigma?

In the first edition of this book (Snee and Hoerl, 2003), we profiled four companies that implemented Lean Six Sigma: GE and W. R. Grace were successful, and Royal Chemicals and Diversified Paper were less success-ful. The names Royal Chemicals and Diversified Paper are fictitious, but the companies behind them are real. They help us identify the success factors for deploying holistic improvement. Furthermore, the experi-ences of the organizations discussed in Chapter 4 illustrate how to lever-age the improvement system to be more holistic. We return to this point later in this chapter.

The discussion of Snee and Hoerl (2003) relates to the status of the companies in the 1999–2002 time period. These initiatives, which were called Six Sigma at the time, contained strong Lean components, includ-ing process simplification, waste reduction, and cycle time reduction. To be consistent with previous chapters, we refer to these initiatives using Lean Six Sigma terminology.

On the surface, GE and Grace are as different as two companies might be. GE is recognized throughout the world, and its 2001 revenues were about $130 billion. Both the giant conglomerate and its previous CEO, Jack Welch, have been studied and reported on by business schools and in journals for 20 years. Grace is a small company with a few niche mar-kets. Many consumers, not to mention business scholars, will likely be unfamiliar with it.

Yet both firms achieved remarkable financial results from Lean Six Sigma. In fact, on some metrics Grace, can be considered even more successful than GE. What did they have in common that led to such success?

Some Common Misconceptions

We should first note what the two companies do not have in common:

- They are at opposite ends of the size spectrum.

- They are not in the same industry.

- They did not use the same Lean Six Sigma deployment provider.

The myth that Lean Six Sigma works only for large companies has likely persisted because business journals, books, and articles tend to focus on sizable companies such as GE ($130 billion in revenue), Bank of America, and AlliedSignal. The successes of small companies, such as Grace ($2 billion in revenue), typically are not visible to the general pub-lic. In reality, big companies have more layers of middle management, which can make effectively implementing Lean Six Sigma more difficult. Change is often easier to introduce in smaller companies.

Another misconception is that Lean Six Sigma applies to only certain industries, such as electronics. This theory is also inconsistent with the available evidence. As of this writing, successful implementations have occurred in all major areas of the economy, from electronics, to healthcare, to insurance, to power generation, to consumer credit, and so on (Snee and Hoerl, 2005).

Lean Six Sigma is a methodology for improving processes, to make them more efficient internally (bottom-line benefits) and more effective at satisfying customers (top-line growth). All businesses need to improve their processes to achieve, maintain, and enhance competitiveness. Even nonprofit organizations and government agencies need to improve their processes to better achieve their objectives. Who would want to invest time or money in an organization that says it has no desire to improve?

GE and Grace also used different Lean Six Sigma providers who recommended slightly different paths to deployment. Providers of Lean Six Sigma training and consulting services often argue over which the "true" Lean Six Sigma methodology is. Trade journals are full of ads from providers claiming that only their unique approach will lead to success. The evidence does not validate these claims. GE and Grace used different providers, but both flourished. Several providers have a long list of successful and very satisfied clients; clearly, no single provider can claim to have a monopoly on winning with Lean Six Sigma.

Success Starts at the Top

If company size, type of industry, and provider were not the determining success factors at GE and Grace, what were? The most obvious commonality in their cases is that, in both companies, success started at the top. Jack Welch led GE's Lean Six Sigma charge with relentless energy and passion. Grace CEO Paul Norris had seen what Lean Six Sigma could do at AlliedSignal and was committed to making it work at his corporation. These CEOs' commitments should be measured not in speeches or quotes from the annual report, but rather in the time, attention, and money they gave to the effort. In both cases, the senior leaders personally drove Lean Six Sigma implementation:

- They ensured that the leadership team was fully on board and had a well-constructed game plan for implementation.

- They provided resources, in terms of people and funding, to properly support the effort.

- They expected, and even demanded, results from the effort.

- They were willing to change internal policies and procedures to support implementation.

Beyond the CEOs, leadership was evident in the designation of overall Lean Six Sigma leaders and the active participation of the rest of the corporate executive teams. In fact, we could argue that getting effective leadership from the top, not just buy-in or support, was the most critical success factor. Many other case studies would help validate this hypothesis (see Harry and Schroeder, 2000).

Lean Six Sigma Requires Top Talent

Another similarity that helps explain GE and Grace's successes is that both put top talent into the Lean Six Sigma initiative. A company might be able to fool market analysts with an impressive PowerPoint presentation, but once the names of individuals going into Lean Six Sigma roles are announced, fooling the rank-and-file employees will be impossible. People generally know their peers well and can immediately evaluate the level of staffing for the Lean Six Sigma effort: Is this top talent, whoever was available, or people who can't do anything else? Many improvement initiatives have failed not because they weren't technically valid, but because they weren't viewed as business critical and thus didn't get the organization's top talent.

An Infrastructure to Support the Effort

Both companies developed an appropriate supporting infrastructure, the network of processes, systems, and organizational structure required to support Lean Six Sigma. This includes designating a leader, identifying specific roles and responsibilities for those involved, obtaining formal systems for utilizing human and financial resources, creating formal processes for project selection and review, and so on. This support network is often formalized by creating a function called the Lean Six Sigma organization, but it does not have to be. Of course, in Lean Six Sigma 2.0, this would be the improvement organization, with Lean and Six Sigma both included.

Any new initiative is likely to die on the vine if it means continued extra work for everyone involved. Creating the appropriate infrastructure supports the effort in the long term because the organization has legitimatized it and ensured that it will be able to obtain needed resources and attention. Lack of a supporting infrastructure is a key reason many Total Quality Management (TQM) initiatives in the late 1980s and early 1990s failed (Snee and Hoerl, 2003).

GE and Grace took certain key actions to create the supporting infrastructure:

- Designated an overall leader for the effort

- Developed formal implementation plans that were reviewed with senior management

- Designated Champions and full-time Master Black Belts (MBBs) and Black Belts

- Introduced formal project selection and review mechanisms

- Formally integrated Lean Six Sigma into the budgeting process, both costs and anticipated savings

- Implemented focused training systems for key roles

- Modified HR, reward and recognition, business planning, financial, and other business systems to support Lean Six Sigma implementation

Proper project selection and regular managerial reviews are particularly important. Both GE and Grace avoided a common problem that plagues many improvement initiatives: huge projects that begin with great intentions and spend large amounts of money but then, months or even years later, have little tangible benefit to show for the effort. Senior management tends to lose faith in such projects, resulting in disenchantment with the initiative and eventual failure. Both companies implemented formal processes that ensured selected projects had these continued characteristics:

- Were strategically important
- Were tied directly to the bottom line or to key customer issues
- Could be completed in a reasonable time frame (three to six months)
- Had the resources to succeed

Similarly, project review processes were set up at different organizational levels. These reviews ensured that appropriate progress was being made and that any barriers to success were identified quickly so they could be addressed by the project Champion. Project selection and review processes such as these minimize the chance that projects will drag on indefinitely, with no tangible results. Figure 5.1 summarizes these common attributes of successful case studies.

Why Were Others Less Successful?

Remember the keys to Lean Six Sigma success at GE and Grace: leadership, top talent, and infrastructure. Using these same criteria, let's look at the less successful efforts at Royal Chemicals and Diversified Paper (remember, these are fictitious company names but real companies).

Very Successful Case Studies	Less Successful Case Studies

• Committed leadership
• Use of top talent
• Supporting infrastructure
  • Formal project selection process
  • Formal project review process
  • Dedicated resources
  • Financial system integration
	• Supportive leadership
	• Use of whoever was available
	• No supporting infrastructure
	  • No formal project selection process
	  • No formal project review process
	  • Part-time resources
	  • Not integrated with financial system

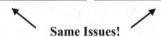

Same Issues!

Figure 5.1 Common attributes of very successful and less successful case studies

How Committed Was Senior Leadership?

This answer should be obvious. Royal Chemicals and Diversified Paper did not share the key attributes of GE and Grace. Neither company had committed leadership; at best, leaders were supportive. At Royal Chemicals, open skepticism questioned whether Lean Six Sigma would work. Similarly, Diversified Paper had no clear corporate leadership.

Now that Lean Six Sigma has achieved a great deal of notoriety, it is sometimes seen as a silver bullet and that that will immediately begin to produce positive results. Such perceptions can cause companies to jump on the bandwagon without carefully considering the commitment required to be successful. As the old saying goes, we need to look before we leap.

Many employees questioned Royal Chemicals' motivation for selecting Lean Six Sigma in the first place. Some felt that it was only a ploy to make Royal a more attractive buyout opportunity. Using a pilot implementation to see if Lean Six Sigma worked clearly demonstrated a lack of confidence on the part of leadership. The leadership team determined that it was too busy for a two-day leadership training session, and then several leaders skipped the reduced one-day session. At that point, we could have safely predicted that this implementation would meet with minimal success.

Similarly, Diversified Paper's decision to allow each business unit to decide whether and when it would deploy Lean Six Sigma tells most of the story. Optional initiatives are not business critical by definition. The leadership decision to restrict Lean Six Sigma to manufacturing operations suggested a lack of understanding of what Lean Six Sigma is all about. Unfortunately, there is no substitute for strong leadership.

Who Was Selected for Key Lean Six Sigma Roles?

Another common problem with these two companies' initiatives was that they did not consistently utilize top talent in their Lean Six Sigma efforts. Certainly, they had some top talent in the Black Belt ranks. However, both Royal Chemicals and Diversified Paper also assigned people to key roles, including Black Belts, who were not viewed as top talent. Diversified Paper generally restricted MBBs and Black Belts to members of the Quality organization. There could well be top talent in the Quality organization, but it is highly unlikely that all the top talent in the company resides there. These companies missed the important point that Lean Six Sigma results happen through people.

A Lack of Supporting Infrastructure

As noted, any new initiative needs a new supporting infrastructure to maintain momentum until it has been institutionalized. This infrastructure of systems, processes, and organizational structure was quite visible and effective at GE and Grace. However, those trying to implement Lean Six Sigma at Royal Chemicals and Diversified Paper were left to fend for themselves. For example, there was no formal process for selecting projects. This led to the selection of poor projects and contributed to a lack of organizational alignment and support for the projects that were selected. If leadership has not agreed on the logic for each project selected, it is much less likely to provide ongoing support for these projects. This lack of support was particularly debilitating at Diversified Paper. Black Belts there were unable to obtain the resources needed to address the root causes of problems that their projects uncovered.

Nor was a formal, consistent, project review system in place. When this system breaks down, or if it is never implemented, as in these cases, the project momentum slows and projects drag on indefinitely. In the case of Royal Chemicals, lack of appropriate project reviews led many projects to disregard the entire Lean Six Sigma process. After nine months of effort, only one project was completed.

Another piece of infrastructure that was missing in the efforts at Royal Chemicals and Diversified Paper was a well-designed training system for each role. Each role (Black Belts, MBBs, Champions, senior leaders, and, eventually, Green Belts) must receive the appropriate training. Additionally, an ongoing system must exist to provide refresher courses and advanced or specialized training, as well as to bring new resources on board.

Royal Chemicals was clearly in need of specialized training for continuous processes, but it opted for generic training because it was cheaper. MBBs at Diversified Paper did not receive MBB training; they got only Black Belt training. Neither leadership team invested in the level of training required. Both companies also viewed training as a one-time event rather than an ongoing process of capability development. Of course, any job is difficult if you have not received the training and development required; this is even more true with a radical change initiative such as Lean Six Sigma.

This training system becomes more critical when we expand to a more holistic system with multiple methodologies. Chapter 8, "Sustaining Momentum and Growing," details the appropriate training system required to support Lean Six Sigma 2.0 deployment.

Another important system that was missing in the less successful case studies was a financial system for estimating and measuring benefits from projects. For example, Diversified Paper did not have a standardized financial system to measure project benefits, so other business units did not believe the savings claimed from successful projects. This prevented them from taking notice and getting on board.

Yet another infrastructure failure was that neither organization named a corporate Lean Six Sigma Leader, an overall Corporate Champion. A leaderless initiative is like a rudderless ship; it goes wherever the prevailing winds and currents take it. That's the reason virtually every major corporation has an overall financial leader (CFO), an overall legal leader (CLO or general counsel), an overall human resources leader, and so on. Such infrastructure is critically important to developing and deploying strategic direction in these areas. Figure 5.1 summarizes the common attributes of the less successful case studies.

The Keys to Successful Lean Six Sigma Deployment

By comparing the successful case studies to the unsuccessful ones, and incorporating the learnings from the holistic case studies in Chapter 4, we can see the keys to successful deployment. We have discussed a few companies' experiences here, but these conclusions are corroborated by many other companies' experiences, not to mention research in organizational change (Harry and Schroeder, 2000; Weisbord, 1989).

The keys to success can be grouped into the four broad, overlapping categories (see Figure 5.2):

- Committed leadership
- Top talent

- Supporting infrastructure

- Improvement methodology portfolio

Note that we add a fourth critical success factor here, the improvement methodology portfolio (as discussed in Chapter 2, "What Is Holistic Improvement?", and illustrated in the experiences of the companies profiled in Chapter 4).

Let's take a more detailed look at each of these categories.

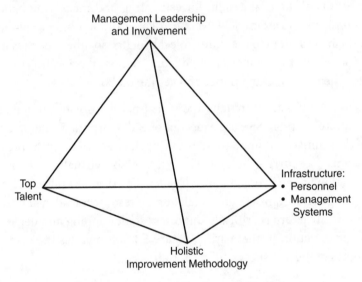

Figure 5.2   Holistic improvement system critical success factors

Committed Leadership

By *committed leadership,* we mean leaders who have the conviction to make difficult decisions and personally lead the organization in the chosen direction without wavering. Such commitment goes well beyond supporting or favoring Lean Six Sigma or holistic improvement.

History provides many examples of committed leadership. For example, historians tell us that when Hernán Cortez landed in Mexico in 1519 to begin the Spanish conquest of the Aztecs, there was considerable dissension in the Spanish ranks regarding whether it was possible for 500 soldiers to defeat the entire Aztec Empire. Most soldiers, and even

Cortez's senior officers, felt that the more prudent course of action would be to sail back to Cuba to obtain more troops.

Cortez's solution to this dilemma was not to hold a prolonged debate, but rather to burn and sink his own ships! With the Spanish ships destroyed, his army had no choice but to go forward toward the Aztec Empire; there would be no more debate or indecision.

Although we do not find Cortez's mission of conquest and destruction praiseworthy, he did provide a classic example of leadership commitment. In his mind, there was no alternative to conquest and no thought of ever turning back. Senior leaders should realize that this is the level of commitment required to make Lean Six Sigma, and especially Lean Six Sigma 2.0, successful.

The following is a checklist we have found useful for measuring leadership commitment:

- Clear, unwavering direction on deploying Lean Six Sigma

- Commitment of required resources, including personnel

- Development of a strategy for deployment—a game plan of tangible goals and objectives

- Frequent and clear communications to the organization

- Personal involvement

- Willingness to revise company policies and procedures to be supportive (for example, management bonus plans)

- Reward, recognition, and celebration of successes

- Insistence on tangible results

As discussed, if there is not a clear commitment for Lean Six Sigma, the effort will gradually be sabotaged until it loses all momentum. If the financial and human resources are not provided, the initiative will never get off the ground. Similarly, lack of a strategic deployment plan is an indication that senior leadership does not view Lean Six Sigma as being strategically important.

The issue of personal involvement is a critical one. Many people feel that dollars measure senior leadership's commitment; the more funding they provide, the more committed they are. Although there is some truth to this, we have found that personal time is an even better barometer of leadership commitment.

Leaders can always get more money. However, even CEOs have only 24 hours in a day; they can't get any more time than that. Given the many demands on their time, they are forced to prioritize, and only the most critical issues receive their commitment. Lean Six Sigma either makes the grade or it doesn't.

GE and other companies have found that some systems and policies need to be revised to stay consistent with the direction of Lean Six Sigma. One obvious example is GE revising its reward and recognition system so that management bonuses would be heavily weighted by Lean Six Sigma results.

Other examples include allowing additional headcount to backfill for Black Belts and MBBs, rethinking career progression paths, incorporating Lean Six Sigma as a criterion in performance evaluations at all levels, and adding Lean Six Sigma as a line item in budgets. This final point also relates to the last item in the previous list.

Just as financial resources need to be provided to properly implement Lean Six Sigma, financial benefits need to be expected as a return. Having financial savings from the Lean Six Sigma effort as a line item in the budget sets clear direction that to whom much is given, much is expected. Conversely, if leadership does not demand financial benefits, the organization will quickly see that this is an optional initiative. Why worry about Lean Six Sigma if you can get fired for not delivering on other things?

Top Talent

Top talent is important to the Lean Six Sigma effort for three major reasons:

- The better the talent, the better the results.
- Top talent attracts more top talent.
- Top talent becomes the next organizational leaders.

The first item on the list is fairly obvious: The better the talent is, the better results they will achieve with the effort. This is true in any initiative—for example, sports teams with the best records tend to have the most talented players. If this is obviously true, why don't improvement efforts tend to obtain the top talent in general?

One answer is that assigning top talent to Lean Six Sigma causes significant stress to the system. These folks have to stop what they are currently doing, their work needs to be reprioritized, and many replacements have to be found. Naturally, the replacements often do not perform as well as the top talent on these important projects.

Weak leaders generally follow the path of least resistance, even if it is not the path to success. It takes committed leaders to choose the more difficult and stressful path. Our experience has been that only companies that have taken the more difficult path have fully benefited from Lean Six Sigma. Certainly, GE and Grace followed this path and accepted the additional stress and difficulties it required. Note also that obtaining top talent applies to filling not only the full-time roles, such as MBBs and Black Belts, but also the roles of other members of the Black Belt project teams. This also involves finding functional support needed to address the root causes identified by the team.

The second reason that selecting top talent is so critical, is somewhat more subtle. If top talent is selected for key roles, this sends a very clear message to the organization that management is serious about Lean Six Sigma and creates suction for the initiative. By *suction,* we mean that people will naturally be drawn to Lean Six Sigma, will want to be involved with it, and might even start to compete with one another for MBB and Black Belt positions.

We are not fans of internal competition, but we do think it is healthy to have more people vying for Lean Six Sigma roles than there are positions to fill. We need to repeat our earlier point that the organization knows the talent, so no words leadership says here will make a difference. After leadership announces the names of the involved individuals, the organization will immediately know whether top talent was selected. The names will speak for themselves.

The third reason for selecting top talent for Lean Six Sigma roles, is to develop the future leaders of the company. Today's top talent will likely become tomorrow's leaders, and we need to ensure that these leaders fully understand and embrace Lean Six Sigma. Having ex–Black Belts and MBBs in senior leadership positions helps ensure that the culture change is permanent and is a major element of making the transition from an initiative to the way we work (see Chapter 9, "The Way We Work"). Deploying Lean Six Sigma 2.0 makes leaders more holistic thinkers.

Furthermore, the experience of being dedicated to disciplined continuous improvement work will produce better leaders. As Jack Welch writes in his autobiography (Welch, 2001, p. 339):

> We've always had great functional training programs over the years, particularly in finance. But the diversity of the company has made it difficult to have a universal training program. Six Sigma gives us just the tool we need for generic management training since it applies as much in a customer service center as it does in a manufacturing environment.

Supporting Infrastructure

As noted, the presence of a supporting infrastructure was a key reason GE and Grace achieved major success, and the lack of one was a major reason Royal Chemicals and Diversified Paper achieved minimal success. Even committed leaders and top talent will have difficulty succeeding without a proper infrastructure.

In practice, of course, these items tend to go together. Committed leaders will ensure that the required supporting infrastructure is developed; uncommitted leaders won't. The most critical infrastructure elements follow:

- An organizational structure for Lean Six Sigma deployment that includes overall leadership of the effort, a Lean Six Sigma Council, and dedicated positions for key roles (MBBs, Black Belts, and so on).

- Lean Six Sigma planning systems (development and managerial review of implementation plans, budgets, human resources plans, and so on, on at least an annual basis). This is nothing more than what is typically done for each business unit in a major corporation, but it is often overlooked for improvement initiatives.

- Project selection and review processes.

- Training systems for key roles.

- Modification of human resources, reward and recognition, business planning, financial, and other business systems to support Lean Six Sigma implementation, as needed.

Related to the first point in this list, formal roles, assigned leadership, and dedicated resources are needed to get the initiative going, overcome inertia, and maintain momentum. No major corporation operates its finance department without a designated leader or a finance committee, with unclear roles, or with resources doing finance in their spare time. If such a disorganized approach fails for finance, why would we expect it to work for Lean Six Sigma?

When Lean Six Sigma becomes ingrained into the organization, it will be possible to scale down the level of dedicated resources. This is similar to the safety department in a well-managed company, which typically has few full-time resources because everyone in the company works on safety every day.

The second item in the previous list addresses the need to have Lean Six Sigma formally managed like any other activity of the company. The Lean Six Sigma effort needs to plan, develop a budget, have clear objectives, obtain resources, and so on. Similarly, if leadership takes Lean Six Sigma seriously, it will want to review and potentially revise these plans. Good companies spend a lot of time planning, which means they spend less time fighting fires and solving crises. As UCLA basketball coaching legend John Wooden noted, "Failing to plan is planning to fail." The same principle holds for Lean Six Sigma.

As we have seen, project selection is a critical component of success. Often the battle is lost before we have even begun because poor projects are selected.

We also need a formal project review process. The review process ensures that the projects continue to move in the right direction and at an appropriate pace. As noted, without a regular drumbeat of reviews, projects often get bogged down and move at a glacial pace. Reviews also give leadership an opportunity to make midcourse corrections and quickly learn of barriers that are getting in the way. Furthermore, they serve as a visible symbol that leadership is personally involved.

We refer to the reviews of projects and reviews of the overall initiative as the "secret sauce." In our experience, when reviews happen on a regular basis, good things happen; projects are successful, initiatives stay on course, roadblocks are identified, and so on. Ron Snee once heard an executive admonish his staff by saying that all they had to do was schedule reviews and show up. Good things would happen. They didn't even have to say anything during the review. Holding reviews on a regular basis sends a strong message regarding what is important.

In later chapters, we will provide more detailed advice on project selection, structuring reviews, the different types of reviews required, and their appropriate timing.

At first glance, the need for training systems might seem obvious. Everyone who gets involved with Lean Six Sigma receives training. However, there is a big difference between establishing a formal training system and doing a wave of mass training. A training system is not a one-time event; it is an ongoing set of interconnected processes. It evaluates and documents the business needs, develops or obtains tailored training courses to meet those needs, and then delivers the appropriate type and depth of training to those that need it, at the most appropriate time. This can require a more complex curriculum with several courses of varying breadth and depth, beyond a single one-size-fits-all course. It also requires new people joining the organization to be trained promptly. Chapter 8 covers developing the required training system.

We have commented previously on the need to modify systems, policies, and procedures to be consistent with the Lean Six Sigma direction. For example, to attract top talent to the effort, career progression paths will need to be modified so that MBB and Black Belt roles are clearly seen as accelerators rather than hindrances to career advancement. Similarly, managerial bonus programs, annual performance appraisal systems, communication processes, and the like will need to be modified to drive Lean Six Sigma. These points illustrate why the key success factors of leadership, top talent, and supportive infrastructure must be tightly linked.

Improvement Methodology Portfolio

We discussed the role and importance of moving from a single "best" methodology to a more holistic system that fits the methodology to the specific problem (see Chapters 1, "A New Improvement Paradigm Is Needed"; 2, "What Is Holistic Improvement?"; and 3, "Key Methodologies in a Holistic Improvement System"). We argue that this critical success factor is just as important as the other three listed in Figure 5.2 and is, in fact, the major enhancement needed to move from Lean Six Sigma to Lean Six Sigma 2.0. However, can any organization be excellent in all possible improvement methodologies? Of course not. Therefore, organizations need to identify the right portfolio tailored to its unique situation.

In finance, it is well understood that having a diverse portfolio of investments is much safer than putting all your eggs in one basket. No financial advisor worth his or her salt would recommend putting a client's entire retirement account into one stock. As discussed in Chapters 1–3, organizations also need diversification (multiple methodologies) to effectively address diverse improvement challenges. The improvement system cannot become all things to all people, so it is critical that organizations identify the portfolio of methods they feel are most applicable to their situation in each of the three improvement categories (quality by design, breakthrough improvement, and quality and process management systems).

In Chapter 3, we presented the methods that we have found most effective across a broad spectrum of organizations. This could be considered a draft or generic portfolio. However, we strongly advise organizations migrating to a holistic improvement system to carefully consider their own needs, context, personnel, and so on, in determining their best portfolio. The portfolio should be dynamic, growing and changing over time as the organization gains more experience using different methodologies.

High-Level Roadmap for Lean Six Sigma 2.0 Deployment

Now that we have identified the key factors that separate very successful from less successful deployments of Lean Six Sigma, we can use them to develop a high-level roadmap to maximize success.

By *high level,* we mean that, at this point, we provide only the major steps and their objectives. Subsequent chapters give much more detailed, step-by-step advice for each step. The overall deployment process and the individual steps are intended to be flexible enough that they can apply to organizations of different sizes, industries, cultures, and so on. Figure 5.3 illustrates the recommended deployment process. This roadmap is certainly not the only possible means of deploying Lean Six Sigma 2.0, but it takes into account the experiences of many companies, including lessons learned about the key success factors.

Figure 5.3 shows that this deployment process consists of four macro steps or phases:

- Launching the initiative

- Managing the effort

- Sustaining momentum and growing

- Being the way we work

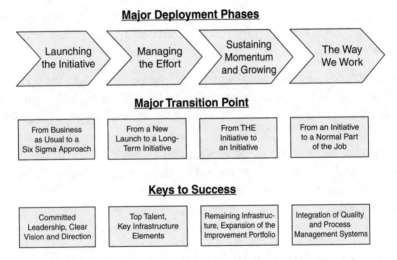

Figure 5.3 A high-level roadmap for Lean Six Sigma 2.0 deployment

Our experience has been that all organizations deploying Lean Six Sigma go through each phase, although they might progress through the phases differently. The process is somewhat different when deploying Lean

Six Sigma 2.0, as we explain in subsequent chapters. Each phase has unique challenges and issues—and, of course, there may be overlap. In some cases, organizations have to re-cycle through previous phases if they have not been properly addressed. So although we have found these steps to be common to all companies implementing Lean Six Sigma, each organization experiences them in a unique way.

A good analogy is child development: All children go through some common stages as they develop from infants, to toddlers, to children, to teenagers, to adults, but each child's experience with these stages is unique.

These four steps have been carefully chosen to align with the major transition points in Lean Six Sigma 2.0 deployment. Unfortunately, no one has gone immediately from being a non-Lean Six Sigma company to being a Lean Six Sigma company (especially to Version 2.0) in one large step. Every organization has had to go through an evolutionary deployment over several years, resulting in several transitions. Organizational transitions often provide major opportunities for breakthroughs—as well as pitfalls.

During transitions, directions change, roles change, circumstances change, and the organization experiences some level of anxiety (if not confusion and fear). It is therefore very important to plan the transitions in Lean Six Sigma deployment and take into account the key success factors discussed previously. Without proper planning, these transitions could turn out to be full of landmines and then derail deployment.

Our four deployment steps are intended to guide organizations through these transitions successfully. Let's take a closer look at each of them.

Launching the Initiative

The first transition occurs when the organization makes the decision to implement Lean Six Sigma. This transition corresponds to our launching the initiative step. Typically, this is Version 1.2 or perhaps 1.3; no organization that we know of has launched Version 2.0 initially. As we explain later, Version 2.0 is a goal to move toward over time. In the following discussion, we assume that one of these earlier versions of Lean Six Sigma is the initial focus.

Implementing Lean Six Sigma significantly changes the status quo of the organization. Current managers might be philosophically opposed to Lean Six Sigma or might want to jockey for position based on political motivations. When migrating to Version 2.0, some employees might remain loyal to their favorite method and resist the holistic approach. Individual contributors in the organization will no doubt have a lot of serious questions. Opinions at this point might be based on hearsay or sound bites from the media that might or might not be accurate. The organization will be looking for clear vision and direction at all levels.

Some of the key issues to address in launching the initiative step include these:

- Setting the overall vision and justification for the deployment of Lean Six Sigma.

- Selecting an external Lean Six Sigma provider, if needed.

- Developing a long-term deployment plan to get to Version 2.0, including objectives.

- Developing a short-term implementation plan, based on the long-term deployment plan. This task includes selecting initial resources and projects.

- Writing a clear communication plan to explain this direction to the entire organization. (As explained in Chapter 7, "Managing the Effort," this is sometimes done in the second phase.)

Of the key success factors discussed earlier, committed leadership is particularly relevant during this step. *Committed* leaders will provide the compelling vision and strong leadership required to properly address the issues; *supportive* leaders hope that someone else takes care of these issues while they focus on whatever they consider to be critically important to the organization. It is very important that everyone in the organization understands why the organization is deploying Lean Six Sigma and knows the long-term vision. Understanding the rationale for change and seeing where the organization is headed are crucial to any change initiative (Weisbord, 1989).

Managing the Effort

After the Lean Six Sigma initiative has been formally implemented, the next key transition occurs when the first set of projects is being completed. At this point, people start wondering where the organization will go from here. If Lean Six Sigma is properly implemented, a wave of enthusiasm will carry the effort through the first set of projects. At this crucial transition point, Lean Six Sigma will either fizzle out as just another short-lived fad or remain properly managed as a long-term business priority.

To successfully move through this transition, you need the involvement of the organization's top talent (change is tough!), as well as initial elements of the supporting infrastructure. These are the most critical success factors for this phase.

Key infrastructure requirements at this step follow:

- Strong leaders in Lean Six Sigma roles

- An effective project selection system

- A multitier project review system

- An approved Lean Six Sigma budget

- Good communication processes

- Formal recruitment and career progression processes for MBBs and Black Belts

- Reward and recognition systems

Sustaining Momentum and Growing

Even after successfully introducing Lean Six Sigma and transitioning to ongoing management of the effort, the effort may lose steam after a couple years. Virtually all organizations implementing Lean Six Sigma have experienced such difficulties. The reasons for this phenomenon are based on business realities and human nature.

In business, the environment is constantly changing due to economic fluctuations, new government regulations, technological breakthroughs (for example, the Internet), and even world political events, such as wars and subsequent waves of refugees (discussed in Chapter 1).

With Lean Six Sigma progressing well, leadership's attention will naturally be distracted toward emerging trends and opportunities in the marketplace. For example, Internet commerce exploded onto the business scene in the middle of Lean Six Sigma deployment at Grace and GE. Similarly, it is human nature to be attracted to the latest hot topic in the business world, such as Big Data analytics, even at the expense of successful initiatives that could be viewed as yesterday's news.

These reasons help explain why so many corporations go through a series of flavor-of-the-month fads without reaping sustained benefits from any of them. If these natural impulses are not checked, Lean Six Sigma will gradually slip in organizational importance. The participation of leadership will fade, Lean Six Sigma will struggle to attract top talent, and it will slowly become a second-tier or back-burner initiative. When the leadership presence, top talent, and infrastructure fade away, so will the benefits. Analysts will eventually ask, "Whatever happened to Lean Six Sigma?" An embarrassed leadership team will likely claim either that the organization is still driving Lean Six Sigma or that it has been successfully integrated into daily operations. Customers and employees will know better.

There is an alternative to this scenario. Certainly, business leaders will have to respond to issues and crises in the marketplace. They do not have the luxury of worrying about only one thing at a time. The tragic attacks of September 11, 2001; their subsequent economic impact; and the growth in hacking of the computer systems of major corporations are examples of unexpected crises that management must respond to. Even under the best of circumstances, the organization will have to transition from Lean Six Sigma being *the* initiative to being *an* initiative. The key to maintaining momentum and growing Lean Six Sigma during this transition is the proper functioning of the rest of the supporting infrastructure.

A good infrastructure ensures that Lean Six Sigma gets the nourishment it needs when the organization must focus on other issues as well. To grow, we also have to continually expand the effort to include all aspects of the organization, including growing the top line. At this point, other elements of a holistic system (that is, Lean Six Sigma 2.0) can start to play important roles. For example, quality by design methodologies are particularly useful for finding and capitalizing on new business opportunities and growing the top line. Design for Six Sigma (DFSS) is one obvious example.

Furthermore, additional elements can be added to the improvement methodology portfolio. If the emphasis has been on Lean projects and Six Sigma projects, perhaps Big Data analytics, Work-Out, or other alternative approaches can be added to better suit different types of problems. We recommend adding methodologies gradually, at a rate that the organization can effectively handle.

To successfully get to this point, organizations will have already implemented several infrastructure elements, such as good project selection and review systems. Other components of the supporting infrastructure that become key in this step follow:

- A well-defined organizational structure, especially a functioning Lean Six Sigma Council. The Council should develop annual objectives and budgets, manage the Lean Six Sigma systems and processes, and provide leadership for the overall effort.

- A training system that passes on the required skills to new employees, as well as continuing education and training for experienced MBBs, Black Belts, and Green Belts. This now needs to incorporate more methodologies than just Lean and Six Sigma, as discussed earlier.

- A system of audits to ensure that previously closed projects are continuing to reap benefits (the purpose of the Control phase in the DMAIC process).

- Quarterly management reviews of the Lean Six Sigma system at the business and corporate levels, to make sure the system is performing as desired.

The Way We Work

The last transition point in deploying Lean Six Sigma 2.0 is perhaps the most difficult. This is the point at which we need to move Lean Six Sigma from being an initiative to being the way we work. In other words, the concepts and methodologies of Lean Six Sigma must become standard operating procedures. Furthermore, we must have a viable improvement methodology portfolio instead of continuing to rely on one or two improvement methodologies.

Organizations can't go on indefinitely with Lean Six Sigma being their primary focus—nor should they. If Lean Six Sigma is deployed properly, it will fundamentally change the way leaders lead and the way work is done. If it can be effectively institutionalized, the organization can continue to reap its benefits without maintaining a separate Lean Six Sigma infrastructure or making prolonged demands on leadership's time and energy. Instead, improvement efforts will be integrated into one holistic system. This allows leadership to focus on other strategically important issues, such as redeveloping its e-commerce strategy or rethinking risk management systems in response to heightened security risks from terrorism or computer hacking.

We believe this is the most difficult transition phase, especially from an organizational point of view. First of all, it is rarely addressed well in the corporate world for any initiative, not just Lean Six Sigma 2.0. Business journals and textbooks are full of case studies in which a variety of initiatives were introduced and produced significant savings. In most companies, however, few traces of the initiative (or the benefits) exist after about five years. Examples include TQM, reengineering, activity-based costing (ABC), and benchmarking. Contrary to some commentators' opinions, this fact does not indicate a deficiency in any of these methodologies. In reality, these initiatives can deliver huge benefits to organizations that deploy them properly.

The deficiency that generally causes this phenomenon is the organization's inability to successfully integrate the key concepts and methodologies of the initiative into its normal mode of operation—to make it the way we work. If this is not done, then as soon as the separate infrastructure is dismantled and leadership moves on to other issues (which it needs to do), the initiative dissolves. This is primarily an organizational challenge instead of a technical challenge.

As noted previously, we do not feel that any organization has yet fully deployed Lean Six Sigma 2.0. Some of the organizations discussed in

Chapter 4 are perhaps furthest along this path. The key to such successes is the ability to integrate the initiative into the culture of the organization so that it is no longer seen as a separate initiative. Furthermore, an organizational challenge exists for integrating all the improvement efforts into one holistic system. It is not sufficient to have three improvement silos that operate independently: one for quality by design, one for breakthrough improvement, and one for quality and process management systems.

How can this be done with Lean Six Sigma 2.0? The best way that we know of is to migrate the breakthrough improvement effort into an ongoing quality and process management system. Breakthrough improvement relies on formal projects and the allocation of dedicated, trained resources. When the infrastructure of Lean Six Sigma matures, we need to integrate these key components into the quality by design effort and the quality and process management systems in place—see Figure 5.4. As we move down this figure over time, the deployment starts to look more organic and less like a separate initiative.

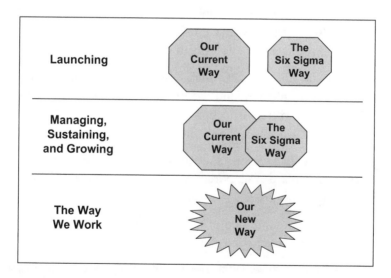

Figure 5.4 Migrating Lean Six Sigma 1.3 to holistic improvement system (Version 2.0)

Obviously, many organizations have deployed successful Lean Six Sigma initiatives and gone through several of the phases noted in Figure 5.3. Would they need to go back to the first phase to migrate to Lean Six Sigma 2.0? Of course not! Organizations that have successful, ongoing Lean Six Sigma initiatives (say, in Version 1.3) mainly need to focus on expanding the improvement portfolio and integrating improvement efforts under one umbrella. These are typically done in Phases 3 and 4, respectively. We recommend that such organizations verify that they have the needed infrastructure and other key elements from Phases 1 and 2, and then focus on expanding methodologies and integration.

Migrating to a holistic improvement system is an evolutionary process that builds on the current state of the organization, wherever that may be. The migration begins with assessing the current state and creating the desired future state. The end result will evolve over time. Some especially important considerations follow:

- Evaluate the process used to identify, select, and manage improvement projects. A broad view must include and assess all aspects of the business. This is particularly true when expanding to an improvement methodology portfolio. When all problems are addressed with Six Sigma, employees might overlook important problems that are not well suited to Six Sigma.

- Tailor the improvement methodology to address the specific types of problems identified by the project selection process. Recall that, with holistic improvement, we first identify the most important projects and only then think about methodologies.

- Assess the management infrastructure. Are all the processes and systems in place to support holistic improvement and successfully sustain it over time?

- Assess the organization of improvement efforts. Is all improvement coordinated and under one umbrella?

- Assess the culture. What needs to be addressed in the organization's culture to support holistic improvement? What are the roadblocks? Does the leadership have the knowledge, skills and will to create and sustain the effort over time?

We recommend that senior management perform an annual review of improvement initiatives and results, to see what's working and identify critical improvement needs for the future. This assessment should address not only process improvement needs, but also organizational needs to support holistic improvement. These include the improvement methodology portfolio, infrastructure, and leadership development.

Summary and Looking Forward

Four common root causes explain why some businesses achieve significant success with Lean Six Sigma and others achieve minimal success. These key success factors are committed leadership, involvement of top talent, and supporting infrastructure.

In this book, we add a fourth critical success factor: the improvement methodology portfolio. This portfolio, which is unique to the organization, enables us to address the improvement needs of all types within a common system.

By integrating these four success factors, we can identify a deployment roadmap toward Lean Six Sigma 2.0 that maximizes the probability of success. Numerous organizations of various sizes and business application areas have successfully followed this roadmap and made significant progress, but we must reiterate that no single organization has fully achieved Lean Six Sigma 2.0.

The next four chapters will provide detailed guidance on how to succeed in each step of this deployment roadmap. Chapter 6, "Launching the Initiative," begins with the first step. The other three phases are discussed in Chapters 7–9. Chapter 10, "Final Thoughts for Leaders," provides summary advice on achieving success and avoiding pitfalls.

References

Harry, M., and R. Schroeder. (2000) *Six Sigma: The Breakthrough Strategy Revolutionizing the World's Top Corporations*. New York: Doubleday.

Snee, R. D., and R. W. Hoerl. (2003) *Leading Six Sigma: A Step-by-Step Guide Based on Experience with GE and Other Six Sigma Companies.* Upper Saddle River, NJ: Financial Times/Prentice Hall.

Snee, R. D., and R. W. Hoerl. (2005) *Six Sigma Beyond the Factory Floor: Deployment Strategies for Financial Services, Health Care, and the Rest of the Real Economy.* Upper Saddle River, NJ: Financial Times/ Prentice Hall.

Weisbord, M. R. (1989) *Productive Workplaces.* San Francisco: Jossey-Bass.

Welch, J. F. (2001) *Jack: Straight from the Gut.* New York: Warner Books.

6

Launching the Initiative

"A journey of a thousand miles must begin with a single step."
—Lau Tsu

hapter 5, "How to Successfully Implement Lean Six Sigma 2.0," provided an overall deployment process for holistic improvement, beginning with Lean Six Sigma. This approach is based on the lessons learned from the case studies in Chapter 4, "Case Studies in Holistic Improvement," as well as the realization that attempting to launch a true holistic improvement system initially would be daunting. We now delve into the first phase of the deployment process, a step referred to as launching the initiative. This is probably the most important phase.

If Lean Six Sigma is poorly launched, reorganizing and regaining momentum will be difficult. People will have already become skeptical, and resisters will have ammunition. Migration to a full holistic improvement system will be unlikely. Taking into full consideration the key points discussed in this chapter will help organizations hit the ground running on their initial implementation.

We define the launch phase of Lean Six Sigma to be roughly the period between making the decision to deploy and completing the initial wave of Black Belt training. At the end of this phase, you should have the following in place:

- An overall deployment plan (strategy)
- The initial wave of projects
- Trained Black Belts and other key players

These are the key deliverables for the launch phase, and they should be considered in that order. Before developing the deployment plan, most organizations need to decide which major deployment strategy to utilize. This decision affects virtually every aspect of the deployment plan, so it must be addressed first, followed by the three main launch topics.

Full or Partial Deployment?

Once organizations have decided to implement Lean Six Sigma, they are faced with the question of, "How do I get started?" The most obvious answer is to adopt the approach of companies such as GE and W. R. Grace (Snee and Hoerl, 2003) and institute a CEO-led, company-wide, top-priority initiative. We believe that this kind of full deployment is the best strategy. Table 6.1 lists the advantages and disadvantages of a full deployment approach.

Table 6.1   Full Deployment Versus Partial Deployment

Full Deployment	Partial Deployment
Strengths	**Strengths**
• The organization knows what is going on	• Requires limited resources
• Vision and direction are clear	• Requires limited management attention
• Resources are more easily assigned	• Can be started by middle management
• Returns are large and come in the first 6-8 months	• Easy to get started
Limitations	**Limitations**

• Top management commitment is required up front to get started	• Difficult to obtain:
	   • BB assigned full time
	   • Functional resources

• Priorities have to be redefined to include the Lean Six Sigma work	• Tough to get management attention
• Management will have to change how they work	• Organization doesn't believe management is committed to Lean Six Sigma
	• Returns are small because only a few BB are involved

Unfortunately, many business leaders below the CEO level are not in a position to take the full deployment approach. Another option is for leaders to deploy Lean Six Sigma in their own realm of responsibility. This could be a division, a business unit, or even a single plant. We refer to deployment on such a reduced scale as partial deployment. Although this is not our first option, it could be the only practical one. Keep in mind, however, that Lean Six Sigma will flourish in the long term only if it becomes a full deployment process. Sooner or later, someone will squash a partial deployment if it does not spread to the rest of the organization. For that reason, the main objective of a partial deployment must be to make a convincing case for full deployment.

Partial deployment usually involves training one to five Black Belts and using their tangible results to make the case for full deployment. It takes little to get started, but if proper planning is not done and adequate resources are not assigned, the effort can quickly run into trouble.

Parikh et al. (2014) report on one successful partial deployment of Six Sigma at Crompton Corporation, a chemical company based in Greenwich, Connecticut. In the first wave, seven Black Belts were trained and given good support. One Black Belt was reassigned and his project was postponed. The other six projects were completed, returning an average of $360,000 in savings per project.

These results encouraged a key business unit of Crompton Corporation to pursue a partial deployment on a much larger scale. This deployment was supported with Executive, Champion, and Site Leadership training and produced project savings similar to those of the initial six projects. Building on this success, the whole Crompton Corporation began a full Six Sigma deployment. The process of moving from partial deployment to full corporate deployment took approximately 18 months. Recall that the ultimate measure of success for partial deployment is that it leads to a successful full deployment. Contrary to popular belief, partial deployment requires more than just good Black Belt training to be successful. Executive, Champion, and Leadership training, as well as good project and people selection, are also needed.

Companies that select the partial deployment route should be aware of the problems they can expect to encounter. The biggest problems include identifying good projects for the Black Belts, getting Black Belts assigned full time, and assigning Champions who will provide good guidance for the Black Belts, including weekly reviews of the projects. Getting functional group support for the projects can be difficult if the organization is not pursuing full deployment of Six Sigma. Completing the Executive, Champion, and Leadership training helps minimize these problems.

The partial deployment approach is most likely to succeed when all of the deployment plan elements for the full deployment are addressed. In other words, success is most likely when partial deployment is essentially a full deployment in one area and looks just like a full deployment to those working in this area. Still, many people feel that doing a partial deployment takes almost as much effort as doing a full deployment, with not nearly the return. This leads some people, including the authors, to conclude that full deployment is overall a better use of resources and also increases the probability of success.

Developing the Deployment Plan

Although there is usually a strong desire to launch Lean Six Sigma as quickly as possible once the decision to deploy has been made, there is significant risk in taking a ready, fire, aim approach—that is, deploying without proper up-front planning. Our experience is that an organization truly needs to begin with the end in mind when deploying Lean Six Sigma. In other words, before you launch, you should have a good idea of the long-term direction. Once the long-term strategy is set, it will be much easier to develop a short-term implementation process that will take you in the right direction.

The long-term strategy is referred to as the deployment plan. Keep in mind that this is the deployment plan for Lean Six Sigma; the ultimate intention is to develop a holistic improvement system, to migrate to Lean Six Sigma 2.0. Of course, the deployment plan does not need to be developed in minute detail. You simply need enough specificity to guide implementation. You will continually re-evaluate, update, and add detail to this deployment plan as you move through the four phases of Lean Six Sigma deployment.

The deployment plan should cover, at a minimum, all the elements listed next. As noted, these elements are not all implemented at once—they work in a phased approach. Think of the deployment plan as a work in progress. The key elements of the deployment plan during the launch phase follow:

- Executive and Business Leadership workshops

- Champion workshop

- Selection of initial projects

- Selection of initial Black Belts and other key roles

- Finance personnel training

- Black Belt and Green Belt training

We consider these elements of the deployment plan to comprise an implementation or launch process, which is the focus of this chapter. Other elements of the deployment plan will be documented at a strategic level now, but details and actual implementation will come during the subsequent phases of deployment.

Our experience has been that most organizations are not ready to develop a proper deployment plan without a more detailed understanding of Lean Six Sigma and facilitation from someone more experienced. For this reason, we strongly recommend leadership workshops to develop this more detailed understanding and to begin development of the deployment plan.

Interestingly, the first draft of the deployment plan will be developed during the Executive and Business Leadership workshops and then will be used to guide development of the other elements of the implementation process. You can see somewhat of a chicken-and-egg relationship here between the implementation process and the deployment plan. The implementation process is needed to develop the deployment plan, but in reality, the implementation process is a subset of the deployment plan.

Required Deployment Plan Elements

- Strategy and goals for Six Sigma

- Process performance measures

- Project selection criteria

- Project identification/prioritization system

- Deployment processes for Champions, MBBs, BBs, and so on

- Roles of management, Champions, MBBs, BBs, and functional groups

- Curricula and training system

- Project and Lean Six Sigma initiative review schedule
- Project reporting and tracking system
- Audit system for previously closed projects
- Reward and recognition plan
- Communication plan

This chapter focuses on how to organize and conduct the workshops that develop the first draft of the deployment plan, with emphasis on elements that are critical to the initial launch of Lean Six Sigma. The next few chapters discuss the other aspects of this plan in detail because those parts become critical in the later stages of deployment.

The Executive workshop should include all members of the executive team because they all have a role to play in Lean Six Sigma deployment. This holds true even if the initiative will involve manufacturing or operations only in the beginning of a partial deployment. All parties are needed to make Lean Six Sigma successful, regardless of the initial focus of the effort. In particular, it is important that the heads of the finance, human resources (HR), and information technology (IT) organizations participate in the Executive workshop and subsequent deployment efforts.

These are three new players that have not typically been involved in previous improvement approaches, such as Total Quality Management (TQM) or quality circles. Finance is responsible for determining the bottom-line impact of the projects and creating the project tracking system that will be used to monitor the tangible results of the effort. HR is responsible for the career development paths of the Champions, Master Black Belts (MBBs), Black Belts, and Green Belts, as well as the reward and recognition systems, communication vehicles, and performance management systems. IT is needed to develop computer systems that collect key process measurement data identified by the Black Belt projects, to improve the cycle time and accuracy of manual systems through digitization, and to automate improvements as part of the project control plan.

Some data acquisition systems might already be in place, but Lean Six Sigma projects often uncover other process measurements that must be improved and that effectively control the process. Frequently, information systems have been put in place for financial (accounting) purposes instead of to aid continuous improvement. Achieving this new purpose often requires new data acquisition systems. Furthermore, as deployment expands to Lean Six Sigma 2.0, there will likely be significant demands on IT to support Big Data analytics.

The Executive workshop is typically two days in length and has the following as its products:

- More in-depth understanding of Lean Six Sigma and holistic improvement
- Defined roles of the members of the management team
- Identification of targeted areas for improvement
- Champions for these targeted areas
- A draft deployment plan

The first version of the deployment plan is finalized in the following weeks by the management team as a regular part of standard management meetings. A key part of this work is refining the list of project areas and associated Champions. In large organizations, it is often appropriate to give the two-day Executive workshop not only for the corporate executives, but also for the leaders of the different strategic business units (SBUs). In such cases, the focus of these additional workshops is the Lean Six Sigma deployment plan within each SBU.

The SBU leaders often attend the original Executive workshop to learn about the process and then assume leadership roles in the SBU-specific workshops. Similarly, it is important to do Site or Functional Leadership training for the management teams in the areas (plant site, functional group, and so on) that are targeted for the initial projects. This ensures that the Black Belts get the support they need to complete their projects in a timely manner. The Site or Functional Leadership training should be completed before the first week of Black Belt training.

The Executive workshop is followed in approximately one month by a three-to-five day Champion workshop for the Champions identified during the Executive workshop. This workshop uses as input the initial deployment plan and the project areas that were outputs of the Executive workshop and were refined in subsequent weeks.

The outputs of the Champion workshop include a deeper understanding of Lean Six Sigma and the roles of the players, a list of chartered projects, and a list of assigned Black Belts. Special attention is focused on the role of the Champion and the way the Champion interfaces with the Black Belts and Green Belts.

This workshop is particularly important because inactive or ineffective Champions are often identified as the root cause of project failures. If this role is not taken seriously or is not properly understood, the Champions can become the weak link in the Lean Six Sigma organization, with devastating consequences.

After their Champion workshop, the Champions meet with the Black Belts to discuss the projects and make any needed refinements. Such refinements are often needed because the Black Belts have detailed data and insights that were not available when the project charters were developed. Project charters are discussed in greater detail shortly. The Black Belts are now ready to attend their training, which usually follows the Champion workshop by approximately one month.

The Black Belts are expected to bring their project charters to the training and work on their actual projects as part of the training. They will learn and deliver results at the same time. Such an approach is consistent with the principles of adult learning. We now take a short detour to look at the elements of the deployment plan; then we come back to Black Belt training and the rest of the implementation process.

Deployment Plan Elements

The deployment plan elements must be addressed regardless of whether a partial or full deployment approach is utilized. However, the elements are not all implemented at the same time. Some are critical at launch, others come into play in the second phase of deployment (managing the effort), and others appear in the third phase (sustaining momentum and growing). At this point, the launch elements need to be covered in detail, but the other elements can be defined at a high, strategic level. Details of these elements will be added at the appropriate time.

Seasoned planners might feel the need to define all deployment elements in detail from the very beginning, but our experience is that trying to do so delays implementation and can result in "paralysis by analysis" as you try to cross every *t* and dot every *i*.

We briefly describe each deployment plan element here and then go into detail on the critical launch phase items. We provide additional detail on the other elements in subsequent chapters.

Strategy and Goals

Strategy and goals make up the first key element. This element is the responsibility of senior management, and it sets the overall vision for Lean Six Sigma deployment. An important element of the strategy is choosing the place where Lean Six Sigma will start and determining the rollout sequence and timing. Obviously, Lean Six Sigma cannot be rolled out everywhere at once. A typical industrial rollout starts in manufacturing. Then, when success is demonstrated, management initiates projects in the other areas of the business and new product development (Design for Six Sigma [DFSS]).

Service businesses, such as insurance or consumer credit companies, typically begin Lean Six Sigma in operations. General business projects and DFSS typically begin six to eight months and one year after manufacturing, respectively.

Two reasons justify starting in manufacturing (operations in service companies), and both relate to the fact that manufacturing tends to have the best measurement systems. First, it is much easier to achieve quick hits if you begin with a good measurement system instead having to take time to create one. Second, the existence of good measurements usually means that everyone is aware of the huge potential savings available in manufacturing and eager to go after them.

Conversely, many people need to be convinced that huge savings are available in the finance department. Starting Lean Six Sigma in manufacturing/operations sets up the initiative for success. Success in manufacturing/operations builds confidence that Lean Six Sigma will work and also produces bottom-line results that help "pay as you go," thereby enabling deployment throughout the organization.

Another decision is when to start Green Belt training, which is typically initiated 8 to 10 months after Black Belt training starts. Black Belts, dedicated to Six Sigma projects 100 percent of their time, are needed to get the initiative moving quickly. Some companies have a goal of training the entire professional staff as Green Belts (part time) as soon as it can be managed.

It is also important to develop one- to two-year goals for Lean Six Sigma and broadly communicate them in the Executive workshop. The goals, which generally include financial targets, should be communicated for the organization as a whole and reinforced within each major part of the organization.

A goal not stated in financial terms is a clear indication that management is not serious about making Six Sigma successful. A financial goal tells the organization's members what is expected of them. For example, in the case of a $1 billion revenue company, a goal of $2 million to the bottom line from Lean Six Sigma communicates a far different message than a goal of $10 million or $20 million. At $250,000 per project, $2 million translates into eight projects, while $10 million and $20 million translate to 40 and 80 projects, respectively. Clearly, much more effort (people, time, and money) will be required to complete 40 to 80 projects than to complete 8. The financial goals will be revised over the course of several years of deployment.

Process Performance Measures

Process performance measures define what's important for success and are used to select projects. A pitfall to be avoided is selecting each project independently. This is analogous to spending 5 minutes starting to clean 10 different rooms in a house, versus spending 50 minutes to completely clean one room. In the first case, it is difficult to see what impact the effort has had; in the second case, there is a visible, tangible success that is now ready to be leveraged elsewhere. The preferable approach is to launch Lean Six Sigma by focusing on a few strategic areas instead of 10 or 20. The process performance measures determined by senior leadership help everyone focus the initial projects strategically.

One model for key measures is Quality, Delivery, and Cost (QDC). This model provides three strategic focus areas for the initial projects. Capacity is added when additional capacity is needed for the market or to run a more efficient operation (for example, moving from a six- or seven-day operation to a five-day operation).

If all the projects affect one of these three areas, you will have significant tangible results when they are completed. Quality obviously relates to customer satisfaction, and an emphasis on it almost always has the fringe benefit of saving money. This invariably follows quality improvement because you reduce the costs of rejecting or reworking defective finished products, dealing with customer returns, shouldering warranty costs, and so on. The only exception that is likely to arise is if delivering the desired quality level requires significant upgrade to equipment or materials. Surprisingly, this is rarely the case. See the discussion of process entitlement later in this chapter.

Delivery relates to the procurement, inventory, and logistics systems. Lean principles, such as moving from a push to a pull system, tend to be particularly useful here. Again, improvement in delivery almost always enhances customer satisfaction, while reducing internal costs (excess inventory, loss of sales from out-of-stock conditions, return of damaged or spoiled product, and so on). Reducing cost means reducing internal sources of waste or rework, regardless of whether this effort directly affects the customer. Improving the internal processes almost always results in better products and services, which ultimately benefits the customer.

In the case of service or transactional processes, the key process metrics are usually some form of accuracy or cycle time measures. Accuracy includes defects in information such as account numbers or financial figures, and it directly relates to both customer satisfaction and rework costs. Cycle time of business processes is a productivity measure, so it also relates directly to costs and, of course, to customer satisfaction (for example, time to approve mortgage loan applications). Interestingly, in the vast majority of cases, attempts to define customer satisfaction or internal cost metrics result in some measure of accuracy or cycle time.

Project Selection Criteria

The process metrics are also used to develop a set of more specific criteria to select projects. The project selection criteria used by one company are summarized in the following list:

- Areas to improve
  - Waste reduction

- Capacity improvement

- Downtime reduction

- Resource consumption (labor and raw materials)

- Effect on customer satisfaction

  - On-time delivery in full

  - Defect levels

- Effect on the bottom line

  - More than $250,000 per project

  - Doable in 4–6 months

  - Benefit realized in less than 1 year

These criteria define areas that are important to improve and that will produce significant bottom-line results. Note that the areas to improve are those that directly affect the customer satisfaction measurements. Project selection criteria also communicate what types of improvements are important to the organization. By communicating these criteria, you alert the organization to what your objectives are and the kinds of projects on which you want to focus. This increases the probability that large numbers of people in the organization will be involved in identifying opportunities for improvement. As noted, you will want to select projects strategically instead of haphazardly.

Project Identification and Prioritization System

These project selection criteria are used in the Champion workshop to develop a set of initial candidate projects. The projects are put in the project hopper and prioritized for assignment to a Black Belt or Green Belt. Project selection is discussed in greater detail later in this chapter.

In later deployment phases, organizations develop an ongoing system to identify potential projects, rank them, and place them in the project hopper so that there is a continuously refreshed list of good projects. Furthermore, as more methodologies are added over time to develop a more holistic improvement system, the specific methodology that is most appropriate for each project needs to be identified.

Deployment Processes for Leaders

Lists of the Champions, Black Belts, MBBs, and Green Belts are also part of the deployment plan. In later deployment phases, these lists will be expanded to become a system for selection, deployment, and advancement for each of these roles. The list of initial Champions is developed at the Executive workshop. At the Champion workshop, the Champions develop the list of initial projects and, based on this, develop a list of candidate Black Belts to lead these projects.

In Chapter 1, "A New Improvement Paradigm Is Needed," you learned that Six Sigma is about improvement, not training. We strongly recommend that the projects be selected first and then the Black Belts be assigned for these projects. The Champions should be selected at the Executive workshop based on the areas targeted for improvement. Selecting the Champions and Black Belts before identifying specific projects increases the risk that important projects will be overlooked. This critical issue is discussed in depth later in the chapter. Furthermore, as more methodologies are added to the portfolio, Black Belts must have sufficient backgrounds in the specific methodologies intended for each project. Few, if any, Black Belts are experts in every methodology.

Roles of Management and Others

Although there are generic job descriptions for Six Sigma titles, such as Champion, MBB, Black Belt, Green Belt, and so on, there is considerable variation in the actual roles these people play in different organizations. In a holistic system, for example, Black Belts are typically knowledgeable in multiple improvement methodologies, but not all of them.

Organizations should take the time to consider the specific roles that each of these positions will play in their deployment. Within reasonable boundaries, management can tailor the roles to a specific organization. The roles of the leadership team, Champions, MBBs, Black Belts, and functional groups should be defined in the Executive workshop and communicated to the organization. The guidelines for each of these roles are discussed later in this chapter.

Curricula and Training System

An overall training system for each of the Six Sigma roles is a key element of the deployment plan. At launch, a training schedule is needed only for the initial wave of Black Belts. This typically focuses on Lean and Six Sigma. As more people in various roles are involved in Six Sigma, new employees are hired, improvement methodologies are added to the portfolio, and the need is found for advanced training in certain areas (DFSS in engineering), a functioning training system with diverse curricula needs to be developed.

A wave of mass training does not make a training system; mass training is an event that usually has no lasting impact. Instead, the company needs a well-thought-out system that identifies all the training needs of all the roles and puts together a sustained, ongoing system to continuously satisfy these needs in the most efficient way possible. This involves a tremendous amount of work, but fortunately, the complete training system is not needed at the launch of Lean Six Sigma.

Project and Initiative Review Schedule

A project review schedule is key for the deployment plan. Experience has shown that an effective schedule involves short (30-minute) weekly reviews by the Champion and monthly reviews with the plant manager, functional leader, or SBU leader, as appropriate. These are needed soon after the kick-off of the initial projects. Chapter 7, "Managing the Effort," discusses this topic in more detail.

A review of the Lean Six Sigma deployment should be done quarterly by the corporate or SBU leader, as appropriate. All the elements of the deployment plan and the associated goals are appropriate agenda items for the quarterly reviews. This review focuses on how well the overall initiative is going; it does not focus on a review of individual projects. This review is critical to sustaining momentum of the Lean Six Sigma effort long term. Chapter 8, "Sustaining Momentum and Growing," discusses this topic in more detail.

Project Reporting and Tracking System

This system documents the results of the projects and provides valuable managerial information. Development of a formal system is not required in initial deployment and is typically emphasized later in the deployment process, such as in the managing-the-effort phase discussed in Chapter 7. The project reporting and tracking system keeps a record of all the improvement projects, providing a corporate memory of what has been accomplished to date. The system generates managerial reports at several levels to keep management informed of progress.

This includes financial results from the tracking system, as well as non-financial information such as the number of projects completed or in progress, the time to completion of projects, status reports, and so on. The tracking part of this system is intended to document the financial benefits of closed projects. Obviously, this system needs to be designed with rigor so that the claimed financial benefits are accurate and credible. For small organizations, or to get started, a simple Excel spreadsheet will do the trick. Dedicated computer systems are eventually needed for larger organizations. Chapter 7 looks at more details of this system.

Audit System for Previously Closed Projects

When your organization gets to the phase of sustaining momentum and growing (see Chapter 8), it will have completed a large number of projects, many of which will claim perpetual benefits—that is, benefits that will recur year after year. For example, if waste levels drop from 10 percent to 5 percent and this improvement is maintained, cost savings from lower waste will be reaped every year. Unfortunately, in many improvement efforts, these lower costs begin to creep up over time, much like weight lost on a diet. To some degree, this is to be expected; it is human nature to revert to old habits once the additional resources and focus brought by Lean Six Sigma move on to other priorities.

Of course, you need to preempt the natural digression back to old ways and rework levels if your efforts are to have lasting impact. Lean Six Sigma has the advantage of a formal step in the DMAIC process, the Control phase, that specifically is targeted to implement controls that prevent backsliding to the previous performance.

As a second layer of protection, an audit system for previously closed projects needs to be implemented. This is not primarily a financial audit system to ensure that claimed benefits are real; financial controls need to be implemented from the very beginning. Instead, this audit system is intended to audit the control plan of previously closed projects and ensure that it is still working. In other words, the audit system checks to make sure the benefits of this project are still being reaped. If not, action is initiated to revisit the project, regain the benefits, and institute an effective control plan. Subsequent chapters discuss this system at greater length.

Reward and Recognition Plan

HR needs to develop a reward and recognition plan to ensure that the organization is able to obtain (and eventually promote) the best possible candidates for Lean Six Sigma roles. We believe in the power of intrinsic motivation (the idea that people do something because they really want to do it) more than solely extrinsic motivation (the idea that people do something because they are coerced or bribed to do it). Therefore, those that have a fire in the belly for improvement will likely perform better in Lean Six Sigma roles than those solely looking for money or promotion.

However, it must be recognized that a total lack of extrinsic rewards for involvement in Lean Six Sigma is essentially a disincentive. Consider rewarding these roles in such a way that top performers will be drawn to Lean Six Sigma. This plan, which is discussed in greater detail in Chapter 7, should be reviewed and revised as needed over time to ensure that the Champions, Black Belts, MBBs, Green Belts, and team members are properly recognized for their contributions. Most successful Lean Six Sigma companies have revised their reward and recognition systems to more effectively support the initiative. A balance of both intrinsic and extrinsic motivation is encouraged.

Communications Plan

A communication plan has to be developed to support the Lean Six Sigma initiative. This is a very important part of the deployment plan because it significantly affects the impression that rank-and-file employees have of Lean Six Sigma and longer-term, true holistic improvement.

Communication about Lean Six Sigma typically utilizes existing media, but sometimes new media must be developed. It is important to use a variety of media because people take in information and learn in different ways. People have variation just as processes do. Some prefer personal contacts, either one-on-one or in groups. Others prefer to read newsletters or memos, while still others respond well to videos, webcasts, or emails. Leadership needs to carefully communicate why it chose to deploy Lean Six Sigma, what they hope to get out of it, and where it will take the organization. The intention to evolve from Lean Six Sigma to holistic improvement is particularly important. One example of such a communication plan was the video Jack Welch made (see Chapter 4). Each employee at GE was expected to watch it. This was followed by frequent emails to all employees with updates on progress of the initiative.

In some cases, such as at GE and Bank of America, the CEO makes a bold statement about Lean Six Sigma at the very beginning. However, we have also worked with organizations that did not feel comfortable making such bold statements. There is often a concern that if too big a deal is made of Lean Six Sigma at the very beginning, unrealistic expectations will be set. Every employee might expect to begin Lean Six Sigma training the next week. Customers might expect better products and services immediately. Confidence in the initiative might fade if people's unrealistic expectations are not fully met. Therefore, many organizations choose to begin the initiative in a fairly low-key manner, without hoopla.

Once actual projects are begun and results start to flow in, the initiative will be more formally and broadly communicated. Leadership will be able to point to tangible savings that have already been achieved and communicate the sequenced rollout of projects and training. The decision of when to begin implementing the communication plan needs to be made at the Executive workshop.

Chapter 7 fully discusses the communication plan. Experience and surveys have shown that every item on this list is important. Moreover, all are needed for success; none is optional. Not paying attention to any of these items can seriously limit the effectiveness of the Lean Six Sigma initiative. As previously noted, however, not all items need to be developed to the same degree of detail in the launch phase. The items that comprise the implementation process are the most critical initially.

Selecting the Right Projects

As noted earlier, the project selection process is started in the Executive workshop where areas for improvement are identified. Initial projects are selected in the Champion workshop based on the improvement areas identified by the executives, project selection criteria, and the project chartering process. This section discusses the characteristics of a good project and how to select one (see Snee, 2001; Snee and Rodebaugh, 2002). Project selection is one of the key success factors for the launch phase.

Six Sigma and Lean Projects

We assume at this point that the initial focus of deployment primarily is on Lean and Six Sigma projects, and that additional improvement methodologies will be added in subsequent deployment phases. Therefore, we focus now on differentiating between projects most suitable to a Six Sigma approach and those most suitable to a Lean approach. Of course, some type of hybrid approach is also an option. Chapter 2, "What Is Holistic Improvement?", also discussed this integration.

In our view, there has been significant confusion—and, at times, animosity—between Six Sigma and Lean in the literature, often because proponents of each have "oversold" their preferred methodology and implied that it can solve all types of problems (Snee and Hoerl, 2007). Of course, a holistic viewpoint is method agnostic, objectively selecting the methodology that is most appropriate to the problem at hand instead of selecting the methodology before knowing the problem. We would therefore like to clear the air and give practical guidance on how to select between these methodologies for a given problem.

Table 6.2   Typical Attributes of Six Sigma and Lean Projects

Six Sigma Projects	Lean Projects
Solution unknown	Solution known
Within the boxes	Between the boxes
Develop $y = f(x)$	Apply Lean principles
Sequential data analysis	Kaizen events

Although both approaches drive breakthrough improvement in results by improving processes, they have some important differences. For example, projects typically fall into two major categories: solution known and solution unknown (Hoerl and Snee, 2013). See Table 6.2.

Note that *solution known* does not imply that the project will be easy. Most brain surgeries address "solution known" problems, such as removing a tumor, but obviously, brain surgery is not easy! This distinction can be helpful in determining the best approach—whether it should be Six Sigma, Lean, or some hybrid. As noted earlier, we believe that the DMAIC framework can be utilized in Lean projects or any other type of breakthrough improvement project (Snee, 2007).

Examples of "solution unknown" projects are decreasing errors in invoices, increasing the yield of a chemical process, decreasing the defect rate of an assembly process, and decreasing the days outstanding in accounts receivables. In each case, we don't know why the problem is occurring—that is, we don't know the root causes. Significant data collection and analysis is likely required to identify these root causes and then figure out what to do about them.

Furthermore, for "solution unknown" projects, these root causes tend to be within the boxes of a flowchart or value stream map—that is, within the value-adding transforms (Snee and Hoerl, 2007). The transform could be a chemical reactor, could make the final decision in processing loan applications, or could perform surgery in a hospital. Development of cause and effect relationships—that is, determining a function relating inputs and process variables to output variables—usually is required. In Six Sigma vernacular, this is often referred to as $y = f(x)$. Experimental design and regression analysis, typically applied in a sequential manner, are particularly useful in developing this function.

The second major category involves projects for which the solution is known at the outset. Implementing a new computer network to conform to corporate security guidelines (risk management), installing a more modern piece of equipment in manufacturing, and moving to a pull-versus-push inventory system are examples of solution-known projects. Most capital projects also fall into this category, and, of course, the case of a pull-versus-push inventory system would be a natural Lean project.

Lean projects are almost always "solution known" because they typically involve applying known, proven principles instead of discovering an unknown solution. Again, this does not mean they are easy! Instead, the challenge is to figure out how to implement these known principles in a particular process, which is why there still is an Analyze phase in Lean projects using a DMAIC framework.

In contrast to Six Sigma projects, Lean projects usually focus on the arrows between the boxes on the flowchart or value stream map. That is, they focus on the flow of material and information between the value-added transforms instead of on the transforms themselves. This is why material flow and inventory projects are so amenable to Lean. Instead of involving sequential data analysis, with each round based on the results of the previous analysis, they often involve Kaizen events in which dramatic improvement is made at one point in time. For example, a manufacturing line could be shut down and then physically rearranged over a couple days to provide better material flow, line of sight, and U-shape workstations to reduce waste and increase throughput (Womack and Jones, 2003).

An organization's improvement plan typically includes diverse projects with both "solution known" and "solution unknown" problems, issues within the boxes and also between the boxes, and those that are data intensive and also more suitable for Kaizen events. This is why diverse improvement methodologies are needed. At this stage, we consider primarily Six Sigma and Lean.

Often some combination of Six Sigma and Lean projects is required to make the full extent of improvement. McGurk (2004) and Snee and Hoerl (2007) discuss an effort to improve the manufacturing organization for a biopharmaceutical product that required a hybrid approach. The organization had developed a new blockbuster drug and was subsequently creating a manufacturing organization to produce it. In pharmaceuticals, as in many industries, the transition from new product development (quality by design) to manufacturing (breakthrough improvement and also quality and process management systems) is fraught with pitfalls. In this case, it soon became clear that the current manufacturing process was not going to meet the demand of the market. An assessment found that process improvement was needed.

Batch release was very slow, keeping acceptable product from reaching patients in a timely manner. Reduction of batch release cycle times using Lean techniques resulted in a reduction of 35 to 55 percent, depending on the specific product (Snee and Hoerl, 2005). This improvement sped up product release and also significantly reduced inventory ($5 million in one-time savings) and manufacturing costs ($200,000 per year).

Product batch yields were also below expectations (entitlement), requiring more batches to be produced to meet market demands. Six Sigma techniques were used to increase process understanding, and through further analysis, raw material quality was found to be the major issue. Working with the supplier to improve the raw material quality increased batch yields by 20 percent. Ultimately, integrating both Six Sigma and Lean projects made the transition from development to manufacturing successful. Attempting to make all needed improvements through a single methodology would not likely have achieved the same results.

Of course, even at this point, other methodologies might be needed and applied, such as Nike projects (Just Do It!), capital projects, risk management projects, and so on. In particular, because both Six Sigma and Lean are oriented toward breakthrough improvement, other methodologies will (and should be) used for quality by design and also for quality and process management systems. We discuss integrating all of these efforts under one umbrella as a true holistic improvement system (Lean Six Sigma 2.0) in Chapter 9, "The Way We Work."

Champions might not have depth in the technology of Six Sigma and Lean, so input from MBBs can be extremely helpful in assigning an improvement methodology to prioritized projects. Although MBBs wear multiple hats, including as trainers and mentoring Black Belts, they are typically in the best position to determine the most appropriate methodology for a given project. This is because of their technical depth and experience. Therefore, MBBs should play an important role in the project selection and prioritization process, along with Champions and business leaders.

For both Six Sigma and Lean projects, it is essential that you carefully identify and document the process that contains the problem. This is typically done with flowcharts or value stream maps, which contain more detail than flowcharts (Monden, 2012). The process provides the focus and context for the improvement work. Process identification is usually easy in manufacturing, where you can simply follow the pipes, but it is much less obvious in finance or marketing. A Black Belt or Green Belt who utilizes the Six Sigma and/or Lean methodology then completes the project. Of course, there is no guarantee that every problem will be successfully solved, but with proper project, methodology, and people selection, we can expect a very high (80–90 percent) success rate.

To use Six Sigma or Lean, you also need one or more measurements that quantify the magnitude of the problem and can be used to set project goals and monitor progress. These measurements are usually called critical to quality (CTQ) measures. Lean Six Sigma takes a disciplined, rigorous approach to problem identification, diagnosis, analysis, and solution. With the integration of Lean and Six Sigma, it is well suited for the diverse array of project types discussed earlier. Of course, more methodologies are needed to create a true holistic improvement system. This is the focus of subsequent chapters.

Selecting Good Lean Six Sigma Projects

Now we turn our attention to selecting the best projects. The characteristics of a good Lean Six Sigma project follow:

- Constitutes breakthrough improvement
  - Not routine problem solving
- Clearly connected to business priorities
  - Linked to strategic and annual operating plans
- Focuses on a problem that is of major importance to the organization
  - Represents a major improvement in process performance (for example, greater than 50%)
  - Represents a major financial improvement (for example, more than $250,000 per year)
- Has a reasonable scope (doable in 3–6 months, or less for Lean)
- Uses clear quantitative measures of success
  - Baseline, goals, and entitlement well-defined
- Has the support and approval of management

Lean Six Sigma projects should obviously constitute breakthrough improvement. A common mistake is to force-fit Six Sigma or Lean to a problem that is better addressed through routine problem solving or perhaps a quality by design methodology. Projects should be clearly linked to business priorities, as reflected in the strategic and annual operating plans. It is also important to include projects that address critical problems that must be solved for the organization to be successful in the next year.

A project should represent a breakthrough in terms of major improvements in both process performance (for example, greater than 50 percent) and significant bottom-line results (for example, greater than $250,000). Determining financial impact is the responsibility of the financial organization, working in cooperation with the Black Belt and Champion.

This approach to measuring project impact sets Lean Six Sigma apart from most other improvement approaches because the financial impact is identified for each project by the finance department. Finance should know what the project is worth to the bottom line before work begins. This makes it an active participant in the improvement of the organization. In many organizations, this is a new role for finance personnel. Of course, finance and other functions will still have their own projects to improve their own processes.

The projects should be doable in three to six months, often less for Lean (Monden, 2011). As Bill Gates pointed out (1999), it is critical that projects be completed in this time frame to keep the organization and resources focused on the project. Organizations typically lose interest in projects that run longer than six months. Projects requiring more than six months of effort can usually be divided into subprojects of shorter duration, with the projects being conducted sequentially or in parallel. For this approach to work, strong project management is needed to coordinate the set of projects.

Additionally, clear quantitative measures of success are needed, the importance of the project to the organization should be clear, and the project should have the full support and approval of management. These three characteristics are needed so that the organization sees the importance of the project, provides the needed support and resources, and removes barriers to the success of the project. People are more likely to support a project that they can see is clearly important to the organization.

Of course, other than the first item, these are generic attributes of a good project. Organizations still need to develop their own specific project selection criteria. Compare these generic attributes to the more specific project selection criteria from one company provided in the earlier section "Project Selection Criteria."

The specific criteria defined areas that were important to improve for this company, and projects based on these criteria did, in turn, produce significant bottom-line results. Note also that the areas to improve included customer satisfaction measurements. Project selection criteria communicate what types of improvements are important to the organization.

Project ideas can come from any source, such as process assessments, customer and employee surveys and suggestions, benchmarking studies, extensions of existing projects, and so on. Many organizations struggle to find high-impact projects. Some sources that we recommend follow:

- Rework and scrapping activities

- Excessive in-process and finished product inventory

- Overtime, warranty, and other obvious sources of waste

- Products with major backlogs—need for more capacity

- High-volume products (small improvements can have huge impact)

- Problems that need solutions to meet the annual operating plan

- Major problems with financial impact (customer or environmental crises)

- Large-budget items, receivables, payables, treasury, taxes (follow the money)

Collectively, these ideas focus on major sources of waste, major problems (customer and environmental), major opportunities (capacity limitations in sold-out markets), and places where the money is going. Budget statements and cost of quality studies are also good sources for identifying opportunities (Conway, 1992, 1994).

Experience has also identified some characteristics of projects to avoid, or at least to further refine. Briefly stated, you should avoid, or redefine, projects that fall into any of these classifications:

- Fuzzy objectives

- Poor metrics

- No tie to financials

- Too broad a scope ("boiling the ocean")

- No connection to strategic or annual plans

- Too many objectives

For example, for the project to succeed, the objectives need to be very clear. Such clarity is usually reflected in the process performance metrics and goals associated with the project. The process metrics should be clearly defined and should have baseline and entitlement values identified. In the case of nonmanufacturing projects, the most useful process performance metrics are typically accuracy, cycle time, and cost. Cost is usually directly related to accuracy and cycle time metrics.

The project must be tied to the bottom line in some way. The project scope should be for improvements that are attainable in three to six months. An unrealistic scope (often referred to as a "boiling the ocean" project) is probably the most commonly encountered cause of project failure. Projects that are not connected to business priorities or that have too many objectives also need further refinement.

The Concept of Process Entitlement

Entitlement is one of the most important concepts in breakthrough improvement, and it is particularly useful in project selection. It is defined as the best performance that you can reasonably expect to obtain from a process (Harry and Schroeder, 2000). As the term implies, leadership is essentially entitled to this level of performance based on the investments they have already made.

Knowing the process entitlement defines what's possible. If entitlement is 500 units per day and the baseline performance is 250 units per day, you can easily see that there is a lot of room for improving this process.

On the other hand, if current baseline performance is 480 units per day, there is little room for improvement. If higher production rates are needed, a search for a totally new process could be in order (that is, a quality by design approach, such as DFSS).

As an analogy, the concept of par for a golf hole is intended to represent the entitlement for a very good golfer. That is, for such a golfer, par represents what score is possible and reasonable to expect. On one hole, a golfer might score less than par, but it is unrealistic to expect such performance on every hole, or even on average. Of course, all golfers have their own unique capability, so the official par doesn't represent process entitlement for the average duffer. Proper analysis and/or calculations would reveal the appropriate individual entitlement, which would be better than par for professionals and much worse for most golfers. Note that standard golfing handicaps are usually based on average performance, which is not the same concept as entitlement.

It is not uncommon to learn in situations where capital is being requested to increase capacity that baseline production is not actually near entitlement once it is carefully calculated. Six Sigma and/or Lean projects might subsequently be instituted to increase the capacity of the current process with solutions that don't require capital. Most companies deploying Lean Six Sigma have been able to cancel existing capital expansion plans because of capacity that has been freed up through Lean Six Sigma with no capital expenditures. For example, if a chemical plant with six production lines is running at a 25 percent waste level, reducing the waste levels to 10 percent (60 percent reduction) creates additional capacity of $6 \times 15\% = 90\%$ of a production line, or essentially creates a new line with no capital expense.

Entitlement should be determined for all key process performance measures (yield, cost of poor quality, capacity, downtime, waste, and so on). It may be the performance predicted by engineering and scientific fundamentals, nameplate capacity provided by the equipment manufacturer, or simply the best prolonged performance observed to date.

Entitlement can also be predicted from empirical relationships. In one instance, it was observed that a process operating at a cost of $0.36 per unit had at one time operated at $0.16 per unit (correcting for inflation). This suggests that the process entitlement (as determined by best prolonged performance) should be $0.16 per unit. On further investigation, it was observed that there was a linear relationship between defects and cost per unit of the form:

$$Cost = \$0.12 + 3(\text{defects})/1{,}000{,}000.$$

Therefore, if defects could be reduced to very low levels (essentially zero), the true process entitlement could be as low as $0.12 per unit.

Entitlement is used in project selection as follows:

1. Look at the gap between baseline performance (current state) and entitlement (desired state).

2. Identify a project scope that will close the gap and can be completed in three to six months.

3. Assess the bottom-line impact of the project and compare it to other potential projects.

4. Select the most reasonable improvement methodology and assign a Black Belt or Green Belt with the requisite background.

The gap between baseline and entitlement is rarely closed in the course of a single project. It is not uncommon for several projects to be required. In each instance, the business case for the project is determined, the project is prioritized relative to the other potential projects, the methodology is selected, and a Black Belt or Green Belt is assigned as business priorities dictate.

Entitlement defines the performance level it is possible for a process to attain. It provides a vision of possible process performance, thereby providing a performance level to target. It tells you how close the current performance (baseline) is to the best possible performance. It also provides a benchmark that you can use to compare your process to other processes in your company or to processes in other companies. It is prudent to compute process entitlement values before doing any benchmarking studies, to provide a basis of comparison.

Keep in mind that process entitlement can, and often does, change as you learn more about it. In most cases, the process entitlement calculations are simply estimates of the true entitlement, and you can update and enhance them over time. After a few Lean Six Sigma projects, it is not uncommon for a process to be performing beyond the entitlement level initially determined for the process. Changing the estimate of process entitlement as you better understand the process is a natural result of Lean Six Sigma projects, and the need to do so should not come as a surprise.

Developing the Project Charter

The project charter has a critical impact on project success. This one-page document summarizes the key aspects of the project. In effect, it defines what management wants done and what the Black Belt and Champion have agreed to accomplish. It forms a contract for all parties involved in the project.

Experience has shown that many continuous improvement projects fail because of misunderstandings among the team or with the project leader, the customer, or management. For example, a team might proudly present a completed project that developed a web-based system for underwriting U.S. commercial credit lines for a leasing company. Management might have expected an internationalized version, however, and would then view the project as inadequate because it cannot be used in either Europe or Asia. A clear, concise project charter avoids such misunderstandings and helps protect the project team from being second-guessed.

The charter is typically drafted by the Project Champion, refined by the Project Champion and Black Belt, and approved by the leadership team. It is not unusual for the charter to be revised a few times as the problem is better understood and data becomes available. Somewhere near the end of the Measure phase, the charter should define the scope of work that the project will accomplish. If such commitment is not made, it will be hard for the project to satisfy expectations. If the expectations defined by the charter are constantly changing, however it will be like trying to hit a moving target.

Figure 6.1 shows a template we have used for project charters that is similar to the template of Harry and Schroeder (2000). All the information that the project charter requires must be reported in the template. Blank entries are not acceptable.

Product or Service Impacted		Expected Project Savings($)	
BlackBelt/GreenBelt		Email	
Champion		Business Unit	
Start Date		Target Completion Date	

Element	Description					
1. Process:	Process in which opportunity exists.					
2. Project Description:	Project's purpose					
3. Objective:	Key process metrics impacted by the project	Process Metric	Baseline	Goal	Entitlement	Units
		Metric 1				
		Metric 2				
		Metric 3				
4. Dollar Savings ($)	Expected financial improvement					
5. Team members:	Names and titles of team members					
6. Project Scope:	Which part of the process will be investigated?					
7. Benefit to External Customers:	Who are the final customers, what are their key measures and what benefits will they see?					
	Key completion dates.	Project Start				
	M- Measurement	"M" Complete				
	A- Analysis	"A" Complete				
	I- Improvement	"I" Complete				
	C- Control	"C" Complete				
	Other milestones					
		Project Complete				
9. Support Required:	Will any special capabilities, hardware, etc. be needed?					

Figure 6.1   Six Sigma project charter form

Be on the lookout for potential problems. The process you are trying to improve should be clear (Charter Element 1). The process provides the focus and context for the work. A clear process definition helps the Black Belt see where the work will focus and what needs to be accomplished. Identifying the process is often difficult for persons and organizations that are not skilled in thinking about their work as a series of interconnected processes.

The scope should be clear and attainable in three to six months, or less for Lean projects (Charter Elements 2 and 6). Many projects fail because the scope is too big for the allotted time. Answering the question, "Can we get this work done in three to six months (or whatever required time frame)?" is an effective way to test whether the project is properly scoped.

Keen attention should be paid to the process metrics (Charter Element 3). These measurements focus the Black Belt on the aspects of process performance that need to be improved and the quantitative goals for the project. They are also used to calculate the financial impact of the project.

Leaving this section of the charter blank is not acceptable because the project will not succeed without the metrics. The project should not proceed until data is available to properly define the project and calculate business impact.

The baseline, goal, and entitlement values for each of the key process metrics should be entered in the charter. Some of these values might be estimates at this point, to be re-evaluated during the Measure phase. You should include the metrics you want to improve as well as the metrics you don't want to negatively influence. For example, if the project is a capacity improvement project and it is particularly important that product quality not deteriorate, then the charter should address both capacity and quality metrics.

It is important to determine the anticipated business impact of the project (Charter Element 4). This should identify both hard dollars (cost savings and profits from increased sales) that flow to the bottom line and any soft dollar benefits, such as cost avoidance. Many organizations that deploy Lean Six Sigma, including GE, consider only the hard benefits when publishing savings from the effort. Even when only hard benefits are reported, you should document planned soft benefits in the charter. Leaving this section blank is unacceptable because, without quantitative knowledge, there will be no way of knowing what the project is worth and whether it is the right project on which to be working.

Our experience suggests that, in most cases, the project team should be small and not have more than four to six members (Charter Element 5). It is important that the team members be identified by name in the charter to ensure that each is available to work on the project. The team can include specialists and technical experts, as needed. All core team members should be available for at least 25 percent of their time. A common pitfall is having team members that are overloaded and not available to work on the project.

Another key item is the project schedule (Charter Element 8). As noted earlier, the project should be scheduled for completion in three to six months. Some will try to resist such an aggressive schedule. Projects scheduled for competition in more than six months is another way a project can fail. The scope of projects taking longer than six months should be reduced, or serious consideration should be given to dividing the work into more than one project.

Once the project charter has been developed, you are in a position to select the Black Belt and Champion who will be responsible for conducting the project. The critical step of selecting the right people for your Lean Six Sigma initiative is addressed in the next section.

Selecting the Right People

Finding the right people for the key Lean Six Sigma roles is another ingredient for success during the Launch phase and is part of the implementation process. Leadership is the key characteristic to keep in mind when selecting the people who are to be involved in Lean Six Sigma. Recall that there is no substitute for leadership.

Achieving the desired results requires changing the way you work, and that means changing how you think about your work. Leaders are required to move everyone successfully from the old way of working to making Lean Six Sigma, and eventually holistic improvement, an integral part of your new way of working. Everyone involved in Lean Six Sigma is a leader (Champions, MBBs, Black Belts, Green Belts). To increase your odds of success, select your top talent—your best performers, who are capable of providing the needed leadership.

Deploying Lean Six Sigma is not an easy task; breakthrough improvement is the goal. For the longer term, you want Lean Six Sigma 2.0 to be your holistic improvement system. You want your senior managers to be skilled in using Lean Six Sigma to help run your business. Placing only technical specialists (engineers, statisticians, quality professionals, and so on) in key Lean Six Sigma roles is a serious mistake. Such major culture change requires persons experienced and skilled in leadership.

The need for leadership is evident in the roles of corporate and unit leadership, Project Champion, Black Belt, and MBB, as summarized in Table 6.3.

Table 6.3 Lean Six Sigma Leadership Roles

Corporate Management	Unit Management	Project Champions	Black Belts	Master Black Belts	Functional Support Groups
Create and deploy strategy and goals	Establish project selection criteria	Facilitate project selection	Learn and use the Lean Six Sigma methodology and tools	Develop and deliver Lean Six Sigma training	Provide data and aid in data collection
Define boundaries—what's in and what's out	Approve projects—ensure linkage to strategy and key needs	Create project charter	Develop and maintain project work plan	Assist in the selection of projects	Provide team members
Communicate purpose and progress	Select Project Champions	Facilitate identification of resources—BB, team, $$, functional resources	Provide leadership for the team	Coach and council Black Belts	Support with expertise in the department, such as financial value of projects
Provide resources—people, time, and $$	Provide needed resources and training	Remove barriers	Meet weekly with the Project Champion	Ensure the success of "mission critical" projects	Identify opportunities for Lean Six Sigma projects
Ensure training plan is in place	Review Black Belt and Green Belt projects monthly	Review projects weekly	Communicate support needs to functional groups	Support the efforts of Champions and Management Team	Help with benchmarking
Ensure recognition plan is in place	Establish and use communications process	Verify project deliverables for each phase of DMAIC	Ensure that the right data are collected and properly analyzed		Set boundaries (legal, company policy, environmental)
Quarterly review of overall initiative	Review the entire process every 3-6 months	Communicate purpose and progress of projects	Identify and communicate barriers to Champion		Provide reality check, diversity of ideas, perspective
Periodic reviews of plant and business initiatives	Establish reward and recognition structure	Approve project closure	Provide monthly updates to Champion and Master Black Belt		
Support initiative with rewards and recognition	Link rewards to performance	Identify next project for the BB/GB	Responsible for delivering results ($$)		
Publicly celebrate successes	Be accountable for the success of the effort	Celebrate, recognize, and reward BB and team Accountable for project results			

The role of the leadership team depends on the size of the company. In large companies, there should be a leadership team at the corporate level as well as a leadership team for each of the business units and functions.

The key elements of the corporate leadership role follow:

- Providing strategy and direction

- Communicating purpose and progress

- Enabling and providing resources

- Conducting reviews

- Recognizing and reinforcing

The Leadership Team

Table 6.3 also summarizes the role of the unit leadership team. We define the unit as the entity responsible for identifying the improvement opportunities and chartering the Lean Six Sigma projects. This could be a division, a facility, or a function. The unit leadership team (often called the Lean Six Sigma Council) leads the overall effort within the unit.

In the case of a manufacturing facility, the leadership team is typically the plant manager and selected members of his or her staff. In the case of the finance function, the leadership team might be the CFO and selected members of his or her staff. A key difference between the roles of the two leadership teams is that the unit-level team has responsibility for the projects.

Champion

Each project has a Champion who serves as its business and political leader. Some organizations have used the term *Champion* to refer to the overall leader of the Lean Six Sigma effort. The Project Champion is typically a member of the unit leadership team, has responsibility for the successful completion of projects, and is held accountable for the results of the projects. Key tasks for the Champion role follow:

- Facilitating the selection of the project

- Drafting the initial project charter

- Selecting the Black Belt and other resources

- Removing barriers to the successful completion of the project

- Holding short weekly reviews with the Black Belt regarding the progress of the project

The Champion has direct contact with and provides guidance and direction for the Black Belt. In some cases, the Black Belt is a direct report of the Project Champion. In other situations, the Black Belt also reports to an MBB. As Figure 6.2 shows, a unit typically has more than one Project Champion, with each directing one to three Black Belts. The Project Champion role is usually part time, but it can be a full-time responsibility in some organizations. In most cases, the part-time role works best because it involves more managers in the Lean Six Sigma improvement process.

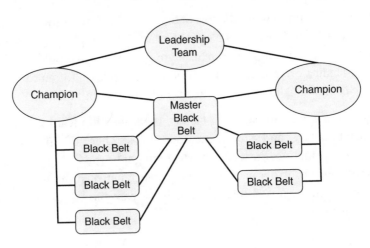

Figure 6.2   Linkages between roles

Black Belt

The Black Belt leads the team that works on the project. Keep in mind that we are not restricting the term *Black Belt*, or other traditional Six Sigma terms, to Six Sigma projects, per se. In a Lean Six Sigma initiative, we use these same titles for Lean or hybrid projects, and as more methodologies are added to the holistic improvement initiative, we continue to use Six Sigma infrastructure and terminology. This is one of the reasons we refer to a true holistic improvement system as Lean Six Sigma 2.0.

Therefore, although all Black Belts in a Lean Six Sigma deployment should have competency in both Lean and Six Sigma, some Black Belts will naturally be more experienced in Lean, while others will be more experienced in Six Sigma. When selecting a Black Belt to lead a specific project, that Black Belt should obviously have a strong background in the particular methodology intended for this project. This need to match Black Belts with the best background to specific intended methodologies for a given project will become even more important as more improvement methodologies are added to the deployment.

In terms of selecting candidates for the role, a Black Belt should have these characteristics:

- A technical leader in the area of the project
  - Helpful for the first project
  - Less important for subsequent projects
- Respected by the organization
- Computer literate
- An analytical thinker, not afraid of numbers
- Skilled in basic statistics
- A team leader, with soft skills
- Skilled in project management
- A positive thinker with a can-do attitude

Black Belts get things done. They are hands-on workers, work full time on their projects, and do much of the detailed work. They should be selected on the basis of what they can do, not on the basis of what they know (Hoerl, 2001). Black Belts also act as mentors for Green Belts, as do MBBs.

Green Belt

Green Belts might lead their own project under the direction of a Champion or MBB, or they might work on a portion of a Black Belt project under the direction of the Black Belt. Green Belts work part time, devoting typically 25 percent of their time to the project. Green Belt projects are typically less strategic and more locally focused than Black Belt projects. A Green Belt project is typically worth $50,000 to $75,000 per year to the bottom line and should be completed in three to six months.

Because Green Belts work on improvement projects in addition to their existing job responsibilities, several companies (such as GE) have as an objective that eventually all professionals will be at least Green Belts. Some Green Belts will become Black Belts, so it is advisable for some of the Green Belts to have many of the Black Belt characteristics.

Master Black Belt

The MBB is the technical leader who enables the organization to integrate Lean Six Sigma within its operations. Ideally, the MBB should have strong leadership and technical skills and be politically savvy, with a good understanding of the business, since he or she will work closely with Champions and the leadership team. As with Black Belts, MBBs should understand both Lean and Six Sigma, but they might specialize in one or the other.

The MBB has typically completed several Black Belt projects and two to five weeks of training beyond the four weeks of Black Belt training. He or she helps the Champions select projects and reviews their progress. The MBB provides training and mentoring for Black Belts, as well as training for Green Belts in some instances. As with Black Belts, the MBBs should be full time.

MBBs play other roles as well. They should help lead mission-critical projects as needed. This work not only contributes to the success of the organization, but it also enables the MBB to further develop process improvement skills. MBBs should be responsible for ensuring that baseline and entitlement data is available and up-to-date for all key processes; this is especially important for effective project selection. MBBs are in an excellent position to identify and distribute best practices for process improvement and management and to distribute them around the organization. Many organizations develop an MBB network that meets periodically to share these best practices around the company.

In essence, MBBs are intended to combine technical skills beyond those of the Black Belt with managerial and leadership skills similar to those of a Champion. Most companies hire external providers to deliver the initial Lean Six Sigma training. The MBBs should gradually take over the responsibility for this training. Experience has shown that Lean Six

Sigma is internalized most quickly in companies that develop their cadre of MBBs rapidly.

Functional Support Groups

The functional support groups, such as HR, Finance, IT, Legal, Engineering, Quality Assurance, and so on, assist the Lean Six Sigma effort in four key ways:

- Provide data as needed by the Black Belt
- Provide unique expertise
- Provide members for the Black Belt project team
- Help identify improvement opportunities

The functional groups are typically involved in more aspects of the organization's work than are other groups. As a result, they see where improvements are needed in cross-functional processes. For example, the finance organization interacts with procurement, manufacturing, marketing, logistics, sales, and R&D; therefore, they can more easily pinpoint cross-functional issues that need to be addressed.

Many companies overlook the role of the functional support groups and, as a result, slow the progress of the Lean Six Sigma initiative. Sometimes Black Belts can't get the expertise and team members when they need them; worse yet, poor planning results in no resources to implement improvements. Careful planning and attention to the availability of functional resources as early as possible are time and effort well spent.

Forming Teams

An important question is, "How do I form the team that will work with the Black Belt or Green Belt?" The short answer is to appoint no more than six people who are familiar with the process and will be involved in implementing the Lean Six Sigma solution.

In our experience, the team should not have more than four to six persons. Larger teams are generally ineffective because they have trouble finding a meeting time when all can attend. Large teams also often have trouble reaching consensus, and responsibility could be diluted. If it seems that the task is too great to be done by four to six people, the project is probably too large and should be split into two or more smaller projects. These smaller projects can still be coordinated at periodic coordination meetings between the Project Champions.

The team needs to include people who are familiar with the process, can contribute to identifying the solution, and will be involved in its implementation. Experts and consultants, even internal or external customers and suppliers, can also be ad hoc members of the team and participate when needed. The core members of the team should be available 25 percent of the time to work on the project. The team receives any needed training delivered just in time by the Black Belt or MBB, as appropriate.

The best approach to forming the team is for the Black Belt to create it in consultation with the Project Champion and the managers to whom the prospective team members report. The process might look like the following:

1. The Black Belt and Champion discuss potential team members.

2. The Black Belt or Champion gets the approval of the team members' management for them to be on the team.

3. The Champion addresses any barriers identified, getting higher management involved as needed.

4. The Black Belt and the team work on the project.

As in any partnership, the Black Belt and Champion work out who will do what in the team-forming process. An MBB can become involved, if needed. It is important that both the Black Belt and the Champion build support for the project with all the involved stakeholders. People are more likely to support a project when the purpose and value are understood, their role in the project is clear, and they see how they will benefit from the successful completion of the project. The Project Champion has the responsibility to see that any problems or barriers identified are resolved.

Where Do I Find the Resources?

This is the question most commonly asked when managers first hear about Lean Six Sigma, and every leader of the deployment should have a ready answer. In short, help can come from re-evaluating employees' responsibilities and from hiring from outside.

To increase their capabilities and move up the learning curve more quickly, some companies hire an experienced MBB or vice president of Lean Six Sigma to lead the implementation effort. Some hire experienced Black Belts from other companies to lead projects or hire new employees to backfill for Black Belts and MBBs.

By far the most popular resource strategy for companies deploying Lean Six Sigma is to re-evaluate existing work programs and reprioritize how they utilize their resources. As a result, Lean Six Sigma is deployed using existing resources. This strategy is used most often, but it is not initially the favorite of managers, who must rethink priorities and deal with personnel changes. Fortunately, this stress decreases as managers learn to deploy Lean Six Sigma and see it improve the performance of their organization.

Over time, managers find many different ways to backfill for the employees that have become Black Belts or MBBs. Some projects will already be in the Black Belt's assigned area of responsibility, so even without Lean Six Sigma, they would likely have worked on this problem. If necessary, the Black Belt's previous responsibilities can be assigned to other employees and contractors. Some work can be postponed, and some work is non-value-added and can be eliminated. Resource sharing can be hard for some to do, but it is an effective way to create resources.

In short, look for two characteristics: underutilized capacity and unrecognized capability. Some employees are not working to their full potential. Some employees can handle bigger workloads. Some are doing tactical work that could be better done by others, freeing these employees to do more strategic work, including Lean Six Sigma. Many times engineers are seen creating budgets, writing talks or making PowerPoint slides for others, or doing paperwork instead of improving processes. We met one overworked and highly stressed vice president of sales who was reviewing *every* sales contract written by the company. Clearly, a lot of time could be freed by delegating the review of smaller contracts to subordinates.

We should add a warning here: The strategy of deploying Lean Six Sigma by adding these new responsibilities on top of existing workloads is almost guaranteed to fail. In all the organizations we are familiar with, most employees are already quite busy; adding Lean Six Sigma responsibilities will result in oversights on the existing work, on Lean Six Sigma, or on both. Adding more food to a plate that is already completely full only creates a mess. Something will have to be taken off the plate in order to add more. Eliminating work is difficult, but leaders are able to make these tough decisions relative to prioritization.

What Training Do I Need?

Lean Six Sigma requires people to think and work in different ways. This requires that they be trained in the new way of thinking and working. A lot of training has to be done as spelled out in the implementation plan. The key groups to be trained are executives, business teams, site leadership teams, functional leadership teams, Champions, MBBs, Black Belts, and Green Belts.

The Executive, Business Team, Site Leadership Team, and Functional Leadership Team workshops are typically one or two days and focus on what Lean Six Sigma is, how it will be deployed, and the roles of the groups involved. These are active workshops in which work is done on the deployment and implementation plans, not as passive overviews. A draft deployment plan with carefully selected areas for initial projects is a key output of these workshops. Figure 6.3 illustrates the intended process of direction from the Executive workshop, cascading down through the organization to the Black Belts and individual projects.

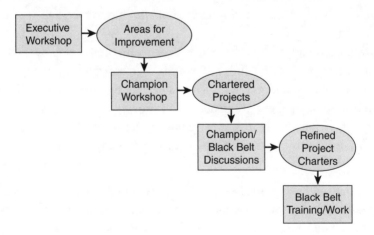

Figure 6.3 Cascading of direction

The Champion workshop is typically three to five days. Its focus is on developing a deeper understanding of Lean Six Sigma, deployment in the organization, and roles of the Project Champion and the Black Belt. Project Champions are trained to guide the work of the Black Belts. The Champion also spends time learning the DMAIC process and understanding the Six Sigma and Lean tools the Black Belt will be using.

Black Belt training typically lasts four weeks, with each week focused on a phase of the DMAIC process. The usual sequence is Week 1, Define and Measure; Week 2, Analyze; Week 3, Improve; and Week 4, Control. The recommended outlines for finance and manufacturing-oriented courses proposed by Hoerl (2001) are shown in the following two lists. These have been modified to incorporate Lean principles and key tools. Note that these outlines also include Design for Six Sigma (DFSS). Some companies teach DFSS separately; others prefer to integrate it with DMAIC training. Both approaches can work.

Sample Black Belt Course for Finance

(This course is in three weeks, with Week 3 being a Black Belt course in addition to an existing Green Belt course.)

Week 1

- Lean and Six Sigma concepts
- The DMAIC and DFSS (Design for Six Sigma) improvement strategies
- Project selection and scoping (Define)
- Flowcharting and value stream mapping
- 5S
- QFD
- Sampling principles (quality and quantity)
- Measurement system analysis (also called "gage R&R")
- Process capability
- Basic graphs

- Hypothesis testing
- Regression

Week 2

- DOE (focus on two-level factorials)
- Pull versus push systems (just in time)
- Kaizen events
- Mistake-proofing (poka-yoke)
- Design for Six Sigma and tools
  - Requirements flow-down
  - Capability flow-up (prediction)
  - Piloting
  - Simulation
- FMEA
- Control plans
- Control charts

Week 3

- Power (impact of sample size)
- Impact of process instability on capability analysis
- Confidence intervals (vs. hypothesis tests)
- Implications of the Central Limit Theorem
- Transformations
- How to detect "Lying with Statistics"
- General linear models
- Fractional factorial DOEs

Sample Black Belt Course for Manufacturing

(The superscripts refer to the week in which the material would appear)

Context[1]

- Why Lean Six Sigma?
- DMAIC and DFSS processes (sequential case studies)
- Six Sigma and Lean principles
- Project management fundamentals
- Team effectiveness fundamentals

Define[1]

- Project selection
- Project scope
- Project plan development
- Multigenerational projects
- Process identification (SIPOC and value stream mapping)

Measure[1]

- QFD
  - Identifying customer needs
  - Developing measurable critical to quality metrics (CTQs)
- Sampling (data quantity and data quality)
- Measurement system analysis (not just gage R&R)
- SPC Part I
  - The concept of statistical control (process stability)
  - The implications of instability on capability measures
- Capability analysis

Analyze[2]

- Basic graphical improvement tools (Magnificent 7)
- Management and planning tools (affinity, ID, and so on)
- Confidence intervals (emphasized)
- Hypothesis testing (de-emphasized)
- ANOVA (de-emphasized)
- Regression
- Multi-vari studies
- Conceptual designs in DFSS

Improve[3-4]

- 5S
- Pull versus push systems (just in time)
- Kaizen events
- DOE (focus on two-level factorials, screening designs, and RSM)
- Piloting (of DMAIC improvements)
- FMEA
- Mistake-proofing (poka-yoke)
- DFSS design tools
  - CTQ flow-down
  - Capability flow-up
  - Simulation

Control[4]

- Control plans
- SPC Part II
  - Control charts
- Piloting of new designs in DFSS

Green Belt training typically lasts two weeks, with Week 1 focused on the Define, Measure, and Analyze phases of DMAIC, and Week 2 focused on the Analyze, Improve, and Control phases. A recommended outline of topics for manufacturing Green Belt training follows:

Sample Green Belt Course for Manufacturing

(The superscripts refer to the week in which the material would appear)

Context[1]

- Why Lean Six Sigma?
- DMAIC (sequential case studies)
- Lean and Six Sigma principles
- Project management fundamentals
- Team effectiveness fundamentals

Define[1]

- Project selection
- Project scope
- Project plan development
- Process identification (SIPOC and value stream mapping)

Measure[1]

- QFD
- Customer needs identification
- Development of measureable critical to quality metrics (CTQs)
- Sampling (data quantity and data quality)
- Measurement system analysis (not just gage R&R)
- SPC Part I
  - The concept of statistical control (process stability)
  - The implications of instability on capability measures
- Capability analysis

Analyze[1-2]

- FMEA
- Basic graphical improvement tools (Magnificent 7)
- Confidence intervals (emphasized)
- Hypothesis testing (de-emphasized)
- ANOVA (de-emphasized)
- Regression
- Multi-vari studies

Improve[2]

- 5S
- Pull versus push systems (just in time)
- Kaizen events
- DOE (focus on two-level factorials)
- Piloting (of DMAIC improvements)
- Mistake-proofing (poka-yoke)

Control[2]

- Control plans
- SPC Part II
  - Control charts

Black Belt and Green Belt training topics and areas of emphasis must be based on the specific needs and targeted applications of the organization. The sample curricula presented here form a base of reference or starting point, not the final answer for all organizations. Alternative curricula, as well as guidelines for conducting effective training, can be found in Hoerl (2001) and its associated discussion. Note that as the organization moves to a holistic improvement system, more improvement methodologies will be added, requiring more thought about the training system. We do not recommend that everyone be trained in every method; this is simply too expensive and time consuming. We discuss this issue in greater detail in subsequent chapters.

Key to the success of Black Belt and Green Belt training is the practice of working on real projects during the training. It is our firm belief that a real, significant project should be the admission ticket for the training: "No Project, No Training." As noted earlier, if the projects are completed, the resulting benefits should more than pay for the training.

Organizing and conducting Six Sigma training requires careful planning, coordination, and execution. It is so important for the training leaders to have experience in deploying similar efforts that most companies hire outside Lean Six Sigma consultants to provide this service initially. Experienced providers have the knowledge, experience, capability, and capacity to do what is needed to create a successful deployment. Once the initiative has been successfully launched and internal MBBs obtain sufficient experience, they should begin to assume leadership of this effort.

Selecting a Lean Six Sigma Provider

Now that you have learned what is required to properly launch Six Sigma, you are in a position to decide whether to hire an external provider (consulting firm) to help with the training and initial deployment of Lean Six Sigma. Almost all companies get external help of some kind, which makes good business sense. Hiring a Lean Six Sigma provider enables a company to learn from those who have gone before and move up the learning curve more rapidly.

The consultant's costs should be more than covered by the returns of the higher number of projects that can be completed using the expertise of a seasoned consultant. Black Belt projects can also produce bottom-line results before the training is completed because quick fixes are often found in the Measure and Analyze phases of the DMAIC process. It is not unusual for 30 to 50 percent of the projects to produce bottom-line savings before the training is complete and for these benefits to more than cover the training costs.

This point is so important that it is worth repeating: In our experience, employing an outside Lean Six Sigma provider is cost effective and can help an organization move up the learning curve more rapidly. Another alternative is to recruit experienced individuals who have led deployments elsewhere to help guide your deployment.

Using an outside provider is also a high-yield strategy because executives and managers tend to listen to those from the outside more readily than to the company's employees. It is difficult to be a prophet in your own land, even when the knowledge to do the work exists within the organization. When hiring an external consultant, look for a proven track record of bottom-line results (contact previous clients), good rapport with your own leadership team, and common vision of how the deployment should proceed—including how to transition work from the consultant to internal resources over time. Unfortunately, even bad consultants can give a convincing sales pitch!

Summary and Looking Forward

The Launch phase of Lean Six Sigma is roughly the period between making the decision to deploy Lean Six Sigma and completing the initial wave of Black Belt training. This typically lasts six to nine months. The purpose of this phase is to ensure that you hit the ground running in Lean Six Sigma deployment. The key deliverables follow:

- An overall deployment plan (strategy)

- The initial wave of projects

- Trained Black Belts, and other key roles, in place

As noted in Chapter 5, committed leadership is the key success factor in this phase. It takes committed leadership to actively participate in leadership workshops, persevere through completion of the deployment and implementation plans, allocate the human resources and funding required for the effort, and address any resistance from within the organization. Leaders need to provide clear vision and direction. Other important success factors follow:

- Selection of good initial projects

- Selection of the right people for key roles

- Full-time allocation of Black Belts and MBBs

- Effective, tailored training for key roles

- Support from functional groups, as needed

Even in a successful launch, there will be a need to transition Lean Six Sigma from being a program fueled to some extent by excitement and adrenalin, to a formally managed initiative. Excitement and adrenalin last only so long! Sooner or later, reality sinks in and a more formal infrastructure is needed to ensure that the initiative is managed for the long haul. In the next chapter, we discuss how to make this transition.

References

Conway, W. E. (1992) *The Quality Secret: The Right Way to Manage*. Nashua, NH: Conway Quality, Inc.

Conway, W. E. (1994). *Winning the War on Waste*. Nashua, NH: Conway Quality, Inc.

Gates, William H., III. (1999) *Business @ The Speed of Thought*. New York: Warner Books.

Harry, M., and R. Schroeder. (2000) *Six Sigma: The Break-through Management Strategy Revolutionizing The World's Top Corporations*. New York: Currency Doubleday.

Hoerl, R. W. (2001) "Six Sigma Black Belts: What Do They Need to Know?" *Journal of Quality Technology* 33, no. 4: 391–435.

Hoerl, R.W., and Snee, R.D. (2013), "One Size Does Not Fit All: Identifying the Right Improvement Methodology", *Quality Progress*, May 2013, 48–50.

McGurk, T. L. (2004) "Ramping Up and Ensuring Supply Capability for Biopharmaceuticals." *BIOPHARM International* (January): 1–4.

Monden, Y. (2011) *Toyota Production System: An Integrated Approach to Just-In-Time*. 4th ed. CRC Press, Boca Raton, FL.

Monden, Y. (2012) *Toyota Production System: An Integrated Approach to Just-In-Time*. 4th ed. Boca Raton, FL: CRC Press.

Parikh, A. N., R. D. Snee, and S. O. Schall. (2014) "Creative Thinking: Devising a Six Sigma Deployment when Top Management Isn't Initially on Board." *Six Sigma Forum Magazine* (August): 8–14.

Snee, R. D. (2001) "Dealing with the Achilles' Heel of Six Sigma Initiatives: Project Selection Is Key to Success." *Quality Progress* (March): 66–72.

Snee, R. D. (2007) "Adopt DMAIC: Step One to Making Improvement Part of the Way We Work." *Quality Progress* (September): 52–53.

Snee, R. D., and R. W. Hoerl. (2005) *Six Sigma Beyond the Factory Floor: Deployment Strategies for Financial Services, Health Care and the Rest of the Real Economy.* Upper Saddle River, NJ: Pearson Prentice Hall.

Snee, R. D., and R. W. Hoerl. (2007) "Integrating Lean & Six Sigma: A Holistic Approach." *Six Sigma Forum Magazine* 6, no. 3: 15–21.

Snee, R. D., and W. F. Rodebaugh. (2002) "Project Selection Process." *Quality Progress* (September): 78–90.

Womack, J. P., and D. T. Jones. (2003) *Lean Thinking.* New York: Free Press.

7

Managing the Effort

"Six Sigma works if you follow the process. If Six Sigma is not working, you're not following the process."
—AlliedSignal Manager

I n the previous chapters, we discussed why the holistic improvement paradigm is needed, examined its building blocks, looked at case studies of its implementation, and shared tips on how to get started. In this chapter, we address how to manage the effort over time to realize its promised improved performance and to sustain it for the long term. This phase is of critical importance because, without it, your improvement initiative will dissipate over time, perhaps as soon as within two years. The elements of this phase are introduced and discussed here.

Your improvement initiative is now underway, initially focusing on Lean Six Sigma. The Executive and Champion workshops have been held. A deployment plan has been drafted, and an implementation plan is in place. The initial projects and Black Belts have been selected, and the first wave of training has been held. The initial wave of enthusiasm likely has carried the Lean Six Sigma effort this far. You are now reaching a critical transition point.

Once the first set of projects has been completed and the initiative begins to expand rapidly, you need to make the transition from a short-term launch to a well-managed long-term effort. The initiative will simply become too large to manage informally. You need a formal infrastructure to properly manage improvement deployment from this point onward.

Otherwise, the initiative will become just another short-lived fad. You also need top talent in key leadership roles to implement the infrastructure and manage the effort.

We refer to this next step in the deployment process as managing the effort. Our guiding principle follows:

> If you want something to happen on a regular and sustained basis, you need to have a management system in place to guide and sustain the effort.

Wikipedia (2011) defines a management system as a framework of processes and procedures used to ensure that an organization can fulfill all tasks required to achieve its objectives.

This phase goes roughly from completion of the initial wave of Black Belt training until we have trained everyone we originally intended to train and completed projects in all the areas mentioned in the deployment plan. It typically lasts a minimum of 18 months, although organizations must continue to manage Lean Six Sigma deployment in subsequent phases.

It is now time to put in place those systems and processes that will enable you to effectively manage the effort. You will have worked on many of these systems in the Executive and Champion workshops, and they are part of the deployment plan. At this point, you not only create systems to manage Lean Six Sigma, but you also begin to think about how to make these systems part of your culture—how you do things in your organization. This will help you sustain the benefits and make Lean Six Sigma "the way we work" (see Chapter 9, "The Way We Work"). Furthermore, during this phase, it is important to begin adding more elements of a holistic improvement system so that you expand beyond Lean Six Sigma to Lean Six Sigma 2.0, holistic improvement.

The following list, adapted from Snee et al. (1998), notes the key types of leadership support needed for successful Black Belt projects. Clearly, Black Belts cannot succeed on their own, and there is too much here to manage informally. Fortunately, your deployment plan can help you with each of these infrastructure elements. This chapter focuses on the elements of the deployment plan that are most needed at this point. Specifically, we discuss the following:

- Management project reviews

- A project reporting and tracking system

- A communications plan

- A reward and recognition plan

- A project identification/prioritization system

- Project closure criteria

- Inclusion of Lean Six Sigma into budgeting processes

- Deployment processes for Champions, Black Belts, MBBs, and so on

Implementation of these systems and processes is the key deliverable for this phase. Each of these infrastructure elements is an aspect of good management. When done well and integrated with your current management system, Lean Six Sigma becomes part of your culture. The goal is to make Lean Six Sigma part of how you do your work, not an add-on—eventually, it should not be something extra that you have to do (see Chapter 9). Before we discuss each of the listed elements and provide examples and guidance for its implementation, we comment on the role of managerial systems and processes to set the stage.

Leadership Support Needed for Successful Black Belt Projects

- Chartered project

    - Identified, approved, and supported by management

    - Important to the organization—aligned with priorities

    - High impact (for example, more than $250,000 annual savings)

    - Scope that can be completed in 3–6 months

    - Clear quantitative measure of success

- Time for Black Belt to work on the project
  - Recommend 100 percent dedicated, absolute minimum of 50–75 percent
  - Time for Black Belt to do the training and project work
  - Reassignment of current workload
- Directions to form project team: typically 4–6 team members
  - Access to people working on the process and others to be team members
  - Access to other specialists and subject matter experts
  - Guidance to keep the team small, to speed up progress
- Training for team members as needed
- Priority use of organizational services such as lab services and access to the manufacturing line.
- Regular management reviews of the project
  - Weekly by Champion
  - Monthly by leadership team
- Help with data systems to collect needed process data on a priority basis
  - Create temporary and manual systems as needed
- Communications—inform all persons affected by the project of:
  - Project purpose and value
  - Need to support work of Black Belts
- Finance assistance in estimating and documenting bottom-line savings (in dollars)
- System to recognize, reward, and celebrate the success of the Black Belt and team

Managerial Systems and Processes

Most of this chapter discusses the implementation of managerial systems and processes. Because these terms are often used loosely in business circles, clarification is in order. All work is done through a series of processes. By *process*, we simply mean a sequence of activities that transform inputs (raw materials, information, and so on) into outputs (a finished product, an invoice, and so on).

There will always be a process, even if it cannot be seen and even if it is not standardized. In manufacturing, identifying the process is easy—just follow the pipes! Seeing the process is much more difficult in soft areas such as finance or legal. Understanding processes is critically important to making any improvement, however, because we improve outputs by improving the process. As noted earlier, process thinking is a fundamental aspect of Lean Six Sigma.

By *managerial processes*, we mean those that help us manage the organization, as opposed to making, distributing, or selling something. These typically include budgeting, reward and recognition, business planning, and reporting processes. Design and management of these processes generally define the core responsibilities of middle managers. Ideally, these processes help align all employees with strategic direction, such as by communicating or rewarding Lean Six Sigma successes. Poor managerial processes usually produce a dysfunctional organization, whereas effective managerial processes usually produce an effective and efficient organization.

Figure 7.1 illustrates what IBM considers to be its core business processes (IBM-Europe, 1990). The diagram separates the core processes into three major categories: product processes that involve design, production, and delivery of the organization's products; general business processes that interact with the external marketplace, such as sales and marketing; and enterprise processes, which are the internal support processes that the customer does not usually see but that are required to keep the company running. Producing the company payroll is one example. Most of the managerial processes we discuss in this chapter fall into the category of enterprise processes, although the two other categories also have managerial processes.

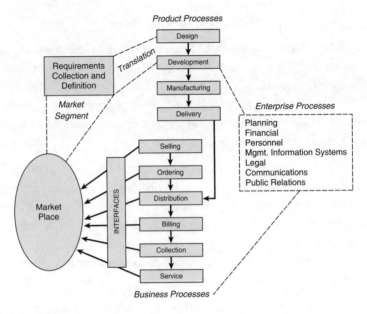

Figure 7.1 IBM core processes

Often you will need to integrate several processes together to form a system. By *system*, we mean the collection of all relevant processes needed to complete some specific work. For example, your body has a cardiovascular system that performs the work of circulating blood. The beating of your heart is one process that is part of the cardiovascular system, but it cannot circulate blood effectively without the action of other muscles or the use of veins and arteries. All muscles, veins, and arteries, along with other parts of the cardiovascular system, must work in harmony for our blood to properly circulate. To return to the business world, most organizations have an overall reward and recognition system. Annual performance appraisal is typically one process in this system, but other processes are also needed to form an overall system.

An understanding of systems is important because you need to make sure that all processes are properly integrated for overall system optimization. It is common in the business word for people to optimize one process at the expense of others, resulting in poor overall system performance. For example, in a company's sales system, four regional managers might compete with each other to land a national account;

the net result could be a less profitable contract for the company. Each regional manager might have attempted to optimize his or her regional sales process, but did so to the detriment of the overall corporate sales system. This is called suboptimization, and it has been one of the central themes of management author Peter Senge's work (Senge, 2006).

Improving systems can have a profound impact on entire organizations. It institutionalizes change because systems and their processes define how you do your work. It goes without saying that top talent in leadership roles is required to properly design, implement, and manage these systems.

In the discussion of Lean Six Sigma deployment, instances will undoubtedly arise when we use the word *system* but the reader feels *process* might be more accurate, and vice versa. This distinction is often gray. The key point is that we need a formal infrastructure, whether a process, a system, or some other mechanism, to effectively manage the effort. The specific term we use is not critical.

The key infrastructure elements are discussed in roughly the order in which they are typically considered in deployment.

Management Project Reviews

Management review is a critical success factor for Lean Six Sigma. Regular management review keeps the effort focused and on track. We know of no successful Lean Six Sigma implementation in which management reviews were not a key part of the deployment process. We refer to management reviews as the "secret sauce"—done regularly and at numerous levels, they significantly enhance the probability of success. I heard one CEO encourage his staff in this way: "Schedule reviews and show up. You don't have to say anything. Good things will happen."

We focus here on management project reviews, and we address management reviews of the overall implementation in Chapter 8, "Sustaining Momentum and Growing." Project reviews should be done weekly and monthly; reviews of the overall initiative are preferably done quarterly or at least annually. We begin with management project reviews because you should already be reviewing the status of the initial wave of projects by this time.

Lean Six Sigma projects are most successful when Champions review them weekly and the business unit and function leaders review them monthly. Such a drumbeat prevents projects from dragging on and gives leadership early warning of any problems. A useful agenda for the Champion review follows:

- Activity this week
- Accomplishments this week
- Recommended management actions
- Help needed
- Plan for next week

This review is informal and is not time consuming—it should take approximately 30 minutes. The idea is to have a quick check to keep the project on track by finding out what has been accomplished, what is planned, and what barriers need to be addressed. Typically, Champions guide only one or two Black Belts, so the time requirements are not great. These reviews help Champions fulfill their role of guiding the project and addressing barriers. Master Black Belts (MBBs) also attend these reviews as needed, and the MBB and Black Belt meet separately to resolve any technical issues that might have arisen.

All current projects are typically reviewed each month as well. This monthly review with the business unit or function leader is shorter than the weekly review, no more than 10 to 15 minutes per project. The purpose is to keep the project on schedule with respect to time and results, and to identify any problems or roadblocks. This review helps the business unit and functional leaders stay involved in Lean Six Sigma and directly informs them of any issues they need to address. A useful agenda for these reviews follows:

- Project purpose
- Process and financial metrics—progress versus goals
- Accomplishments since the last review
- Plans for future work
- Key lessons learned and findings

Notice that this agenda is similar to the agenda for the weekly review with the Champion. In the monthly review, much more emphasis is placed on performance versus schedule, progress toward process and financial goals, and key lessons learned and findings.

As Lean Six Sigma grows, the number of projects could become large, requiring a lot of time for reviews. The review time can be reduced by rating projects as Green (on schedule), Yellow (in danger of falling behind schedule if something isn't done), or Red (behind schedule and in need of help), and then reviewing only those rated as Red and Yellow.

One way to increase the speed, clarity, and understanding of the review process is to use a common reporting format, such as the one in Figure 7.2. This format is similar to templates that GE, AlliedSignal, DuPont, and other companies use. An overall project summary is shown on one page using the four headings of Project Description, Metrics, Accomplishments, and Needs. Additional backup slides to support the material in the summary can be added as needed.

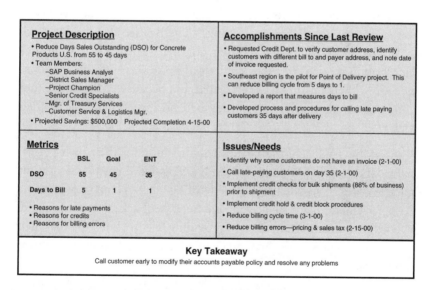

Figure 7.2 Example project status reporting form

A good way to show progress toward entitlement is to use the graph in Figure 7.3 (Rodebaugh, 2001). A separate graph is used for each process measure impacted by the project.

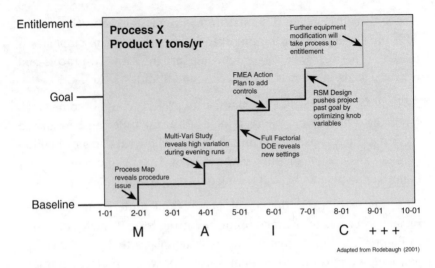

Figure 7.3 Progress toward process entitlement for sample project

We all need feedback so that we know how we're doing and how we can improve. Former New York City Mayor Ed Koch used to ask at every opportunity, "How am I doing?" The Beatles also needed feedback. The rock group's last outdoor concert was held in Candlestick Park (San Francisco) in 1966. The crowd noise was extremely loud, so they knew their music was appreciated, but because of the noise, they couldn't hear themselves sing; they had no direct feedback of their voices.

Without this feedback, the Beatles couldn't monitor their own performance and improve it where necessary. This led them to discontinue outdoor concerts. Feedback provided during reviews is an important aid to improvement. Black Belts want and need feedback, and management reviews are one important form of providing it. Also, knowing that their projects will be reviewed by management provides significant motivation to Black Belts.

In all project reviews, it is important to ask questions to identify the *methods, logic,* and *data* used to support decisions. It is also important to pay attention to both *social* and *technical* issues. Sometimes the social concerns, such as interpersonal and interdepartmental relationships, as well as leadership skills, are more important than the technical issues.

It is also important to do a lot of listening. Open-ended questions (ones that cannot be answered *yes* or *no*) generally lead to more informative answers. Two helpful questions are, "Could you explain that in more detail?" and "Could you help me understand how you arrived at that conclusion?"

When you want to learn how the project—or any activity, for that matter—is progressing, ask two questions: "What's working?" or "What are we doing well?" and then "What do we need to do better?" The answers will take you a long way toward understanding what is going on in the project or activity. A more detailed list of good questions to ask appears in Appendix A, "Ensuring Project and Initiative Success."

The Black Belts, Champions, or a combination of Black Belts and Champions can present the project reports at the monthly reviews. Having the Champions give the reports involves them more deeply in the Lean Six Sigma initiative and increases understanding and ownership. When appropriate, Champions can report on several projects, reducing the amount of time required for the reviews. Project reviews are critical to success. Infrequent review of projects is a good predictor of a Lean Six Sigma initiative in trouble, as in the case studies of Royal Chemicals and Diversified Paper (Snee and Hoerl, 2003).

As noted previously, typically 30 to 50 percent of projects produce improvements that have bottom-line results even before the project is completed. Champions and other leaders should be on the lookout for such situations and make sure that the project, the Black Belt, and the Lean Six Sigma initiative get credit for the results as soon as possible. The weekly and monthly reviews are a good place to identify these opportunities and will speed up the impact of the Lean Six Sigma initiative.

Project Reporting and Tracking

As noted, it is important to have a regular drumbeat of reporting on the progress and results of projects. Developing a formal reporting and tracking system should therefore be an early priority during this phase of Lean Six Sigma deployment. The reporting system provides electronic or paper documents to back up and facilitate the project reviews.

The best reporting structure for Lean Six Sigma projects depends on the needs of the organization. A target frequency follows:

- Weekly highlights from the Black Belt to the Champion. A summary of the weekly review is usually sufficient for this purpose.

- Monthly reports for the business or function leader, typically using information provided by the Champions.

- Quarterly reports for corporate leadership, typically using information provided by the business and function leaders.

The purpose of the reporting system is to keep the various levels of management informed of progress and results of the initiative. These reports also become the raw material for internal and external communications (see the upcoming "Communications Plan" section).

The reports should, of course, be designed to meet the needs of the organization. A good way to report on a project is to create a short summary of the project, analogous to the review template. Such a summary typically contains three parts: the problem/issue description, work done, and the results/impact/implications. Depending on the required length, it is usually appropriate to include a two- or three-sentence description for each of the three areas, plus relevant metrics and graphs. Your summary must include the results obtained in terms of improvement of process performance and bottom-line results. Lean Six Sigma is about getting results.

Typically, the Black Belt enters the project-level information into a computer system that can roll up the results across projects, functions, and business units, and drill down to greater detail on individual projects. Using workflow software, users can track the status of a project portfolio at a high level and also find links to additional, more detailed information, such as PowerPoint presentations or statistical analyses.

A key element of this reporting system is the financial tracking system. Leadership needs to know how the total bottom-line savings are progressing. By tracking the projects, leadership not only knows how the Lean Six Sigma initiative is performing, but also communicates the importance of the initiative to the organization. Recall the old saying: "What we measure and pay attention to gets done."

Project tracking is typically led by finance because of the need to validate the financial data. Some key measures (English, 2001) that are typically tracked follow:

- Hard and soft dollar savings
- Number of projects completed
- Savings per project
- Projects per Black Belt and Green Belt
- Time to project completion
- Number of Black Belts and Green Belts

Leaders want reports of these measures for the whole organization, as well as the ability to drill down by business unit, function, plant or site, region of the world, country, and so on. Keeping track of a few projects is easy; an Excel spreadsheet usually does the trick. As the projects grow in number and as Lean Six Sigma moves throughout the organization, a more sophisticated system is needed. This system can be a database such as Lotus Notes, Microsoft Access, or Oracle, or software specifically designed for tracking Lean Six Sigma projects. We also know of instances when an existing project tracking system (such as for R&D projects) was enhanced to track Lean Six Sigma projects, thereby integrating Lean Six Sigma with existing management systems.

When tracking projects, people commonly ask, "How do I calculate the financial impact of a project?" Although the answer depends on the financial rules of each organization, we can provide some general guidance.

Financial impact is typically divided into hard and soft dollars (Snee and Rodebaugh, 2002). Hard dollars are dollars that clearly flow to the bottom line and will show up on the income statement and balance sheet. Examples include dollars from cost reductions, increased capacity that is immediately sold (because the product is in a sold-out condition), and decreased holding costs from increased inventory turns. As a general rule, companies report only the hard dollars as Lean Six Sigma savings because these are the funds that indisputably affect the profitability of the organization. For example, W. R. Grace reported a

$26 million bottom-line impact in 2000 and an additional $7 million in cost avoidance (Snee and Hoerl, 2003).

Soft dollars are improvements in operations that do not directly affect the bottom line, but typically do so indirectly. Some examples are improving meeting efficiency so that less time is wasted in meetings, preventing problems that typically occur in new product introduction, and simplifying accounting processes so that fewer resources are needed to close the books. In each case, we could calculate a theoretical savings (in soft dollars) from the reduction of either the effort required or typical waste and rework levels. However, we cannot clearly demonstrate how these soft savings will show up on the balance sheet.

To clarify the difference between hard and soft dollars, consider a process that is improved and now requires three fewer people to operate it. If these three people are reassigned to other work, we have a cost avoidance (soft dollars). They are now freed to do more value-adding work to the benefit of the organization elsewhere. However, they are still employed and are still a cost to the organization, so we cannot claim hard dollar savings. On the other hand, if three positions are removed from the employee rolls after reassignment, we have a cost reduction (hard dollars) because we will clearly see this savings on our payroll expenses.

It is not unusual for a project to have both hard and soft dollar savings. It is also not unusual for the financial impact of a project to come from several different places. Black Belts and the financial organization should search for all possible sources of project impacts and capture the true savings, to make sure that no tangible savings are missed. Typically, the finance organization makes the final decisions about what qualifies as hard savings.

Communications Plan

We noted in Chapter 5, "How to Successfully Implement Lean Six Sigma 2.0," that clear communication of the vision and strategy for Lean Six Sigma is a critical responsibility of leadership. Communication has a huge impact on the organization's perception of Lean Six Sigma and, subsequently, on everyone's receptiveness to it. We also noted that many organizations wait until they have achieved some tangible success before making major pronouncements about the initiative, so we did not address the communications plan until this chapter. The information provided here is relevant whenever leadership wants to begin formal communications about the effort.

The project reporting for management described in the previous section is one form of communication. In this section, we discuss communications more generally. We need to answer the following six questions to move toward designing an effective communications plan for Lean Six Sigma: Who? What? When? Where? Why? and How? The answers to these questions follow:

Question	Answer
Who?	Different target audiences
What?	Lean Six Sigma need, vision, strategy, and results
When?	Continual, ongoing
Where?	In a variety of media
Why?	Set the tone, keep the organization informed
How?	Clear, concise, continual using a variety of media

An informed organization will produce a more rapid, effective implementation of Lean Six Sigma. Many studies of change initiatives have demonstrated that people are more likely to embrace change when they understand the rationale, vision, and strategy of the change (Weisbord, 1989).

Fundamental to communicating well is recognizing that a lot of variation exists in both the information to be communicated and the target audiences. For example, the information that we need to communicate to the investment community is likely much different than the information we need to communicate to rank-and-file employees. The communications plan should take this type of variation into account. Communication is a process just like any other process used to run the business. Organizations have a variety of target audiences, each with different needs, wants, and desires. People are individuals who take in, process, and understand information in different ways. Their differences dictate that we utilize different media to communicate the message, even to the same target audience.

Note that leaders communicate by their actions—both what they do and what they say. Each contact, in person or otherwise, is an opportunity to communicate. Communication is a key responsibility of leaders, and they need to communicate their message over and over again, and in different ways, for it to be understood and internalized by the organization. People might have to hear something new at least five times before they internalize it. A message delivered only one time will likely go unnoticed.

The design of the communications plan depends on the organization. We summarize some communication principles here:

- We communicate by what we do and by what we say.

- Use a variety of communication vehicles: face-to-face interaction, video, newsletters, memos, emails, skits, tweets, and pocket cards, among others.

  - Leaders must be seen and heard, as well as read.

- Communication has these characteristics:

  - An on-going process, not an event

  - A two-way process—talk top-down, listen bottom-up

  - A key aspect of leadership and a job responsibility

  - Also horizontal, employee to employee

  - Each contact is an opportunity to communicate.

- Leaders clarify complex issues.

The following are communication methods:

- IT systems that share information throughout the organization, including customer views

- Employee meetings to discuss strategic direction and initiatives

- Periodic reports on the progress of projects and initiatives

- Periodic reviews at all levels

- Act of connecting all initiatives to the strategic plan

- Use of the strategic plan to guide work processes

- Behaviors that match the values of the organization

- Horizontal: employee to employee

- Visual management and measurement

- Process management

  - Communicates how we serve our customers

The next two lists illustrate specific examples of awareness training from one company (first list) and the outline of an overall communications plan in another company (second list). The first company decided to do a two-hour awareness training to introduce the organization to Lean Six Sigma.

Two-Hour Awareness Training for the Organization

- Creation of a standard script and visual aids for use by all managers

- Agenda: presentation followed by a question/answer session

- Feedback and follow-up

- Barriers and issues identified in question/answer session were collected and reviewed by senior management team, and needed actions were taken

Overall Communications Plan

- Plan covers the first 6–9 months

- Themes to be communicated

  - Lean Six Sigma tie to business strategy

  - Building on what was done before

  - Goals

  - Roles of individuals

- Media to be used

  - Corporate and plant newspapers, Lotus Notes, bulletin board postings, staff meetings, corporate television, Lean Six Sigma website

- Topics for first 9 weeks

  - Lean Six Sigma strategy and goals

  - Meet the Lean Six Sigma Champions

  - How other companies are using Lean Six Sigma

  - Customer feedback surveys

  - Lean Six Sigma improvement process

  - How projects are being selected

  - How Lean Six Sigma is different

  - Executive, Champion, and Black Belt training

  - How Lean Six Sigma will affect the organization

- Periodic communications as needed

  - Answers to frequently asked questions

  - Comments from the president

  - Results of Lean Six Sigma projects

  - Success stories and celebrations

  - Lean Six Sigma financial updates

Note that the awareness session followed the principles that communication is a process and is two-way: delivering and receiving. An awareness session usually answers these questions:

- What is Lean Six Sigma?

- Why are we pursuing Lean Six Sigma?

- How will we deploy Lean Six Sigma?

The answers are intended to communicate the organization's rationale for deploying Lean Six Sigma, its vision, and its overall strategy. This is a critically important message and should be an integral part of any communication plan. Our experience is that it usually takes two to four hours for a group of any size to develop a useful awareness of Lean Six Sigma.

The second plan had a time frame of the first six to nine months of deployment. Note that the plan did not contain any awareness training. Those participating in the Executive and Champion workshops were told to do awareness training for their organizations using the materials they had received in the workshops. This unique approach illustrates how organizations differ in their deployment of Lean Six Sigma.

Some organizations prepare presentations for the managers to use to communicate Lean Six Sigma. Other companies ask the managers to prepare their own awareness materials. Both approaches have pros and cons. A common presentation helps ensure a consistent message. However, managers who prepare their own awareness training will develop a deeper understanding of Lean Six Sigma in the process. Because first impressions often last, we recommend using common materials to hit the rationale, vision, and strategy, combined with tailored materials for each organization developed by its own management.

Reward and Recognition Plan

As we noted in Chapter 5, we believe that the most effective motivation is intrinsic motivation—that is, people doing something because they believe in it or want to do it. For example, history shows that mercenary armies have never performed well against armies that believed in what they were fighting for. On the other hand, if there are no tangible rewards for accomplishments in Lean Six Sigma, this omission will essentially be a demotivator. People might say, "I would love to be involved in Lean Six Sigma, but I'm concerned about what it might do to my career."

We must balance intrinsic motivation with extrinsic motivation. Extrinsic motivation means providing a carrot or stick to motivate someone to do something they would not do otherwise, such as rewarding children for cleaning their rooms. Providing extrinsic motivation helps ensure that there are no barriers to top talent getting involved in Lean Six Sigma.

We are all motivated to work on those things that will be beneficial to our career. This fact leads us to consider what reward and recognition system we will use to support Lean Six Sigma. In fact, some companies have the reward and recognition plan for Lean Six Sigma designed even before deployment. Jack Welch said about GE, "As with every initiative, we backed Lean Six Sigma up with our rewards system" (Welch, 2001). This included basing 40 percent of the annual managerial bonus on Lean Six Sigma results, providing stock option grants for MBBs, and requiring Green Belt certification for promotion.

Every successful implementation of Lean Six Sigma we are familiar with has developed a special reward and recognition system to support Lean Six Sigma. Conversely, during previous improvement initiatives (such as TQM), leadership might have stated that it wanted one behavior (such as quality improvement) but rewarded something totally different (such as meeting the financial numbers). Such disconnects between leadership's words and actions are immediately obvious to employees and can lead to cynicism.

The reward and recognition system is a statement by leadership about what it values and is a much more important document than a printed values statement. Leaders must think carefully about the message they want to convey.

As with communications, the form of the reward and recognition plan is greatly dependent on the culture and existing plan of the company involved. Some companies choose to use their existing system because they feel it has the capability to adequately reward the contributions of those involved in Lean Six Sigma. This can be the case in some instances, but in general, a special reward and recognition system should be developed. The following list summarizes the Black Belt recognition program for one company we have worked with. This plan recognizes that Black Belts are critical to our success and that special rewards are needed to ensure that top performers are eager to take this role. Unfortunately, this plan makes no mention of rewarding others involved in Lean Six Sigma work.

- Base pay
  - Potential increase at time of selection
  - Retain current salary grade
  - Normal group performance review and merit pay
- Incentive compensation
  - Special plan for Black Belts
  - Target award at 15 percent of base pay

- Performance rating on 0–150 percent of scale

- Measured against key project objectives

- Participation ends at end of Black Belt assignment

The Lean Six Sigma reward and recognition plan for another company is summarized next. Note the completeness of this plan, including recognition of Green Belts and team members (including MBBs and Champions), as well as an annual celebration event complete with leadership participation.

- BB Selection: Receive Lean Six Sigma pin

- BB Certification: $5,000 certification bonus, plus plaque

- BB project completion

  - $500 to $5,000 in cash or stock options for first project

  - Plaque with project name engraved for first and subsequent projects

- BB Lean Six Sigma activity awards

  - Recognizes efforts and achievements during projects with individual and team awards (cash, tickets, dinners, shirts, and so on)

- Green Belt recognition

  - Similar to Black Belt recognition

  - No certification bonus

- Project team member recognition

  - Similar to BB and GB recognition

  - No certification awards

- Annual Lean Six Sigma celebration event

  - Presentation of key projects

  - Dinner reception with senior leadership

Note also that not all rewards have to be monetary. For many people, peer and management recognition, such as an opportunity to present their project, is a greater reward than money.

In evaluating these reward and recognition plans, as well as those of other organizations, we conclude that the most appropriate plan is company dependent. What works for one company, or even one employee, will not necessarily work for another. Reward and recognition plans are also not static. The points listed here will likely change over time as experience with Lean Six Sigma grows and the reward and recognition needs become clear. The one constant is to make sure you are rewarding the behavior you want to encourage.

Lean Six Sigma goals and objectives should be part of performance plans for all those involved in the Lean Six Sigma initiative. If the company intends for Lean Six Sigma to involve the entire organization, then these goals and objectives must be included in the performance plans for the entire organization. This is consistent with our earlier recognition that we are all motivated to work on the things that will be beneficial to our career. Lean Six Sigma responsibilities should be part of people's individual goals and objectives, and their performance should be evaluated relative to these goals and objectives. Once again, what management measures and pays attention to gets done.

Project Identification and Prioritization

Improvement project management has many aspects. A system is needed for project identification and prioritization to effectively manage the many moving parts.

We discussed initial project selection in Chapter 5. When the Black Belts have completed their first projects, they are ready to take on another project. You don't want to lose any momentum. After this new project has gotten underway, full-time Black Belts will be ready to take on a second project simultaneously. This ramp-up will continue until fully operational Black Belts are handling three or four projects at a time.

Clearly, with a lot of Black Belts working in an organization, you need to plan carefully to ensure that you have important, high-impact projects identified and ready to go when the Black Belts are ready. A frequent mistake companies make is waiting for the Black Belt to finish a project before looking for another one. Such a strategy wastes the time of the Black Belts, a valuable resource. A Black Belt without a project is a sin in the Lean Six Sigma world. Lack of planning also often results in mediocre projects because insufficient thought had been put into the selection process. Good project selection is a key to success.

Now that you have numerous projects and Black Belts, you cannot rely on ad-hoc project selection, but instead must implement a formal selection and prioritization system. Figure 7.4 shows a schematic of an ongoing project selection process and its associated project hopper (Rodebaugh, 2001). Project selection should be an ongoing process that ensures we always have a collection of projects ready for Black Belts to tackle. One strategy for keeping the project hopper "evergreen" is to require that a new project be added to the hopper each time a project is removed and assigned to a Black Belt or Green Belt.

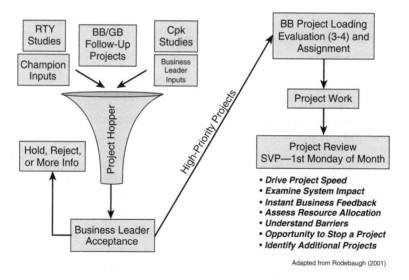

Adapted from Rodebaugh (2001)

Figure 7.4 Project selection and management process system

The project hopper can be thought of as an organizational to-do list and should be managed in much the same way. Projects are continually being put into the hopper, the list is continually being prioritized, and prioritized projects are assigned to Black Belts or Green Belts as these resources become available. By continually searching for projects and reprioritizing the list of projects in the project hopper, you ensure that problems most important to the organization are being addressed using Lean Six Sigma.

When considering project identification, two important sources are often overlooked in Lean Six Sigma but should be considered: Big Data and risk management. A Big Data project (see Chapter 3, "Key Methodologies in a Holistic Improvement System") typically produces several subprojects that should be addressed using Lean Six Sigma. As previously noted, Big Data analytics provide important opportunities for improvement that should be integrated with other improvement efforts instead of creating an isolated "island of improvement" or even becoming a "competitor" to the Lean Six Sigma initiative. Utilizing input from Big Data projects for Lean Six Sigma project selection provides an early opportunity for integration. Similarly, risk management (discussed further in Chapter 9) is a business need that is relevant to all processes and business functions. The associated risk assessments result in several opportunities for improvement that generate projects to be added to the project hopper.

Each business or functional unit should have a project hopper. It is also appropriate to have a corporate project hopper to handle projects that do not naturally fit into the hoppers of the business and functional units. For example, a project to improve integration of business units or functions does not fit squarely within any one business or function. The hopper should always be full, containing at least a six-month supply of projects (a year's supply is even better) and at least one project that would naturally fit into the work of each individual Black Belt. As noted earlier, Black Belts should never be without a full load of projects. It is important to review the hopper contents as part of the quarterly Lean Six Sigma initiative review (discussed further in Chapter 8).

The discussion of initial project selection in Chapter 6, "Launching the Initiative," provided most of the guidelines for project selection. These apply to the ongoing project selection and prioritization system as well. We recommend focusing projects strategically on business priorities and also wherever the organization is experiencing significant pain, such as responding to critical customer issues. Information that is helpful in selecting specific projects is contained in the baseline and entitlement database. This data tells you how the processes are performing today and how they could be performing in the future; it also identifies the sources of important improvement opportunities.

Process baseline and entitlement data should be maintained and updated for all key process performance metrics associated with the manufacturing and nonmanufacturing processes used to run the organization. The job of creating and maintaining this database is typically assigned to an MBB or experienced Black Belt. Depending on the level of complexity, the information technology group might actually develop the system or might assume long-term responsibility to maintain it. This database should be updated every six months or so and be included in at least every other quarterly Lean Six Sigma initiative review (see Chapter 8).

The development and maintenance of such databases is simply good management practice, but our experience is that typically they don't exist at all or they focus solely on accounting information and, therefore, are inadequate for improvement purposes. Lack of good data is probably the greatest challenge Black Belt teams face. This is one reason evaluation of the measurement system is a key element of the Measure phase of DMAIC projects.

When you have spent time and effort developing an adequate measurement system for improvement purposes, you should make sure it is properly integrated with existing information systems and is maintained so that you don't have to re-create the system for future projects.

Project Closure: Moving On to the Next Project

Project closure is an important event. It is the signal that the project is completed, that the Black Belt can move on to the next project, and that you can "ring the cash register" with money flowing to the bottom line. Project closure criteria form an important part of the project identification and prioritization system because they help Black Belts and others move on to their next projects promptly. They should neither linger on projects too long nor leave prematurely before critical controls are in place.

Some perfectionists will not want to move on until they have reached entitlement, even though they have met their original objectives and bigger issues are emerging elsewhere. Other Black Belts or Green Belts might be eager to tackle the next problem and want to leave before critical controls are in place. The key players in this event are the Black Belt or Green Belt, the Champion, the finance representative, and the person who owns the process. The process owner is needed because the process improvements developed by the Black Belt or Green Belt will become standard operating procedure for the process in the future.

The key to project closure is verification of the process improvements and associated financial impact (determined by finance), completion of the process control plan, completion of the training associated with the new way of operating, and completion of the project report that summarizes the work done and the key findings. When this work is done, the Black Belt or Green Belt often makes a presentation to management; the rest of the organization is informed through the project reporting system or other methods of communication (newsletters, websites, storyboards, and so on).

You can manage project closure by having a standard set of steps to close out a project, a project closure form that is an integral part of the project tracking system, and a method for electronically archiving the project in the reporting system so the results are available to the whole organization. This last item is important because Black Belts working in non-standard areas such as risk management find documentation of previous projects in this same area extremely helpful. The specific closure steps and form should be tailored to each organization, but we recommend that the following steps be required:

- Successful completion of each phase of the DMAIC (or DFSS) process

- Finance sign-off on the savings claimed

- A control plan in place and being used by process owner

- Any needed training implemented

- Final Champion and management reviews

Lean Six Sigma Budgeting

Most organizations that implement Lean Six Sigma do not have the implementation costs or benefits in their budget at the time they decide to launch. This happens simply because most didn't realize in the previous year, when the current year's budget was developed, that they would be implementing Lean Six Sigma now. Therefore, Lean Six Sigma is generally launched with special funding allocated by senior leadership. This is certainly acceptable to get started, but as organizations begin to formally manage the effort, it is critically important that Lean Six Sigma be included in their key budgeting processes.

This inclusion is important for several reasons. First, leadership needs to make sure that Lean Six Sigma receives the same degree of financial scrutiny as any other budgetary area. Virtually all public corporations, and most private and even nonprofit organizations, have existing budgeting and financial control systems in place, so they can simply include Lean Six Sigma in these instead of having to create a new infrastructure.

Second, inclusion into the budget helps Lean Six Sigma move from being viewed as a separate, potentially short-term initiative, to being a normal part of how you work.

Third, this budget documents and formalizes leadership expectations of all layers of management. These expectations are clear when each business unit budget shows a line item for financial benefits from Lean Six Sigma, in addition to a line item for expenditures for Lean Six Sigma. Leadership is providing financial resources to implement Lean Six Sigma, but it expects a payoff. Ideally, business unit managers will be intrinsically motivated to enthusiastically deploy Lean Six Sigma because they believe in what it can do. However, just in case some managers are not, knowing that they are accountable for obtaining financial benefits through Lean Six Sigma will provide significant extrinsic motivation to succeed.

Deployment Processes for Leaders

After you have selected your first group of Champions, Black Belts, and other roles in this phase of launching the initiative, these team members will begin working on their initial projects. We explained in Chapter 5 how to go about initial project and people selection. During the phase of managing the effort, however, the number of projects will be growing too quickly to pick Black Belts and others on an ad hoc basis. You need to develop a formal process for selecting Black Belts and other roles and then assigning them to projects.

This process will become even more important later, as Black Belts begin rotating out of their assignments and need to be replaced. It might be appropriate for some Black Belts to remain in their role for many years. However, the world is dynamic, and Black Belts will leave the initiative for a variety of reasons, just as people leave other assignments over time. A few will leave because they are not suited for the work; others will leave because of a transfer or promotion. A few will become MBBs; some will move on to other companies and other careers.

A formal process, typically led by human resources (HR) personnel, must continually look at the improvement needs of the organization (for example, strategy and project hopper contents) and the career development needs of the top performers in the organization, and then select the ones who should take Champion, Black Belt, MBB, or other Lean Six Sigma roles.

This process also looks to move top Green Belts into Black Belt roles, Black Belts into MBB roles, and so on. After about two years into the initiative, Black Belts and others will begin to rotate out of Lean Six Sigma roles and will be looking for big jobs. It is important to have a placement process ready to properly place them into important roles.

As noted in our discussion of reward and recognition, people need tangible evidence that making the commitment to Lean Six Sigma will help their careers. Seeing others get big and important jobs after their Lean Six Sigma assignment is one way to make this happen. Conversely, if you do not place these resources in important positions, you will be wasting the significant leadership development they have received.

HR might primarily manage the people selection process, or this could be managed by a business Quality Council with support from HR. Most organizations soon see the need for an active, formal Lean Six Sigma organization to effectively manage many of these systems and processes (see Chapter 8). The people selection process should follow the criteria given in Chapter 5 for the selection of Black Belts and others. The process of assigning these resources to projects should be based on the project identification and prioritization system. In other words, you should first select the projects and then select the appropriate Black Belts to work on them. Such an approach simplifies the process of assigning Black Belts after they have been selected.

The placement process for those rotating out of Lean Six Sigma roles often presents a greater challenge because big jobs are few in number; there might not be a suitable job waiting for each Black Belt or MBB rotating out. Therefore, many companies make the timing flexible, allowing Black Belts and others to begin looking for their next job after about 18 months, while still in their Lean Six Sigma position. This enables them to wait until they find a good fit and still complete their current project.

Initially, HR might need to help those leaving Lean Six Sigma roles obtain the job they desire. After a while, managers will be actively seeking Black Belts and MBBs with no prompting from HR because they will see how these assignments have grown and matured the people in them. Recall from Chapter 3 that a key benefit of Lean Six Sigma is that it becomes an excellent leadership development system for top talent.

Integrating Lean Six Sigma with Current Management Systems

Organizations should look for every opportunity to integrate Lean Six Sigma management systems with their current management systems. Integration will help make Lean Six Sigma part of their culture, reduce bureaucracy and the amount of effort needed to manage the initiative, and increase its impact. This approach to integration is discussed in detail in Chapter 9, which shows how to make the transition from Lean Six Sigma being an initiative to holistic improvement being the way you work. However, you should begin integrating Lean Six Sigma now, at the point when you implement Lean Six Sigma management systems. The more integration you do now, the less you will have to do later.

For example, Lean Six Sigma reviews can become part of normal staff and management meetings, as long as they are given adequate time on the agenda. As noted, Lean Six Sigma should be part of your budgeting processes, not a standalone item. In some companies, Lean Six Sigma identifies a gap in the communications process that has to be filled by creating new media. We noted previously that the reward and recognition system usually has to be revised to support the needs of Lean Six Sigma, but there will eventually be only one reward and recognition system. Most organizations will need to create a project tracking system. In some instances, existing project management systems can be enhanced to enable Lean Six Sigma project tracking.

In most cases, project closure procedures and supporting forms have to be created and integrated with the project tracking system. The project selection process and its associated project hopper also have to be created in most organizations. Whenever possible, the project selection process should be integrated with the capital project system and other, similar systems. Early focus on integrating Lean Six Sigma managing processes with current systems greatly speeds up acceptance of the methodology and its bottom-line impact, not to mention simplifying the final transition to the way you work.

Summary and Looking Forward

We define the phase of managing the effort to be the period between completion of the initial wave of Black Belt training and the point when you have trained everyone originally intended and implemented all projects identified in your original deployment plan. This phase typically lasts about 18 months, although management of the effort lasts indefinitely.

The critical transition that occurs here is from a new launch to a formal long-term initiative. The effort will become too large to manage informally and will require the implementation of formal management systems and processes. These systems and processes are all infrastructure elements of the deployment plan discussed in Chapter 5.

The key deliverable is implementation of these infrastructure elements, which typically include the following:

- Management project reviews

- A project reporting and tracking system

- A communications plan

- A reward and recognition plan

- A project identification and prioritization system

- Project closure criteria

- Inclusion of Lean Six Sigma into budgeting processes

- Deployment processes for Champions, Black Belts, MBBs, and so on

Obtaining top talent for key Lean Six Sigma roles and implementing this key infrastructure are key success factors in this phase. Top talent is needed to properly design, implement, and manage these systems and processes. Designing management systems is not easy work, and a poor system can negatively impact the entire organization. Other important success factors in this phase include the following:

- Making improvement opportunities possible with a good process baseline and entitlement database.

- Using Lean Six Sigma assignments as a leadership development system.

- Integrating Lean Six Sigma management processes into normal operating procedures. This reduces the effort required to manage the initiative, reduces bureaucracy, and sets the stage for making Lean Six Sigma the way we work.

In the next chapter, we discuss how to sustain the momentum of the improvement initiative over time and expand to a more holistic approach: Lean Six Sigma 2.0. This enables the improvement initiative to grow in its effectiveness, maintaining the bottom-line improvements established by the improvement projects and extending the improvement initiative to new problems and improvement opportunities.

References

English, W. (2001) "Implementing Lean Six Sigma: The Iomega Story." Presented at the Conference on Lean Six Sigma in the Pharmaceutical Industry, Philadelphia, PA, November 27–28, 2001.

Rodebaugh, W. R. (2001) "Lean Six Sigma in Measurement Systems: Evaluating the Hidden Factory." Presented at the Penn State Great Valley Symposium on Statistical Methods for Quality Practitioners, Malvern, PA., October 2001.

Senge, P. (2006) *The Fifth Discipline: The Art and Practice of the Learning Organization*. Revised ed. New York: Doubleday/Currency.

Snee, R. D., and R. W. Hoerl. (2003) *Leading Six Sigma: A Step-by-Step Guide Based on Experience with GE and Other Six Sigma Companies*. Upper Saddle River, NJ: Financial Times/Prentice Hall.

Snee, R. D., K. H. Kelleher, and S. Reynard. (1998) "Improving Team Effectiveness." *Quality Progress* (May): 43–48.

Snee, R. D., and W. F. Rodebaugh. (2002) "Project Selection Process." *Quality Progress* (September): 78–80.

Weisbord, M. R. (1989) *Productive Workplaces*. San Francisco: Jossey-Bass.

Welch, J. F. (2001) *Jack, Straight from the Gut*. New York: Warner Business Books.

8

Sustaining Momentum and Growing

"To improve is to change. To be perfect is to change often."
—Winston Churchill

You have successfully launched your Lean Six Sigma initiative (from Chapter 6, "Launching the Initiative"), and you have been working on putting in place systems that are needed to effectively manage the deployment (from Chapter 7, "Managing the Effort"). Many Lean Six Sigma initiatives begin to hit a lull at this point as other priorities gradually erode the momentum. Now is the time to implement systems and processes that will help you sustain the energy. Sometimes the best defense is a good offense, and growth of the initiative can be a good offensive tactic that helps maintain momentum.

This chapter focuses on the defensive effort needed to sustain impetus and the offensive effort needed to expand the Lean Six Sigma initiative toward a true holistic improvement system. This sustaining and growing phase is defined as the time between completing the training and projects identified in the original deployment plan and transforming Lean Six Sigma from an initiative to the normal way you work, as Lean Six Sigma 2.0. This phase can last several years.

The momentum of Lean Six Sigma is maintained by holding the gains of completed projects and by sustaining the gains of the overall Lean Six Sigma system. Figure 8.1 schematically displays some of the methods discussed in this chapter. As you will see, and as should come as no surprise, the key is consistent implementation of periodic reviews, including audits. It is also important to implement a complete training system (instead of individual training courses), create a formal Lean Six Sigma organizational structure, and develop Leadership Green Belts. Note from Figure 8.1 that all the other elements are done within the context and direction of the Lean Six Sigma organizational structure. This makes up your defensive effort to maintain the momentum you already have.

At this stage, you also want to play offense and extend the deployment into new areas. You can accomplish this primarily by expanding the portfolio of improvement methodologies and also by expanding Lean Six Sigma to the whole organization. For example, expansion across the organization might include introducing customers and suppliers to Lean Six Sigma, and using Lean Six Sigma to increase revenue as well as reduce costs. Quality by design projects, using different methodologies than Lean or Six Sigma, can help drive new revenue. Lean Six Sigma can be applied to top-line growth, but quality by design methodologies are better suited for new product and service development. We first review the key elements of our defensive strategy and then discuss the offensive elements.

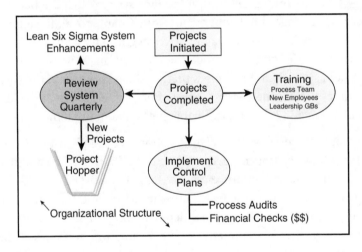

Figure 8.1 Sustaining the gains

Playing Defense: Sustaining Momentum

After a couple years, Lean Six Sigma could become old news and more recent issues or problems might divert managerial attention. All organizations deploying Lean Six Sigma have faced this phenomenon. Leadership's response to it determines whether the deployment will succeed in the long term.

In Chapter 5, "How to Successfully Implement Lean Six Sigma 2.0," we noted that implementing the remaining infrastructure elements is the key to successfully making this transition. Recall that these infrastructure elements were identified as part of the overall deployment plan developed in the phase of launching the initiative (Chapter 6). Some of these infrastructure elements were implemented during the phase of managing the effort (Chapter 7), such as the systems for selecting projects and Black Belts. You now close the loop and implement the remaining infrastructure elements identified in your deployment plan. These elements will enable you to sustain momentum without the same level of personal attention from senior leadership that you have had up to now.

Holding Project Gains

The improvements obtained from Six Sigma and Lean projects are held by implementing the project control plans, ensuring that all employees associated with the process are trained in the new way of operating the process, and performing periodic process and financial audits. A control plan (AIAG, 2008a) contains the information needed to monitor and control a process and to maintain improvements; it is finalized during the Control phase of a DMAIC project. This plan contains specific activities required to monitor and control the process, including answers to the questions of *who, what, when,* and *how.* The control plan also contains the reaction plan, which defines what should be done by whom and who should be informed when something goes wrong.

The control plan is effective when it contains all the information needed to ensure that the process is in a state of control, is in a form easily used by the operators (process workers), and is, in fact, used to operate the process. An evergreen document, it is continually updated to reflect the current methods and measurements used to monitor and control the process. Clarity, completeness, conciseness, and simplicity are key characteristics of effective control plans.

Figure 8.2 shows an example of a control plan adapted from the Automotive Industry Action Group (AIAG, 2008a). Control plans are process specific and have many different forms, as well a variety of information (such as process steps, FMEA findings, measurement system indices such as Gage R&R values, and process capability indices). The right control plan for your process is the one that contains the information needed to monitor and control your process and to maintain the gains of improvements projects.

Prototype	Pre-Launch	Production **X**										
Control Plan Number		Key Contact/Phone					Date (Orig.)		Date (Rev.)			
Part Number/Latest Change Level		Core Team					Customer Engineering Approval/Date (If Req'd)					
Part Name/Description		Supplier/Plant Approval/Date					Customer Quality Approval/Date (If Req'd)					
Supplier/Plant	Supplier Code	Other Approval/Date (If Req'd)					Other Approval/Date (If Req'd)					

Part/ Process Number	Process Name/ Operation Description	Machine, Device Jig, Tools for MFG	No.	Characteristics		Special Char. Class	Product/ Process Spec/ Tolerance	Methods				Reaction Plan
				Product	Process			Evaluation Measurement Technique	Sample		Control Method	
									Size	Freq.		
3	Machine Surface "A"	Rotary Machine	51	Depth of Cut		*	2 ± 0.25"	Depth Gage	5	per hour per fixture	x̄ -R chart	Quarantine adjust and reset
		Holding Fixture #10	52	Perpendicular Cut		*	90° ± 1°	Gage 050	1 pc	every 4 hrs	x̄ -MR chart	Quarantine adjust and reset
		Holding Fixture #10	53		Hold casting in fixture for proper orientation		Fixture free from debris	Visual inspection	1 pc	after each cycle	Air blow-off	Readjust air blow-off

Adapted from Automotive Industry Action Group (2008a)   Advanced Product Quality Planning and Control Plan

Figure 8.2 Control plan example

Part of the control plan and project closure report is a schedule for the process and financial audits. The goal of the process audit is to see whether the process is being operated as directed by the control plan and standard operating procedures, as well as whether the process performance levels are being maintained. An effective way to integrate process audits into the normal work procedures is to make them part of the ISO 9000 audit. Recall that ISO 9000 is a common system used for quality and process management. Both control plans and ISO 9000 audits have provisions for changing the standard operating procedures as more effective means to operate the process are found. Incorporating these audits into ISO 9000 is an effective means of integrating breakthrough improvement with quality and process management as part of an increasingly holistic improvement system.

The financial audits determine whether the projected monetary gains are being realized. These audits, typically done by the financial organization, generally follow the financial performance of a project for 12 months after project closure. They help validate the results, build credibility for Lean Six Sigma, and identify opportunities for improvement. Recall that documentation of financial benefits is a key success factor for Lean Six Sigma. Maintaining the financial gains is equally important.

There also needs to be a concerted effort to ensure that all persons connected with the process, whether old hands or recently assigned, are trained in the new way of working. The adequacy of the training can also be checked as part of the ISO 9000 audit. (The overall training system is discussed later in this chapter.) Some organizations train all process operators as Lean Six Sigma Yellow Belts. Yellow Belt training is usually conducted by the Black Belt, typically lasts two days, and focuses on the Measure and Control phases of DMAIC. Although accountabilities vary considerably based on organizational philosophy and structure, in typical organizations, the operators' (process workers') main responsibilities are to take process data and to control the process.

Quarterly and Annual Reviews

Quarterly reviews conducted by the chief executive monitor the health and effectiveness of the overall Lean Six Sigma system. We noted in

Chapter 5 that management reviews are the "secret sauce" that is needed to keep Lean Sigma deployments on track and sustain the gains. In large organizations, these reviews should also be held at the business and function levels. The goal is to check on the functioning of the overall Lean Six Sigma infrastructure, including all relevant systems and processes.

Table 8.1 is based on the elements of the deployment plan (see Chapter 6), but augmented with some specifics that have been developed since, such as review of selected projects and overall financial results. Table 8.2 shows a typical outline for such a quarterly meeting. The key Six Sigma processes to be reviewed are progress toward financial goals, training progress (particularly in the first two years), and the project selection process (including the project hopper). It is not imperative that all processes be checked in each quarterly review, but certainly all processes should be checked at least once per year.

Table 8.1 Augmented Deployment Plan

• Goals and Strategy
• Budgeting–costs and benefits
• Project selection including financial impact ($$)
• Project hopper review
• Personnel selection
• Training
• Project reviews
• Project reporting
• Project tracking
• Project closure and handoff
• Audits – Process and Financial
• BB, GB, and Champion Performance Management
• MBB, BB, and GB career development including certification
• Communications
• Recognition, Reward, and Compensation
• Lean Six Sigma System review and enhancement

Table 8.2 Sample Quarterly Meeting Outline

- Review Format
  - Presentation of deployment status
  - Questions for clarification
  - Discussion
  - Action Items
  - Review Evaluation - Went well, do differently at next review
- Materials for Quarterly Review
  - Summary status for all projects
  - Trends in key process performance metrics
  - Financial impact assessment
  - Status of communications
  - Assessment of other Lean Six Sigma System elements as needed
  - Actions needed
  - Key learnings

Note: Materials to be discussed at the review should be sent to review team 2-3 days prior to review.

A good strategy is to formally review the critical processes in each of the first three quarterly reviews. The fourth quarter or annual review should probe in more depth, reviewing all the processes and developing an annual plan and goals for the coming year. Obviously, the annual plan and goals should link tightly to the overall strategic plan and goals from the deployment plan.

The annual review is a good time to check the project hopper for sufficient projects to reach the financial goals set for the coming year and determine whether the project portfolio (mix of projects) is sufficient to satisfy the goals of the organization. Do you have the right mix of projects, as categorized by business unit, functional unit, cost reduction versus cost avoidance, strategic versus tactical, revenue enhancement versus cost reduction, and quality improvement?

Consider taking an organizational survey of Lean Six Sigma deployment every 18 to 24 months, to check on deployment progress and identify opportunities for improvement (Snee, 1995). This survey should measure the feelings and attitudes of all employees. Honest, unfiltered feedback from employees is difficult information for senior leadership to obtain but is very important. The results of the survey are useful input for the annual planning sessions. Organizations change slowly, and the 18- to 24-month frequency is usually sufficient to detect improvement needs and any trends that have occurred.

The Training System

To sustain Lean Six Sigma for the long term, organizations need an overall training system, not just a mass wave of training. Portions of this system will already exist by this phase, and Executive, Business Leader, Champion, Black Belt, Master Black Belt (MBB), and Green Belt training will be underway. It is now time to think holistically about the organization's overall training needs relative to Lean Six Sigma and develop an expanding improvement methodology portfolio for years to come.

Key elements of a long-term training system follow:

- Six Sigma awareness training for new people
- Ongoing Champion, MBB, BB, and GB training
- Champion, MBB, BB, and GB refresher training
- Advanced Black Belt training
- Initial MBB training
- Training in different languages
- Curricula for operations, administration/transactional, and new product development processes
- Leadership Green Belt training
- Training in newer elements of the improvement methodology portfolio

Advanced Black Belt training is typically needed because some skills specific to certain technical areas are not part of the general Black Belt training. Examples include mixture experimentation for the chemical, coatings, and foods industries; multidimensional tolerancing for the assembly industries; and advanced process control and process variance component studies for the process industries. Black Belts also might need additional or advanced skills that couldn't be part of their original training because of time limitations. Some examples include advanced regression analysis and modeling techniques, complex multi-vari studies, and advanced design of experiments. Table 8.3 includes supplemental Black Belt materials and topics based on Hoerl (2001).

Table 8.3   Supplemental Black Belt Materials and Topics

• Failure Modes and Effects Analysis – Automotive Industry Action Group (2008b)
• Design of Experiments – Box, Hunter, and Hunter (2005); Montgomery (2012a)
• General Statistics – Walpole, Myers, and Myers (2016)
• Measurement Systems Analysis – Wheeler and Lyday (1989); Automotive Industry Action Group (2010)
• Mixture and Formulation Designs – Cornell (2011), Snee and Hoerl (2016)
• Quality Function Deployment (QFD) – Cohen (1995)
• Regression – Draper and Smith (1998); Montgomery, Peck, and Vining (2012)
• Reliability – Meeker and Escobar (1998)
• Response Surface Methodology – Myers, Montgomery and Anderson-Cook (2016)
• Statistical Process Control – Wheeler and Chambers (2010); Automotive Industry Action Group (2005); Montgomery (2012b)
• Statistical Thinking – Hoerl and Snee (2012)
• Time Series – Box, Jenkins, Reinsel, and Ljung (2015)
Adapted and Updated From Hoerl (2001)

Organizations are dynamic. People move in and out for various reasons. The training system must include processes for training new executives, Champions, Black Belts, MBBs, and Green Belts. Some training is job dependent; for example, engineers and financial personnel need different versions of training. In general, we recommend tailoring training to the degree feasible. Existing executives, Champions, Black Belts, MBBs, and Green Belts can also benefit from brief refresher courses, particularly when they stay in these roles for an extended period of time. New topics or techniques will likely be added to courses over time, and refreshers provide a convenient means for those previously trained to stay up-to-date. To sustain Lean Six Sigma momentum, training needs to be a sustained system, not simply a one-time event.

Multinational companies need to develop training materials and instructors to deliver Lean Six Sigma training in multiple languages. In our experience, you can often deliver Executive, Champion, MBB, and Black Belt training in English in most industrialized countries, but Green Belt training usually needs to be in the native language. Learning Lean Six Sigma is challenging enough without having to struggle with the nuances of a foreign language. Accurate translation of technical material is difficult, and for digital training systems, often unique challenges arise when translating into double-byte languages such as Chinese or Japanese (for which characters are stored as 2 bytes instead of 1 byte).

Expansion of the improvement methodology portfolio is a key aspect of growing the Lean Six Sigma initiative toward true holistic improvement, Lean Six Sigma 2.0. We discuss this in more detail later in this chapter. At this point, we just want to note that the training system will need to gradually expand to incorporate the additional improvement methodologies being added, such as Work-Out, Big Data analytics, or statistical engineering. This is required to address large, complex, unstructured problems.

A training system is much more extensive than a list of courses. A good system includes processes for developing and presenting new courses, keeping track of who has attended courses and passed exams, identifying people in need of specific training, translating materials, qualifying instructors, and providing managerial reports, all on an ongoing basis.

The organization must think carefully about how the training system will be managed over time. In most situations, a Lean Six Sigma provider manages the training system initially, but what happens when the contract expires? Taking over the responsibility for managing the training system from the Lean Six Sigma provider helps make improvement part of the culture—how things are done around here. Many organizations put MBBs in charge of managing the training system (perhaps through a Training Council) because training is a key role of MBBs.

Leadership Green Belt Training

It takes time for your entire management team to acquire the required Lean Six Sigma skills and experience. GE recognized this and decided to train all its professionals as Green Belts; the company also made Green Belt status a condition of promotion for professionals. Jack Welch said, "...with Six Sigma permeating much of what we do all day, it will be likewise unthinkable to hire into the Company, promote, or tolerate those who cannot, or will not, commit to this way of work" (GE Annual Report, 1997).

When management provides support in this manner, Lean Six Sigma becomes an effective leadership developmental tool. Leaders learn how to use Lean Six Sigma to improve an organization and its processes in all businesses, all functions, and all cultures. They see how formal approaches to improvement develop personnel, providing breadth of experience by allowing people to work on a variety of processes, empowering people to improve processes, teaching teamwork, and developing leaders. Leadership Green Belt training also results in all leaders hearing a common message that helps create alignment on the objectives and goals of improvement. Leaders with such perspective ensure that the gains of Lean Six Sigma are maintained.

Iomega reported, "Six Sigma is the best people development tool we have ever deployed" (English, 2001). Through its Six Sigma projects, Iomega (which provides storage products for digital items) developed a common language and a common approach for process design, improvement, and management. DuPont, Honeywell, and Bank of America have also provided Six Sigma training for their leadership.

We focus on Green Belt training as a leadership tool to ensure that all leaders have experienced Lean Six Sigma at the gut level. Green Belt training is needed at the beginning of implementation because, in most cases, none of the senior leaders will have held MBB or Black Belt positions. The need for Leadership Green Belt training will decrease over time as more leaders have Black Belt and MBB experience.

The goal of the Green Belt Leadership training is for the leaders to develop a deeper understanding of Lean Six Sigma and to learn how to use it to improve the organization. Lean Six Sigma training works best when it is project based, but finding appropriate projects for the leaders can be difficult. Training without a project is of less value; it can leave the impression that the leaders are just getting their tickets punched and are not serious about learning the methodology. A similar result can occur if the projects are not viewed as important, or if the leaders don't do a good job and obtain poor results. So we have come full circle, finding that project selection is a potential Achilles' heel of Leadership Green Belt training, just as it is for other types of Lean Six Sigma projects. We offer a few suggestions for finding appropriate projects next.

Focus on the work the leader actually does. This ensures that the project is meaningful, not merely duties added to an already overflowing plate. Recall from the discussion of nonmanufacturing applications that all work can be viewed as a process, but with general business processes, it is much harder to actually see the process. Experienced MBBs should be able to help the Leadership Green Belts see the underlying processes in managerial activities such as budgeting, evaluating performance, and allocating resources. Many senior executives feel that they spend too much time in unproductive meetings. All would appreciate improvements to the meeting process. Implementing and managing the systems and processes that are part of the Lean Six Sigma infrastructure would make excellent leadership DFSS projects.

A senior HR leader could implement a new reward and recognition system. An IT leader could design a new tracking and reporting system. Finance leaders could work on designing the financial auditing system for projects. Large projects such as these might need to be split up into several smaller projects, and additional team members will likely be needed to address details (such as writing computer code). Nevertheless, relevant, important project areas such as these tend to be much more fruitful than projects that are perceived as "moving the water cooler." Table 8.4 gives other examples of topics for Leadership Green Belt projects.

Table 8.4 Sample Topics for Leadership Green Belt Projects

- Reduce the amount of expedited freight usage in the Eastern Region (Business Executive Vice President)
- Improve the customer complaint handling process to reduce response time (Quality Manager)
- Increase the impact of the employee training process (Human Resources Manager)
- Improve the management reporting process to increase the timeliness of reports and to eliminate little-used reports (Assistant Plant Manager)
- Reduce the cost and increase the job offer acceptance rate of the college recruiting process (Corporate College Recruiting Director)
- Speed up the transfer of manufacturing processes from pilot plant to manufacturing in order to reduce amount of backorders (Director of Manufacturing)
- Streamline the operations forecasting process to improve timeliness and accuracy (Planning and Scheduling Manager)
- Reduce the corporate budgeting process cycle time from 12 months to 9 months (Corporate Financial Officer)
- Reduce the cycle time of the new acquisitions process (President)
- Improve shipping contracting process to improve on-time delivery performance (Logistics Vice President)

Our recommendation is that every Green Belt, including senior leadership, should do at least one formal project. We do not believe you can get a gut-level appreciation for Lean Six Sigma without actually doing it yourself. Through careful project selection and mentoring from experienced MBBs, Leadership Green Belts can successfully complete meaningful projects. Although extra mentoring from the MBB can be extremely helpful, the MBB must carefully avoid even the perception that he or she is doing the project for the Leadership Green Belt. People will be watching and will see that leaders are saying one thing, but doing something completely different.

Lean Six Sigma Organizational Structure

By now, you have realized that some Lean Six Sigma infrastructure is needed to sustain momentum. If properly designed and implemented, this infrastructure will be value added, with minimal bureaucracy. Note that we recommend a Lean infrastructure, one that is primarily automated and requires minimal human staffing.

For example, the project tracking and reporting system should be digital so that additional personnel are not required to process paper reports. Despite its Lean-ness, the infrastructure will require some human guidance to manage and improve it over time. Therefore, you will need a formal Lean Six Sigma organizational structure to clarify roles and responsibilities for managing the infrastructure. This organizational structure will likely have begun in the phase of managing the effort, but it needs to be expanded and invigorated now because of the extension of supporting systems and processes in this phase. Eventually, this will become the holistic improvement organization, the umbrella organization for all improvement work.

Organizational structure is particularly important now that the direct involvement of the Lean Six Sigma provider is winding down. In many Lean Six Sigma deployments, the provider handles much of the initial organizational effort. Transitioning to an internal organizational structure is an important step in becoming self-sufficient. It is particularly important that the training system be well managed and that it not miss a beat as the provider's efforts wind down.

If the transition is not properly handled, a leadership vacuum will be created when the provider fades out of the picture. The best way to avoid this is to have a formal, functioning organizational structure, including an active Lean Six Sigma Council led by the overall Lean Six Sigma Leader, to manage the effort going forward. This implies more than just naming Champions, MBBs, Black Belts, and so on. You need a functioning team that works like a well-oiled machine to properly lead and coordinate all aspects of the Lean Six Sigma deployment.

By *active*, we mean that all members must participate regularly. It does little good to list the company's top leaders as council members if they do not participate. As noted earlier, we can also set up Lean Six Sigma Councils within individual business units or functions. The leaders of the business unit and functional councils are usually members of the overall council, resulting in interlocking membership. This aids in communication and coordination across the organization.

For example, when Roger Hoerl was the Quality Leader (Six Sigma Leader) of the GE Corporate Audit Staff (CAS), he also was a participant in the GE Quality Leaders' Council (overall Six Sigma Council). In addition, he led the CAS Quality Council that consisted of the following members:

- The CAS Vice President (head of CAS)
- Head of financial service business audits (GE Capital)
- Head of industrial business audits
- CAS HR manager
- CAS IT leader
- An MBB

This organizational structure worked well for a couple of reasons: (1) It ensured that the CAS Six Sigma effort was aligned with the overall direction of GE's Six Sigma deployment, due to the interlocking membership; and (2) the participation of the key decision makers in the CAS council ensured alignment within CAS.

For example, when the council made policy decisions about certification criteria, training requirements, and so on, all the key leaders conveyed the same message. If the leaders had not participated in these decisions, there would have been potential for second-guessing, misalignment, or organizational conflict at the top. All members, including the vice president, made their active participation in this council a priority. The HR and IT representatives contributed significantly to training, reward and recognition, career development issues (HR), and tracking systems for projects, training, and certification (IT). Lean Six Sigma Councils typically include the Lean Six Sigma Leader, representative (not all) Champions, representative MBBs, and leaders of finance, HR, IT, and any other relevant functions.

Six Sigma Leaders Must Work Together As a Team

It is important not only that an organizational structure be in place to lead and manage the Lean Six Sigma effort, but also that the key players work together as a team. A team functions well when each player does his or her job well and knows the roles and functions of all the other players on the team. Each person must focus on performing his or her role in such a way that the team wins. For example, it is important that the Black Belts understand the roles of the Champion and other Lean Six Sigma team members so they know where to go for help.

Similarly, it is critical that the functional group leaders know the role of the Black Belts so they can provide them with data, expertise, and resources. This attitude helps everyone learn their roles and functions effectively. The Lean Six Sigma Sweep sports analogy can help us deepen our understanding of this requirement.

The "Lean Six Sigma Sweep"

Columnist George Will tells us that "sports serve society by providing vivid examples of excellence." This can be true with Lean Six Sigma. Sports provide vivid examples and analogies that help us understand why Lean Six Sigma is so effective—it provides a strategy, a methodology, and an infrastructure that enables all the leaders to work together as a team to improve the performance of the organization.

When you think of excellence and success in the sports world, many modern examples come to mind, such as the New England Patriots in football and the Golden State Warriors in basketball. However, we choose to look back to an "old school" football team from yesteryear, before the wide-open, passing-oriented game of today emerged. In the times of Vince Lombardi, football games were generally won in the "trenches," through the running game. Lombardi was the coach of the Green Bay Packers team that won five National Football League titles and the first two Super Bowls in the 1960s. Many subsequent successful football coaches were students of Lombardi. How did he do it? His success came from careful thought, detailed planning, lots of practice and hard work, and a clear focus on the goal. These success factors also apply to Lean Six Sigma.

What was Lombardi's methodology? The famous Packer Sweep was Lombardi's signature play and a key component of his success. This was a running play in which the running back carried the ball to the outside behind two lineman (pulling guards). The popular "jet sweep" in today's game is an adaption of the Packer Sweep. Lombardi practiced the sweep more than any other play, refining it until his players knew that they could run it anytime against any opponent. Anyone who has seen video of Green Bay playing during the Lombardi years will recall the sweep in which the guards Jerry Kramer (64) and Fuzzy Thurston (63) pulled out of the line and led the running back Jim Taylor (31) around the end while each of the other players completed his assignment.

Interestingly, Lombardi did not invent this play (he borrowed it from the Los Angeles Rams), but he certainly perfected it. He also developed many variations. On every play, each player knew his job and understood that if each person completed his assignment, the play would be successful. The play was so important to Lombardi's offense that Coach John Madden recalls him devoting an entire one-day seminar to the subject (Madden, 1985). Lombardi discussed the play, its philosophy, its fundamentals, its objectives, each player's role, and why the play couldn't be stopped if each player executed well. Each variation of the sweep was discussed in the same detail.

Many similarities emerge between the Packer Sweep and Lean Six Sigma. First, Lean Six Sigma was not totally original. It built on the work of others and continues to be enhanced as we move toward holistic improvement. Lean Six Sigma works because it emphasizes focus, planning, constant practice (every project is a practice session), and dedicated leadership. The roles are well defined; if each person does his or her job, as defined by the process, the projects will succeed and Lean Six Sigma will achieve its goals.

Lean Six Sigma (ultimately, as holistic improvement via Version 2.0, as discussed in Chapter 2, "What Is Holistic Improvement?") can be the signature business strategy and management process that separates an organization from its competition—providing focus, reducing costs, growing revenues, empowering and developing people, enhancing teamwork, and providing a common corporate language and methodology. In the process, Lean Six Sigma improves an organization's performance, sweeping money to the bottom line, just as Lombardi's Green Bay Sweep gained yards, put points on the scoreboard, won games, won conference titles, and won Super Bowls. We refer to this use of Lean Six Sigma as a signature business strategy as the Lean Six Sigma Sweep.

This analogy actually goes much deeper. There are 11 roles on the Lean Six Sigma Sweep team, just as there are 11 positions on a football team. These roles are detailed in Table 8.5 (also see Chapter 6) and are shown schematically with linkages in Figure 8.3. Although many analogies are possible, we resist the temptation to match the roles on the Lean Six Sigma team with those on a football team. The important point is that these roles must work together as a team just as the players on a football team must work together to be successful.

Table 8.5 Roles on the Lean Six Sigma Sweep Team

- Chief Executive Officer – Provides strategy, goals, promotion, resources, review, recognition, and feedback
- Six Sigma Leaders – Build infrastructure, provide training, coordinate initiative, track progress, identify best practices
- Management Teams – Provide strategy, goals, and resources; identify and approve projects; report progress; provide review, recognition, and feedback
- Champions – Project business and political leader, removes barriers, reviews BB progress, promotes initiative
- Black Belts – Learns methods and tools, completes strategic projects, trains and promotes Six Sigma
- Green Belts – Learns methods and tools, completes tactical projects, promotes Six Sigma
- Master Black Belt – Technical Leader, trains, completes "mission critical" projects, and coaches
- Functional Groups – Provide data, expertise, and personnel for BB and GB teams
- Finance – Determines and tracks financial impact of projects and Six Sigma initiative
- Human Resources – Creates and administers communications process, career development, and recognition and reward systems
- Information Technology – Provides process data collection and management systems

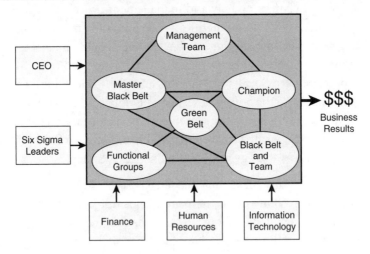

Figure 8.3 Lean Six Sigma Sweep team linkages

If the people in these roles perform their jobs as defined and understand the roles of the others on the team, just as Lombardi required of his players, the Lean Six Sigma Sweep will work. Organizational performance will improve, money will be swept to the bottom line, and the organization will be well down the road to success. In fact, when an organization moves out in front of its competition using Lean Six Sigma and continues to use it and expand it toward holistic improvement, the organization will most likely always be ahead of its competition. It is unlikely that the competition will ever catch up.

We again recall the AlliedSignal manager's admonishment: "Six Sigma works if you follow the process. If it is not working, you are not following the process."

Playing Offense: Growing the Effort

Although your efforts to hold project gains and the benefits of the overall Lean Six Sigma system help sustain momentum, this is basically a defensive strategy. You don't want to lose the benefits you have worked so hard to obtain. As in many aspects of life, however, the best defense is a good offense.

While you work on holding gains, you also want to take proactive steps to grow and expand the deployment into new areas. This is your offensive strategy. Continuing to drive Lean Six Sigma into new areas will keep the initiative fresh and prevent it from losing steam.

Some key areas that can prove particularly fruitful are extending Lean Six Sigma to the entire organization, taking it to suppliers and customers, expanding your portfolio of improvement methodologies, and driving top-line growth to complement the bottom-line benefits already achieved.

Expanding Lean Six Sigma Throughout the Organization

Most Lean Six Sigma initiatives begin in manufacturing or operations because manufacturing typically has better measurement systems than other functions. These measurement systems enable you to get going on improvement projects faster. In addition, the money to be made is more obvious and easier to quantify than in other parts of the organization. Nothing shows that Lean Six Sigma works better than speed and results.

These two ingredients, speed and results, help you demonstrate success and allow the organization to see that "Lean Six Sigma will work here!" In the process, you gain experience in Lean Six Sigma, build confidence that you can deploy it successfully, and produce bottom-line results. Lean Six Sigma is shown to more than pay for itself.

But there is much more to be gained. Many believe that more than half of an organization's improvement opportunity lies outside manufacturing or operations. This additional improvement is a huge opportunity the organization must capture. Organizations typically move Lean Six Sigma in one of two directions after manufacturing/operations: to administrative and transactional processes, or to new product development (R&D). Some organizations might want to improve both areas at the same time. Most, however, move first to the administrative and transactional processes, such as accounts receivable, transportation and shipping, human resources, finance, and other areas listed in Table 8.6.

Table 8.6 Administrative and Transactional Processes

• Supply Chain	• Human Resources
– Logistics, distribution, warehousing	– Recruiting
– Inventory reduction	– Performance evaluation
– On-time delivery	– Retention of "hi-pots" (high
• eCommerce	potential employees)
– Website development (eSell)	• Legal
– Fulfillment (eSell)	– Compliance
– Procurement (eBuy)	– Patent filing
– Digitization (eMake)	• Business Development
• Finance	– Mergers and acquisitions
– Accounts payable	– Due diligence
– Accounts receivable	• Marketing
– Manual account reconciliations	– Advertising & promotions
• Environmental	– Marketing research process
– Waste disposal	• Customer Service
– Emission control	– Response time
	– Issue resolution

Transactional and administrative areas have unique characteristics that are unlike those of manufacturing processes (Snee and Hoerl, 2005):

- The culture is usually less scientific, and people don't think in terms of processes, measurements, and data.

- The work typically requires considerable human intervention, such as customer interaction, underwriting or approval decisions, and manual report generation. Human intervention is, of course, an additional source of variation and errors.

- Transactional and administrative processes are often invisible, complex, and not well defined or well documented. Such characteristics make opportunities for improvement difficult to identify and make projects difficult to define.

- Measurements are often nonexistent or ill defined, resulting in the need to create measurement systems first and then begin to collect the data.

- The process output is often intangible and can be unique. For example, the actual output of a due diligence study is knowledge, possibly documented in the form of a report. Each due diligence study will be unique.

- Similar activities are often done in varying ways. Three people in three different company locations are unlikely to do the same job in the same manner.

The most important of these unique attributes is the frequent lack of process measurements. In our experience, four key measures of the performance of nonmanufacturing processes come up repeatedly: accuracy, cycle time, cost, and customer satisfaction.

- *Accuracy* is measured by correct financial figures, completeness of information, and freedom from data errors.

- *Cycle time* is how long it takes to do something, such as pay an invoice.

- By *cost,* we mean the internal cost of process steps, not the price charged for services. In many cases, cost is largely determined by the accuracy or cycle time of the process; the longer it takes and the more mistakes that have to be fixed, the higher the cost.

- *Customer satisfaction* is the fourth common measurement. For a situation in which the key process outputs are intangible, such as customer service processes, customer satisfaction (often measured through surveys) will likely be the primary measure of success.

Fortunately, there are more similarities than differences between manufacturing and nonmanufacturing processes. One of the key similarities is that both types of processes have "hidden factories," places where the defective product is sent to be reworked or scrapped (revised, corrected, or discarded in nonmanufacturing terms). In reality, every process has a hidden factory (see Figures 8.4 and 8.5). Nonmanufacturing examples include performing manual account reconciliation in accounting, revising budgets until management will "accept" them, and shipping product back to online retailers because a mistake was made in the order. Find the hidden factory, and you have found one good place to look for opportunities to improve the process.

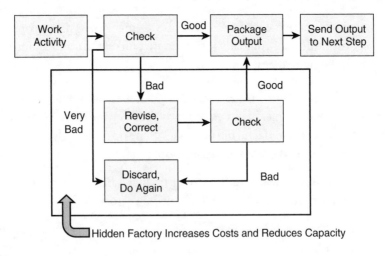

Figure 8.4   Every process has a hidden factory: a nonmanufacturing view

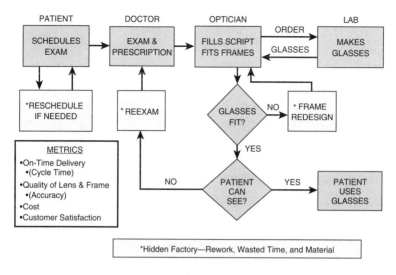

Figure 8.5 Eyeglasses fitting process

Use of Lean Six Sigma in new product development (R&D) is commonly referred to as Design for Six Sigma (DFSS). This is another area in which you must expand the effort because the entitlement of a process is often determined in the Design phase. The goal is to improve the product development process so that the organization can get new and better products to market quicker and at less cost to both the consumer and the company.

The strategy is to build the Lean Six Sigma methods and tools into the company's new product development process (usually a stage-gate process). Close interaction with marketing also greatly improves the development process and, therefore, the new products and services that are ultimately produced. The payoff on DFSS projects usually has a longer time frame because of the time required to get a new product to market. The training is still project focused (no project, no training) and is done at both the Black Belt/MBB and Green Belt levels. More will be said about DFSS when we discuss top-line growth later in this chapter.

Using Six Sigma to Improve Supplier Performance

You will quickly learn that the average level and variability of quality (not to mention the cost) of materials from suppliers have a big effect on the quality and cost of your products and services. It is not unusual for 40 to 60 percent of the final cost of a company's product to derive from the costs of materials purchased from suppliers. You cannot overlook such a high cost or the effects of variation in materials on the performance of processes, so you might wonder how to get suppliers to use Lean Six Sigma to improve their performance, ultimately improving yours.

You will have more credibility going to suppliers with a recommendation to use Lean Six Sigma once you have used it in your organization and demonstrated that it works. For this reason, supplier Lean Six Sigma programs typically don't start until after the first or second year of a deployment.

The first step in getting suppliers to use Lean Six Sigma is to determine how the quality and cost of supplier materials are affecting the performance of your organization. One way to accomplish this is to track supplier materials as they flow through your processes and determine the scrap, waste, downtime, and yield loss they cause. You will no doubt also see that a large portion of the loss comes from your company's processes, thereby identifying additional opportunities for internal improvement.

We do *not* recommend focusing improvement efforts on "beating up" suppliers without a clear understanding of how their materials affect your process. This misguided step is popular because it requires no change or hard work on the part of your organization. A more effective method is to first focus Lean Six Sigma on what you can control and then, as you learn about root causes coming from materials, integrate suppliers into your improvement efforts.

This approach works in both manufacturing and nonmanufacturing environments. For example, a newspaper company initiated a Lean Six Sigma project to reduce errors in the paper. Such errors were generally found before publication, but finding and fixing them was an expensive form of rework. Data from the project ultimately revealed that the root causes of many errors were in the information obtained from external sources, such as wrong facts, wrong names, and wrong figures (Hoerl and Snee, 2012; see Chapter 10, "Final Thoughts for Leaders"). Armed with this information, the newspaper communicated to reporters and copy editors which information sources (suppliers) could be trusted and should be used. Other sources needed to initiate improvement efforts to be trusted and used in the future.

When you know the magnitude of the problems coming from suppliers, you can set an improvement goal for them to attain. A common goal is a 5 percent reduction per year in price, adjusted for inflation. The intent is for the price reduction to be based on supplier improvement projects that reduced the supplier's own costs. In this way, both the supplier and the customer benefit financially. The price reduction goal could be mandatory, or suppliers that meet this price reduction goal could receive preferential treatment.

If these goals are based on actual data and can be achieved via a win–win approach, communicating such expectations is not simply "beating up" suppliers. When it makes business sense, companies also might find it appropriate to develop unique improvement goals for different organizations or processes within a given supplier.

Next, you have to determine which suppliers you are going to approach with encouragement to use the Lean Six Sigma approach. One way is to do a Pareto analysis of the key sources of costs, such as supplier-caused scrap, rework, and other losses. Focus on the materials and suppliers that are associated with the highest costs; the biggest problems usually represent the biggest opportunity. You might also want to approach key suppliers that you would like to form a long-term strategic relationship with.

Companies have introduced suppliers to Lean Six Sigma in a variety of ways. One way is to identify a few high-impact projects and form customer–supplier teams to complete the projects using Lean Six Sigma. If the supplier doesn't have Black Belts available to work on the project, then the customer supplies the Lean Six Sigma expertise and any needed training. Tremendous progress is made when both the customer and the supplier have one or more Black Belts on the project team.

Another approach is for the company to make available supplier training programs that are partially funded by the customer and that make available both Champion and Black Belt training, at a minimum. An effective way to create such a program is to start with a few good projects and then use their success to expand the program. It is essential that the supplier's management be involved in the program. An executive work-shop is a good way to help build this involvement because it communi-cates what Lean Six Sigma is and the benefits the supplier organization can expect to receive.

Clearly, careful planning is needed to have a successful Lean Six Sigma supplier program. Any financial arrangements must be defined and agreed to up front so that the expectations of both parties are met. The goals and objectives have to be carefully thought out and clearly communicated.

Additionally, Lean Six Sigma must be positioned as a *how* instead of a *what*. In other words, your purpose is not to have the supplier use Lean Six Sigma. Instead, your purpose is for suppliers to make tangible improvements that positively affect you and your organization. Lean Six Sigma is just a means to help them accomplish this objective. If the sup-plier can obtain the desired results without Lean Six Sigma, this should be acceptable. Of course, desiring improvements without a method to achieve them is little more than daydreaming. Lean Six Sigma can be an effective methodology for achieving customer and supplier goals once those goals have been clearly defined and communicated.

Expanding the Improvement Portfolio

As we discussed in Chapters 1–3, holistic improvement integrates differ-ent methodologies under one overall improvement system. An organiza-tion needs diverse methods and tools at its disposal to be able to address the diverse nature of problems it will face. A key distinction of holistic improvement over approaches based on only one methodology is that it is method agnostic. That is, it starts by diagnosing the problem that needs to be solved and then selects the best improvement methodology for that particular problem. It does not force-fit a preselected methodology to a problem for which it is not well suited. This is a common shortcoming with virtually all other improvement approaches, including Six Sigma and Lean.

Furthermore, holistic improvement integrates the three main categories of improvement—quality by design, breakthrough improvement, and qual-ity and process management systems—under one umbrella. Such integra-tion makes the overall improvement effort more coordinated, integrated, and, ultimately, optimized. In most organizations, these three types of improvement reside in different organizational silos, resulting in a lack of coordination, isolated efforts ("islands of improvement"), and, in many cases, outright competition for resources and management's attention.

Given these points, it might seem logical to implement a holistic improvement initiative from the beginning. This makes sense on paper, but in practice, it turns out to be too large an effort to launch at one time. As an analogy, strong middle school students don't skip high school and go directly into college. A few students have done so successfully, but in general, it is a poor strategy and is not recommended. A much more pragmatic approach is to initially launch a Lean Six Sigma initiative and then gradually expand it to become holistic—to evolve toward Lean Six Sigma 2.0. This is the approach we have assumed in previous chapters.

Now that you have launched a Lean Six Sigma initiative, have transitioned to managing it through formal infrastructure (systems and organizational structure), and are now expanding the effort, you are in a good position to make significant progress toward holistic improvement. A key step in this direction is to expand the portfolio of improvement methodologies. So far, most projects will have utilized Lean and/or Six Sigma. Going forward, we would like a broader portfolio to allow the organization to attack problems that are not well suited for either Lean or Six Sigma, such as routine problem solving.

Three key questions must be answered:

1. How do we go about adding methodologies?

2. How do we modify the infrastructure developed in previous phases, given a broader portfolio of improvement methodologies?

3. How do we determine the most suitable methodology for a given project?

We address these three questions next.

Which Methodologies to Add?

In thinking about which methodologies to add, it is good to revisit the concept of holistic improvement. We have reproduced Table 2.2 and labeled it here as Table 8.7. Note that we need to think about methodologies in each of the three categories listed: quality by design, breakthrough improvement, and quality and process management systems. As we discuss later in this chapter, DFSS is a logical next step because it brings quality by design into the mix and is a natural extension of Lean Six Sigma. No doubt Black Belts will have already identified design projects that require a somewhat different approach than DMAIC. We return to DFSS shortly.

Table 8.7 Holistic Improvement System Needs and Sample Approaches

Quality by Design	Breakthrough Improvement	Quality and Process Management Systems
Needs	**Needs**	**Needs**
• Business innovation	• Meet annual and strategic plans	• Quality & process management system
• Process design/redesign	• Better product/process performance	
• Product design/redesign	• Better organizational performance	• Risk management system
• Organizational design/redesign	• Mission critical problems	• IT system
		• Measurement system
		• Training system
Approaches	**Approaches**	**Approaches**
• Innovation/Creativity	• Six Sigma	• ISO/Baldrige
• DFSS	• Lean Enterprise	• Total Productive Maintenance
• TRIZ	• Statistical Engineering	
	• Big Data Analytics	• "Internet of Things"
	• Work-Out	• Kepner-Tregoe

Note that the methodologies listed in Table 8.7 are just a sample of recommended approaches that have proven effective within diverse organizations. Each organization should develop its own list, based on its particular needs, taking into account the methodologies and systems it already has in place. Consider Table 8.7 as a reference point or benchmark to begin building upon.

In the breakthrough improvement category, Work-Out is a logical methodology to add at this point. The organization will likely already have undergone improvement projects that did not require the rigor of Lean Six Sigma. The knowledge of the folks in the room might have been sufficient to solve the problem, producing bottom-line results more quickly. Furthermore, Work-Out does not use any sophisticated tools—just sound meeting management, including formal methods for idea generation and prioritization (Hoerl, 2008). Therefore, the additional training required to add Work-Out to the portfolio is relatively minor.

When the project does not require any tools, but can be considered a quick fix, we often refer to it as a "Nike project" (Just Do It!). Nike projects can still be important and impactful; they just don't require the same degree of rigor and formal tools. Obviously, Nike projects are easy to add to the portfolio.

Your organization might or might not have a Big Data analytics group. If it does, now is a good time to begin informal networking to better coordinate these improvement efforts. Reorganizations are difficult and fraught with pitfalls, so we recommend leaving a formal reorganization for the fourth phase, the way we work. If no Big Data organization currently exists, it is a good idea to begin seeking individuals with the right skills (potentially, MBBs) who might begin such an effort. As previously noted, analyzing massive data sets provides a great opportunity for additional improvement beyond Lean Six Sigma.

Most organizations have a formal quality group active in ISO 9000, Malcolm Baldrige, or other quality management approaches, but routine problem solving still might need to be added to the improvement portfolio. As noted in Table 8.7, Is–Is Not analysis, often referred to by the authors names Kepner–Tregoe, is an effective methodology for addressing special cause problems. By *special cause problems*, we mean situations in which performance has deteriorated, but we don't know why. Black Belts need to quickly identify the root cause of the problem so the organization can fix it and return performance to normal levels. Kepner–Tregoe does require training, but not as rigorous as Six Sigma or Lean.

In summary, the following improvement methodologies are potentially the most logical to add to the portfolio now:

- DFSS
- Work-Out
- Nike projects
- Big Data analytics (exploratory)
- Kepner–Tregoe

The other methodologies in Table 8.7, as well as others your organization identifies, can then be added gradually over time as you migrate toward holistic improvement. Recall that the improvement portfolio should be dynamic, evolving over time as new methods become available and potentially replace older methods that are no longer relevant. Managing the improvement portfolio is a critical responsibility of the Lean Six Sigma Council, often referred to as the Quality Council.

Implications for Infrastructure

Several elements of the existing infrastructure need to be modified to accommodate a broader improvement portfolio. For example, the training system now has more methodologies to consider. We recommend that the training system *not* try to train every employee, or even every Black Belt or MBB, in all methods in the portfolio. This training commitment would be monumental and very expensive. Instead, the training system needs to have the appropriate level of resources in each methodology to match the organization's current needs. For example, we feel that everyone needs to be familiar with the basics of Six Sigma and the Lean principles. However, very few need to be competent in Big Data analytics.

Similarly, more R&D scientists and engineers will need training in DFSS relative to employees in manufacturing or finance. Even MBBs cannot be expected to specialize in all methodologies, although there will need to be a critical mass of MBBs who are well versed in each improvement methodology added to the portfolio. Such a critical mass might not exist at the time the methodology is added to the portfolio, so training will be required to develop it.

Recall that developing and managing a training system is much more challenging than conducting a mass wave of training. Mass waves of training rarely have lasting value (Snee and Hoerl, 2005). This is why we recommend chartering the Training Council at this point if it is not already in existence. Obviously, this council requires heavy involvement from HR, as well as a core group of MBBs who collectively understand the full set of methodologies and know who in the organization needs to be trained in each.

Another system that needs to be modified is the project selection and prioritization system. Until now, the main objectives were to identify and prioritize potential projects and put them in the project hopper. As noted in Chapter 6, some thought was needed regarding whether a Lean, Six Sigma, or perhaps hybrid approach was most logical so that an appropriate Black Belt could be assigned to lead the project. Now that we have a broader improvement portfolio, more thought needs to go into selecting the project methodology and the most appropriate Black Belt.

Going forward, once projects are identified, they also need to be mapped to the most appropriate methodology. For example, should this be a Six Sigma project or is it more suited to Kepner–Tregoe? The choice of methodology is important, so the project selection process must incorporate MBBs who collectively understand the full range of potential project types. You will notice that the MBB role becomes more critical as we migrate from Lean Six Sigma to holistic improvement.

After the project methodology has been chosen, a Black Belt with a strong background in the chosen methodology is needed. We certainly encourage cross-training to develop Black Belts with broad backgrounds, but as with MBBs, not every Black Belt will be competent in every improvement method. Recall that we strongly recommend selecting projects first and then assigning Black Belts, not vice versa.

Selecting the Most Appropriate Methodology

Identifying the most appropriate improvement methodology can be challenging. Despite the fact that holistic improvement is a method-agnostic approach, people will no doubt still have their favorites. Therefore, it is often helpful to develop tools to guide the selection of methodology in an objective manner. Hoerl and Snee (2013) developed one such tool, which is shown in Figure 8.6 with minor updates. The two main questions that teams need to answer in using this approach are whether the solution is known or unknown (we discussed this previously) and whether the problem has relatively high or low complexity.

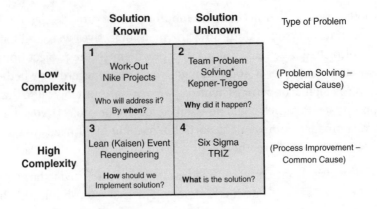

	Solution Known	Solution Unknown	Type of Problem
Low Complexity	**1** Work-Out Nike Projects Who will address it? By **when**?	**2** Team Problem Solving* Kepner-Tregoe **Why** did it happen?	(Problem Solving – Special Cause)
High Complexity	**3** Lean (Kaisen) Event Reengineering **How** should we Implement solution?	**4** Six Sigma TRIZ **What** is the solution?	(Process Improvement – Common Cause)

*Structured team problem solving, using the "Magnificent 7" Tools, for example

Figure 8.6   Selecting the most appropriate improvement methodology

The answers to these two questions identify the most appropriate cell in the matrix, which lists the logical questions that need to be answered in that cell and the potential methods to do so. High complexity is usually associated with quality by design or breakthrough improvement—achieving a new level of performance. Low complexity is usually associated with routine problem solving—fixing something that is broken. Note that *reengineering* is a more general term for DFSS projects. It was generally intended to represent the redesign of existing processes, often with the intent of automating something that was previously done manually.

Team problem solving is a generic term for any structured approach to solving problems. The so-called Magnificent 7 tools noted in Figure 8.6 are listed here:

- Cause-and-effect diagram
- Pareto chart
- Check sheet
- Run chart
- Histogram
- Scatter diagram
- Stratification

Figure 8.6 is intended to only highlight alternative improvement approaches; it is not intended to be comprehensive.

For solution-known, low-complexity problems (potentially Nike projects), we just need to know who is going to complete the project and by when. If the solution is not known, the root cause (the *why*) needs to be identified (potentially with Kepner–Tregoe) and then fixed. As noted previously, Lean tends to work best for solution-known problems that involve some degree of complexity—those that require breakthrough improvement. Because of the complexity, we still need to determine how to implement the known solution. This will rarely be trivial for Lean projects, including Kaizen events.

The "sweet spot" for Six Sigma is solution-unknown, high-complexity problems. In such cases, we need to perform significant data gathering and analysis to identify root causes and, subsequently, potential solutions to them. For even higher-complexity problems (for example, the large, complex, unstructured problems discussed in Chapter 1, "A New Improvement Paradigm Is Needed"), a statistical engineering approach might be more appropriate.

Of course, Figure 8.6 is just one example of a tool that might be used to help identify the most appropriate methodology for a given project. In Chapter 6, we discussed how to determine whether the issue is "within the boxes" or "between the boxes" of the flowchart when considering Six Sigma or Lean. This principle can also help in selecting the best methodology. Organizations should further develop their own tools to make this critical decision. More research is clearly needed in methodology selection for a given problem.

Growing the Top Line

A common question when implementing Lean Six Sigma is, "I can see how to use Lean Six Sigma to reduce costs, but how can I use Lean Six Sigma to increase revenues?" Expanding the improvement portfolio to incorporate more quality by design methodologies will certainly help, but it often goes unnoticed that Lean Six Sigma can also grow the top line. In general, revenues are increased by these actions:

- Obtaining new customers (find more)
- Getting current customers to buy more (get more)

- Regaining old customers who have left to do business with your competitors (keep more)

Fortunately, Lean Six Sigma can be applied in many ways that directly tie to one or more of these revenue-increasing areas. For example, consider the following specific approaches, with the principle revenue-increasing areas noted:

- Use DFSS to create new and better products (find, get, and keep more). DFSS is obviously a quality by design approach, but it is also a form of Six Sigma.

- Increase capacity (productivity) when the product line is sold out (find and get more)

- Improve product quality and price (find, get, and keep more)

- Improve the service processes that touch the customer, such as delivery, billing, and customer service (get and keep more)

- Show customers how to benefit from Lean Six Sigma (get more).

- Institute "at the customer, for the customer" projects (get and keep more).

- Successfully complete strategic sales and marketing projects (find, get, and keep more).

Developing new and better products and services are obviously key to growing the top line. This is why integrating breakthrough improvement with quality by design is so important. These two types of quality improvement need to be well integrated to keep them from residing in separate silos. DFSS is the Six Sigma approach to accomplishing this objective. We have seen that DFSS is typically started about one year after initiating the DMAIC methodology for improving existing processes, and after gaining confidence that Lean Six Sigma will work in the company.

Conceptually, we can consider product design a process and apply Lean Six Sigma in a straightforward manner to improve it. In most cases, however, organizations want to apply Lean Six Sigma to the design of a specific new product or service. Although it applies equally well here, Lean Six Sigma requires a different roadmap that is more tailored to design.

If a team applies the DMAIC roadmap to designing a new product, it will likely stumble in the Measure phase because there is no existing process on which to take measurements.

GE developed the DMADV roadmap, and many others have adopted it since then, to apply to design projects. As we explained in Chapter 3, "Key Methodologies in a Holistic Improvement System," the Define stage is analogous to Define in DMAIC, although it is typically more complicated because we are designing a new product or service, not improving an existing process. In the DMADV Measure phase, we determine the CTQ characteristics and ensure that we have measurement capability, but we do not measure an existing process unless the new design is an enhancement of a current design.

The Analyze phase focuses on conceptual design, in which we use creative "out of the box" thinking to determine the most promising high-level design to satisfy CTQs. For product designs, we might develop prototypes. The details of this design are completed in the Design phase, where we make calculations to predict final design capability. If these calculations are not promising, the team must repeat the Analyze phase and the Design phase to improve the design capability. In the Verify phase, we pilot the new design under realistic conditions to obtain real data verifying the design capability.

For example, an organization that is designing a manufactured product would utilize a pilot run in a real manufacturing facility, using regular workers and raw materials for the Verify phase. This contrasts with a prototype made under ideal conditions that might be used to prove the design concept in the Analyze phase. Similarly, an organization that is designing a web-based insurance application and underwriting system would utilize people with computer skills similar to the targeted market to access the system during normal business hours using standard platforms. In many cases, we go through a mini-DMAIC cycle here to improve design flaws observed in the pilot. If major discrepancies in capability arise, organizations might need to loop back through the Analyze phase and Design phase again.

This approach to DFSS maintains the key technical elements of DMAIC:

- Disciplined approach
- Use of metrics throughout the process

- Use of analytical tools

- Emphasis on variation

- Data-based decision making

Lean Six Sigma can be used to improve the top line in ways besides DFSS. One way is to find situations in which a product is in a sold-out condition today or is forecast to be sold out in the near future. Here you can use Lean Six Sigma in a traditional manner (DMAIC) to increase capacity (productivity). Whereas Six Sigma is often thought of as primarily a quality improvement methodology, Lean tends to focus more on productively. Its integration provides a more balanced approach that applies equally well to improving quality or productivity. When we increase capacity closer to the theoretical maximum capacity (capacity entitlement), we have the opportunity to sell more to new or existing customers, resulting in top-line growth. When an organization has reached the theoretical maximum capacity, it will likely need quality by design approaches, such as DFSS or capital projects, to further increase output.

Often customers will buy more if the quality of the product improves or price is reduced. In these situations, companies can use Lean Six Sigma to improve quality and decrease internal costs. They can then pass on part of the cost savings to the customer if desired, thereby increasing volume without having to sacrifice margin. The company also might be able to obtain new customers because of the improved quality and decreased price. Better yet, some customers that the company previously lost because of poor quality or high price might return.

In many instances, the key problem is a service issue, such as customer response time (CRT), or the time between placing an order and receiving the product or service. Resolving service issues can require analyzing the entire process: order, manufacture, delivery, bill, and return. The root cause of the problem could lie in some or all of these steps.

A point often missed is that manufacturing is only one step in the process of serving the customer. We know of one instance in which the CRT for a piece of heavy equipment was 12 months. A look at the sub-process cycle times revealed that the physical manufacture took only three months, so reducing manufacturing time to just a few days still left 75 percent of the cycle time untouched. Clearly, sometimes moving outside of manufacturing is needed to obtain significant reductions in total cycle time.

Variation in CRT is as important as, if not more important than, the average level of CRT. For example, if a customer receives two orders, one 30 days early and one 30 days late, the average CRT is perfect, but neither order was on time! In some instances, early orders are worse than late ones because the customer is not prepared to handle the early delivery and might tell the shipper to return the order to the vendor. Noting this, GE focused on reducing variation as a way of creating greater customer satisfaction (see the "Message to the Shareholders" in the 1998 GE Annual Report).

The opportunity to increase revenues by improving quality or service requires input from the customer. Price reduction is universally appreciated! Organizations need to determine the key problems that, if fixed, would result in the customer buying more. Asking the customer, "What changes can I make in my products or services that would allow you to buy more from me?" is not without risk. It can lead the customer to expect that any improvements requested will be made. Of course, noncustomers or previous customers can also be asked the same question, to try to win their business as well.

Another way to use Six Sigma to grow the top line is to introduce customers to Lean Six Sigma and show how it can help them improve. The theory is that customers with a better bottom line will be happier customers with a closer working relationship and will then repay the company by buying more of its products and services.

Helping customers solve their problems as a method of developing better business relationships is not new; various companies have been doing this for many years. What is new is using Lean Six Sigma in working with customers in this way. GE developed such an approach by having its Black Belts work with customers to solve their problems. GE called the program Six Sigma at the Customer for the Customer.

Welch (2001) reported that, in 2000, GE helped 50 GE Aircraft Engine customers complete 1,500 projects that saved $230 million. Also in 2000, a total of 1,000 projects were completed for GE Medical Systems customers, returning $100 million to the customers' bottom lines. Many of these projects were done primarily by GE Black Belts as at the customer, for the customer projects.

Lean Six Sigma can also be applied to strategic sales and marketing processes. DMAIC projects in these areas will primarily improve top-line growth, but they might have secondary benefits for cost savings as well. Such projects are generally initiated as part of the effort to spread Lean Six Sigma across the organization, as discussed earlier. Potential applications include these:

- Improving the impact of advertising (more bang for the buck)

- Improving marketing research studies, which drive DFSS projects

- Increasing sales force effectiveness

With the exception of improving capacity, all the approaches discussed require close working relationships with customers. This aspect of Lean Six Sigma improvement differs somewhat from the improvements from cost reduction projects. Of course, all Lean Six Sigma projects have a link to customers in one way or another; some links are just stronger than others.

Summary and Looking Forward

Sustaining momentum and growing occurs between completing all the training and projects identified in the original deployment plan and completing deployment across the organization. Deployment is considered complete when you are ready to make the transition from Lean Six Sigma as an initiative to holistic improvement as the normal way you work—that is, to move to Lean Six Sigma 2.0.

This phase can last several years. It consists of both a defensive strategy (sustaining momentum) and an offensive strategy (growing the effort). Keys to the defensive strategy are taking proactive steps to hold the gains from completed projects and also hold the gains from the overall Six Sigma initiative.

Implementing the remaining infrastructure elements is the critical success factor in this defensive strategy. These elements include the following:

- Process and financial audits to verify the benefits

- Lean Six Sigma system reviews
- A comprehensive training system (versus a mass training event)
- A formal Lean Six Sigma organizational structure

The offensive strategy consists of expanding the effort across the organization, involving strategic suppliers and customers, expanding the improvement portfolio, and using Lean Six Sigma to grow the top line. Utilizing a DFSS approach to new product and service design is a critical success factor because it influences each of these elements of the offensive strategy. By definition, it also helps bridge the quality by design work in the organization with the breakthrough improvement work. Using the philosophy that often the best defense is a good offense, organizations want to make sure they are aggressively deploying Lean Six Sigma in new areas to ensure that they maintain momentum and reach the entire organization and all its activities.

When Lean Six Sigma has become the modus operandi across the organization and is well integrated with both quality by design and also quality and process management efforts, the company will be well positioned to make the transition to "the way we work." This transition will ensure that benefits are permanent and also that the organization achieves true holistic improvement, or Lean Six Sigma 2.0. Organizations that can accomplish this transition will no doubt be recognized as world-class leaders in improvement. We discuss how to make this difficult transition, including organizational changes, in the next chapter.

References

Automotive Industry Action Group. (2005) *Statistical Process Control Reference Manual.* 2nd ed.

Automotive Industry Action Group. (2008a) *Advanced Product Quality Planning and Control Plan.* 2nd ed.

Automotive Industry Action Group. (2008b) *Potential Failure Mode and Effects Analysis Reference Manual.* 4th ed.

Automotive Industry Action Group. (2010) *Measurement System Analysis Reference Manual.* 3rd ed.

Box, G. E. P., W. G. Hunter, and J. S. Hunter. (2005) *Statistics for Experimenters.* 2nd ed. Hoboken, NJ: John Wiley and Sons.

Box, G. E. P., G. M. Jenkins, G. Reinsel, and G. M. Ljung. (2015) *Time Series Analysis: Forecasting and Control*. 5th ed. Hoboken, NJ: John Wiley and Sons.

Cohen, L. (1995) *Quality Function Deployment: How to Make QFD Work for You*. Reading, MA: Addison-Wesley.

Cornell, J. A. (2011) *A Primer on Experiments with Mixtures*. Hoboken, NJ: John Wiley and Sons.

Draper, N. R., and H. Smith. (1998) *Applied Regression Analysis*. 3rd ed. New York: John Wiley and Sons.

English, Bill. (2001) "Implementing Six Sigma: The Iomega Story." Presented at the Conference on Six Sigma in the Pharmaceutical Industry, Philadelphia, PA, November 27–28, 2001.

General Electric Company (1997). *Annual Report*, Fairfield, CT: General Electric Company.

General Electric Company (1998). *Annual Report*. Fairfield, CT: General Electric Company.

Hoerl, R. W. (2001) "Six Sigma Black Belts: What Do They Need to Know? (With Discussion)." *Journal of Quality Technology* 33, no. 4: 391–435.

Hoerl, R. W. (2008) "Work-Out." In *Encyclopedia of Statistics in Quality and Reliability*, edited by F. Ruggeri, R. Kenett, and F. W. Faltin, 2103–2105. Chichester, UK: John Wiley and Sons.

Hoerl, R. W., and R. D. Snee. (2012) *Statistical Thinking: Improving Business Performance*. 2nd ed. Hoboken, NJ: John Wiley and Sons.

Hoerl, R. W., and R. D. Snee. (2013) "One Size Does Not Fit All: Identifying the Right Improvement Methodology." *Quality Progress* (May): 48–50.

Madden, J. (1985) *Hey, Wait a Minute! I Wrote a Book*. New York: Random House.

Meeker, W. Q., and L. A. Escobar. (1998) *Statistical Methods for Reliability Data*. New York: John Wiley and Sons.

Montgomery, D. C. (2012a) *The Design and Analysis of Experiments*. 8th ed. Hoboken, NJ: John Wiley and Sons.

Montgomery, D. C. (2012b) *Statistical Quality Control*. 7th ed. Hoboken, NJ: John Wiley and Sons.

Montgomery, D. C., E. A. Peck, and G. Vining. (2012) *Introduction to Linear Regression Analysis.* 5th ed. Hoboken, NJ: John Wiley and Sons.

Myers, R. H., D. C. Montgomery, and C. M. Anderson-Cook. (2016) *Response Surface Methodology,* 4th ed. Hoboken, NJ: John Wiley and Sons.

Snee, R. D. (1995) "Listening to the Voice of the Employee." *Quality Progress* (January): 91–95.

Snee, R. D., and R. W. Hoerl. (2005) *Six Sigma Beyond the Factory Floor: Deployment Strategies for Financial Services, Health Care, and the Rest of the Real Economy.* Upper Saddle River, NJ: Financial Times/ Prentice Hall.

Snee, R. D., and R. W. Hoerl. (2016) *Strategies for Formulations Development: A Step-by-Step Guide Using JMP.* Cary, NC: SAS Press.

Walpole, R. E., and R. H Myers. (2016) *Probability and Statistics for Engineers and Scientists.* 9th ed. Englewood Cliffs, NJ: Prentice Hall.

Welch, J. (2001) *Jack, Straight from the Gut.* New York: Warner Business Books.

Wheeler, D. J., and D. Chambers. (2010) *Understanding Statistical Process Control.* 3rd ed. Knoxville, TN: SPC Press.

Wheeler, D. J., and R. W. Lyday. (1989) *Evaluating the Measurement Process.* 2nd ed. Knoxville, TN: SPC Press.

9

The Way We Work

"With Lean Six Sigma permeating much of what we do, it will be unthinkable to hire, promote, or tolerate those who cannot, or will not, commit to this way of working."

—Jack Welch, former CEO, General Electric

In Chapters 7, "Managing the Effort," and 8, "Sustaining Momentum and Growing," we discussed managing the Lean Six Sigma initiative, sustaining the gains, expanding the initiative by incorporating additional improvement methods, and expanding to all parts of the enterprise (including suppliers and customers). A central theme was the need to integrate Lean Six Sigma activities with quality by design and quality and process management efforts.

In this chapter, we take Lean Six Sigma one step further and discuss how to integrate it into daily work processes. The changes an organization makes in its work as a result of Lean Six Sigma 2.0 comprise its control plan for the overall initiative and ensure that it maintains the gains it has achieved. The desired end game is that holistic improvement becomes such an integral part of the way the organization manages that there is no longer a need for a formal Lean Six Sigma initiative. Instead, there is a holistic improvement organization that is a stable and integral part of the company, analogous to finance, human resources, marketing, and so on.

The recognition that Lean Six Sigma 2.0 has been institutionalized into your culture is not based on a Gantt chart or a predetermined deadline. You will know that you have achieved true holistic improvement when you see the key elements of Lean Six Sigma 2.0 being used on a daily basis. Some examples include the following:

- Continuously working to find better ways of doing things

- Recognizing the importance of the bottom line and finding ways to improve it

- Thinking of everything you do as a process

- Working to reduce variation and risk

- Using data to guide your decisions

- Using diverse methods and tools to make your processes more effective and productive

- Integrating quality by design activities with breakthrough improvement and quality and process management, all within one organizational umbrella

These key elements will be clearer as we discuss ways of making Lean Six Sigma 2.0 part of daily work processes.

In our experience, the best way to make holistic improvement a reality is by integrating Lean Six Sigma with other improvement approaches, including quality by design and quality and process management. This integration results in the creation and management of an overall improvement system. This system is then responsible all types of organizational improvement. This includes ISO 9000 and the Malcolm Baldrige Award assessment, in the area of process management, as well as new product development and DFSS, in the area of quality by design.

Creating a Holistic Improvement System

As discussed previously, we often see diverse improvement activities compete for resources and management attention, resulting in unhealthy "islands of improvement." From the beginning of Lean Six Sigma deployment, the long-term goal has been to combine all improvement initiatives into one holistic improvement system that has Lean and Six Sigma as integral components. Furthermore, the supporting management systems and structure required to sustain this system over time need to be put in place. When this work is done, true holistic improvement, or Lean Six Sigma 2.0, has been achieved. Table 9.1 re-emphasizes the needs and methods of the overall improvement system that we initially presented in Chapter 2, "What Is Holistic Improvement?".

Table 9.1 Holistic Improvement System Needs and Sample Approaches

Quality by Design	Breakthrough Improvement	Quality and Process Management Systems
Needs	**Needs**	**Needs**
• Business innovation	• Meet annual and strategic plans	• Quality & process management system
• Process design/redesign	• Better product/process performance	• Risk management system
• Product design/redesign	• Better organizational performance	• IT system
• Organizational design/redesign	• Mission critical problems	• Measurement system
		• Training system
Approaches	**Approaches**	**Approaches**
• Innovation/Creativity	• Six Sigma	• ISO/Baldrige
• DFSS	• Lean Enterprise	• Total Productive Maintenance
• TRIZ	• Statistical Engineering	• "Internet of Things"
	• Big Data Analytics	• Kepner Tregoe
	• Work-Out	

The intent is for improvement to become a core business function within the management system, on equal footing with finance, human resources, information technology, marketing, manufacturing, and so on. Going forward, the company would have no individual improvement initiatives, such as Lean Six Sigma and ISO 9000, but would instead have one holistic improvement system that is a permanent part of the management system. We discuss more details of this organization shortly. First, however, we discuss the lynchpin of the holistic improvement system: the improvement project portfolio.

The Improvement Project Portfolio

Key to making such a holistic improvement system work is having all improvement ideas come through one organization, to be prioritized based on their potential impact on the organization instead of based on organizational or political boundaries. During the organization's annual planning process, all potential improvement projects are placed into one improvement project hopper, which is then prioritized based on business need and impact. Only the highest-prioritized ideas are funded and placed into the improvement project portfolio—that is, the portfolio of projects selected for implementation.

The improvement organization then selects the most promising improvement methodology for the project, which could be Six Sigma, Work-Out, Lean, or some other approach. An appropriate Black Belt who is knowledgeable in that methodology is assigned, and the company provides additional resources, including funding and team members. Note that there is still competition between potential projects, but it is a healthy competition of ideas within one organization, with all ideas on an equal planning field. Note also that the project could simply be a "Nike project" (Just Do It!), which requires only project management and not a formal improvement methodology.

The improvement project portfolio needs to be dynamic; as one project finishes, a new project is added. Of course, much can change after the annual planning is completed, so relative priorities of projects could also change as new situations occur or new information becomes available. The annual planning simply sets the stage at the beginning of the year.

Some guiding principles for developing and maintaining the improvement project portfolio follow:

- Improvement and growth occur project by project.
- A project is a problem scheduled for solution.

- Projects come from many different sources and should be managed by a common system.

- Effective project management skills are needed for successful projects.

- Projects should be linked to the strategic needs and priorities of the organization.

- Continual review, assessment, and evaluation of the combined list of projects will keep it up-to-date.

- As in investment portfolios, the focus should be on balancing the overall portfolio to best achieve the organization's objectives.

The organization's improvement portfolio generally includes a mixture of projects in the three main categories shown in Table 9.1:

- Quality by design projects, which typically offer the potential for innovation and top-line growth

- Breakthrough improvement projects, often intended to drive significant bottom-line improvement

- Projects intended to enhance the organization's quality and process management excellence

Table 9.2 shows a simple example of an improvement project portfolio of 14 projects. (Note that actual portfolios typically are much longer than Table 9.2, which is for illustrative purposes only.) Putting all improvement projects in a single list aids the budgeting process and focuses the organization on what needs to be done, given the available resources.

Table 9.2 Holistic Improvement System Needs and Sample Approaches

Project	Category	Methodology
Increase Capacity of Process Z	Breakthrough Improvement	Six Sigma
Relocate Milling Process	Quality by Design	Lean Process Design
Upgrade DCS Software	Quality and Productivity Mgt	Project Management
Speed Up Acquisition of Environmental Permits	Breakthrough Improvement	Lean
Automate Packaging Line	Quality by Design	Lean Process Design
Increase Yield of Process XX	Breakthrough Improvement	Big Data Analytics
Reduce Downtime of Mixer M	Breakthrough Improvement	Six Sigma
Reduce Manufacturing Cost of Product P	Breakthrough Improvement	Statistical Engineering
Improve Steam Trap Performance	Breakthrough Improvement	Six Sigma
Install New Pump on Line K	Quality and Process Mgt	Project Management
Reduce Plant B Reactor Cycle Time	Breakthrough Improvement	Six Sigma
Reduce the Impurity of Product 741	Breakthrough Improvement	Six Sigma
Process Monitoring System for Products T and S	Quality and Process Mgt	Statistical Process Control
Reduce Cycle Time of Batch Record Release	Breakthrough Improvement	Work-Out

In some cases, planners charter a breakthrough improvement project to assess whether the solution proposed by the quality by design project (which can require significant capital) is actually the best solution. For example, a Six Sigma project could achieve the same level of improvement without significant capital investment. Planners might want to make sure the process is at entitlement before they spend significant capital to upgrade it or expand capacity.

The Improvement Organization

As noted earlier, in a holistic improvement system, all improvement projects are managed by one organization, which we refer to as the improvement organization. Some companies refer to this as the *quality organization*, but this term can be limiting because of how traditional quality organizations are structured. For example, most employees do not think of the quality organization being responsible for innovation or growth. Using the term *improvement organization* can help employees understand that this group has broader accountability than traditional quality organizations.

Typically, quality by design activities are managed by marketing or perhaps research and development (R&D), and quality and process management activities are managed by the quality or process control organizations. As previously discussed, this often leads to unhealthy competition based on politics and organizational boundaries instead of fostering a competition of ideas on a level playing field. Therefore, a new organization should be created to both provide such a level playing field and offer a strategic view of improvement across the "islands of improvement."

In our view, the quality organization (as well as Lean or Six Sigma organizations, if they exist) needs to be incorporated into the improvement organization. We do not recommend incorporating marketing or R&D into the improvement organization, but projects and activities that are intended to drive top-line growth through innovation and new products and services should be managed within the improvement organization.

A Chief Improvement Officer (CIMO—*CIO* is already taken by Chief Information Officer; *IM* stands for *Improvement*), on the staff of the Chief Executive Officer (CEO), should lead the improvement organization. Being on the CEO's staff is critical because improvement work also is critical. In addition, this improvement work needs to be carefully coordinated with other functional groups, such as R&D, marketing, manufacturing, human resources (HR), and so on.

Furthermore, this coordination needs to start at the strategic level—that is, at the CEO staff level. The CIMO need not be the top technical person in the improvement group, just as the Chief Financial Officer (CFO) is not necessarily the top financial analyst. Instead, the position of CIMO requires significant vision and leadership skills, in addition to the ability to understand improvement. Several organizations, including GE and DuPont, have set a similar precedent by naming a senior Six Sigma executive who reported directly to the CEO.

The CIMO needs to have a proper leadership team, just as a CEO, CIO, or CFO needs a proper leadership team. Improvement is inherently a technical discipline, so the team needs strong technical expertise. It could be led by a Chief Master Black Belt (CMBB) or other appropriate title. This individual, with his or her own team, is then responsible for overseeing the training system and determining the proper mix of improvement methodologies to be included. Furthermore, this group determines which improvement method should be applied to each prioritized project. As discussed in previous chapters, holistic improvement does not mean that a given organization will utilize every improvement method in existence; instead, each organization needs to determine the best portfolio of methods for its own needs.

The CMBB cannot be expected to be an expert in all improvement methods within the portfolio. Therefore, he or she needs a critical mass of expertise for each methodology within the portfolio. Cross-training (that is, having individuals with expertise in multiple methods) is an obvious advantage. Furthermore, the CMBB needs to create a culture in which technical experts are open minded about improvement approaches instead of pushing each project toward the methods that they personally know best. Again, the culture needs to be one of starting with the problem and then objectively determining the best approach to solving it, not selecting favorite methods in advance.

It should be obvious that the improvement organization needs to maintain close connections with the other functional groups, including R&D, finance, marketing, HR, IT, and operations, whether the company's operations are primarily manufacturing, banking services, hospital operations, or something else. These other functional groups no doubt will insist on having input on the decisions regarding the prioritization of improvement projects. Therefore, representatives from these groups should be regular participants at the CIMO's staff meetings and at meetings to prioritize potential improvement projects. In this sense, the improvement organization should not have its own agenda, but should focus on the existing strategy and priorities of the company.

The proper size of the improvement organization obviously depends on the size of the company. However, keep in mind that this is the organization to maintain and improve the holistic improvement system over time, not to put it into place. That is, when the company moves from an initiative to a way of working, the level of resources needed should go down. Creating the system requires significant momentum and resourcing, which should be gradually reduced once the system is in place. As an analogy, constructing an office building requires a lot more resources than maintaining and improving it over time. Recall that the improvement organization is responsible for managing the overall improvement system, not for completing each project. All employees are expected to participate in improvement projects. Therefore, the responsibility for improvement is widely shared across the company.

Integration of Quality and Process Management Systems

Earlier chapters discussed launching a Lean Six Sigma initiative, with the intention of evolving this to a more holistic approach over time by gradually incorporating additional improvement methods. In Chapter 8, we discussed the need to expand the effort, including growing the top line by incorporating quality by design methods, such as Design for Six Sigma (DFSS). This can include other individual methods as well, such as the Theory of Inventive Problem Solving (TRIZ) and Quality Function Deployment (QFD). Quality and process management systems are often the last to be formally incorporated within the holistic improvement system. This is because many people do not think of quality or process management systems as "improvement" and because most companies already have a well-established quality organization.

The ISO 9000 quality system requires detailed documentation of process management and control procedures. Thus, the line between quality management and process management is often blurred. We therefore combine them into the "third leg" of the improvement stool, which we refer to as quality and process management systems. These systems include the set of procedures, methods, requirements, operating manuals, training, and so on that you use to manage a given work process. The work process itself can be an operational one, such as an assembly line, or a managerial one, such as the budgeting process. Every process has a process management system, although, in many cases, it is ad hoc, undocumented, inconsistent, and totally ineffective. Effective work processes almost always have a good process management system, which helps explain why the process is effective.

We take a strategic view of quality and process management systems, seeing them as an additional set of methods that can be used for improvement. For example, formally competing for the Malcolm Baldrige National Quality Award (MBNQA) or obtaining ISO 9000 certification can drive significant improvement. However, the investment required to do so is non-negligible. Therefore, we argue that the anticipated payoff from these investments needs to be compared with the anticipated payoff from other potential improvement efforts, such as quality by design or breakthrough improvement projects.

As discussed previously, we feel that this can best be accomplished by integrating the quality and process management organizations into the overall improvement organization. Fortunately, some natural synergies exist between major quality methodologies (particularly ISO 9000 and the Malcolm Baldrige Award), and quality by design and breakthrough improvement approaches (particularly Six Sigma). We highlight some of these natural synergies shortly.

Such synergies can produce a multiplicative rather than additive impact by implementing multiple projects in a coordinated fashion. This is why the project improvement portfolio is not simply a laundry list of projects, but should be actively managed to take advantage of such synergies. Furthermore, these synergies clarify why it is so important to house these quality initiatives within the improvement organization instead of having them sit outside as competitors to improvement.

Synergies with ISO 9000

ISO 9000 is widely used by diverse companies around the globe (ISO 9000 Standards, 2015). Many customers, particularly in the

European Community, require ISO certification as a condition of doing business. Fortunately, many breakthrough improvement methods, such as Lean and Six Sigma, support ISO 9000 and help an organization satisfy the ISO 9000 requirements. In this sense, implementing Lean Six Sigma and implementing ISO are synergistic: The effort required to implement both is less than the sum of the efforts required for each individually. Furthermore, ISO 9000 is an excellent vehicle for documenting and maintaining the process management systems involving Lean, Six Sigma, and other breakthrough improvement methods. In other words, ISO 9000 can help make improvement the normal way you work.

ISO 9000 requires having a continuous improvement process in place (see Figure 9.1). However, ISO does not dictate what the process improvement system should look like. The holistic improvement system, including quality by design and breakthrough improvement methods, can provide the needed improvement process. ISO 9000-2015 requires that you measure (M), analyze (A), and improve (I). These are three phases of the Lean Six Sigma 2.0 DMAIC process improvement methodology. ISO 9000 also helps create the process mind-set that is required for holistic improvement to be successful.

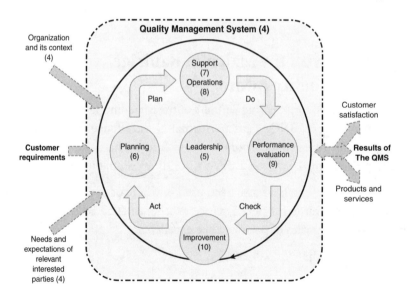

Figure 9.1 ISO 9000 2015 model of a process-based quality management system

When expanded to working with suppliers, as we discussed in Chapter 8, holistic improvement also supports each of the ISO 9000 quality management principles:

1. Customer focus

2. Leadership

3. Engagement of people

4. Process approach

5. Improvement

6. Evidenced-based decision making

7. Relationship management

ISO 9000 can also provide valuable support to the holistic improvement system. ISO audits can be expanded to include monitoring the performance of processes improved via breakthrough improvement, or can be introduced through quality by design. Such monitoring should include the use of control plans developed for these improvement projects. In this manner, ISO 9000 becomes a key methodology to ensure that the overall holistic improvement system is maintained over time.

Synergies with the Malcolm Baldrige National Quality Award

The criteria used for selecting winners of the Malcolm Baldrige National Quality Award (MBNQA) for performance excellence form a widely used tool for improving corporate performance. The Baldrige National Quality Program (2017) identifies outstanding companies in this area.

The Baldrige criteria have also been used in whole or in part to establish various state awards for performance excellence. The Baldrige criteria have seven categories of performance excellence:

1. Leadership

2. Strategy

3. Customers

4. Measurement, analysis, and knowledge management

5. Workforce

6. Operations

7. Results

Obviously, a holistic improvement system supports all the categories of the Baldrige criteria. In addition, the use of holistic improvement can significantly enhance the performance of the organization so that it better satisfies the Baldrige criteria. Conversely, as we explain shortly, pursuing the MBNQA often leads directly to identifying the most important improvement projects needed in holistic improvement. Again, there is a synergistic relationship between holistic improvement and the MBNQA.

Many companies use the Baldrige criteria to identify their best opportunities for improvement, even without formally applying for the award. Leadership typically charters a team to perform an organizational assessment; they identify, categorize, and prioritize the opportunities, and assign them to improvement teams for solution. These improvement teams generally have annual goals and report on progress monthly to leadership. Obviously, such project teams should be part of the overall improvement project portfolio. This project is intended to identify promising improvement projects that will subsequently also be part of the improvement project portfolio.

This approach can effectively turn the opportunities identified by the Baldrige assessment into projects that produce high-impact and lasting organizational improvements (Snee, 1999a). Baldrige assessments are typically done every 18 to 24 months because organizational change tends to occur slowly. When an organization uses such assessments, its outputs should be given high priority for selection into the project improvement portfolio.

A word of caution applies here: The most difficult aspect of using holistic improvement to capture the opportunities identified in a Baldrige assessment is properly defining the projects. The opportunities identified by the Baldrige criteria are frequently areas of opportunity that have a broad scope, making project definition challenging. A good approach is to perform an affinity analysis (Hoerl and Snee, 2012) to first group the areas of opportunity into logical categories and then put the resulting categories through the project prioritization process to identify good candidate improvement projects.

Synergies with Risk Management

Risk management in the form of risk identification and mitigation has become an increasingly important approach to process improvement and management. As we discussed in Chapter 1, "A New Improvement Paradigm Is Needed," commercial organizations are faced with more significant risks than at any time in history. These include terrorism, litigation resulting from faulty products or processes, environmental disasters, computer hacking of confidential records, and allegations of social misconduct (sexual harassment, racial discrimination, utilization of overseas "sweat shops," and so on). We consider risk management to be a key element within quality and process management systems, and we therefore feel it should be integrated into the improvement organization.

In Table 9.3, we show how holistic improvement methods and risk management are synergistic. A guiding principle is that *risk increases as variation increases*. This principle suggests that we should be looking for every opportunity to reduce variation. Statistical thinking and methods, in particular, are aimed at identifying, characterizing and reducing risk. ISO 9000 procedures also focus on minimizing variation in work processes.

NOTE

In Table 9.3, ISO has another standard, ISO 31000, that specifically focuses on risk management.

Table 9.3 Synergies of Holistic Improvement Methods and Risk Management

Holistic Improvement Method	Risk Identification and Mitigation
Innovation	Creatively identifies unique approaches to reduce risk Creates robust products and processes
Design for Six Sigma	Uses formal improvement methods to take the unique approaches identified above from idea to actual deployment. Creates robust processes and products.
TRIZ	Identifies innovative problem-solving solutions for key risks. This holistic approach to problem-solving results in reduced risk.

Holistic Improvement Method	Risk Identification and Mitigation
Six Sigma	DMAIC addresses major sources of variation that increase risk. FMEA is used to identify how the process can fail. Processes are mistake-proofed. Standard operating procedures (SOPs) include use of checklists. Control plans and statistical process control methods are used to sustain improvements and reduce variation.
Baldrige Assessment	Enhances the Baldrige criteria categories for performance excellence: leadership, strategy, customers, measurement, analysis and knowledge management, workforce, operations, and results. These individually and collectively result in reduced risk. Risk assessment is included in each of the Baldrige categories, enabling the identification of potential failures.
Big Data Analytics	Databases are designed to include data on all sources of variation and incorporate state-of-the-art security systems.
Statistical Engineering	Creates improvement project scope to ensure that all potential root causes are addressed by the project (big picture).
ISO 9000	Involves ISO 9000 quality management principles: customer focus, leadership, people engagement, process approach, improvement, and evidenced-based decision making and relationship management. The individually and collectively result in reduced risk. The ISO companion standard, ISO 31000, focuses specifically on risk management.
Total Productive Maintenance	Uses predictive maintenance methods to reduce equipment failures and improve safety. Uses FMEA to identify how the process can fail.
Lean	Uses lean principles to optimize the flow of information and materials throughout the process ensuring customers receive the desired products, services, and information on time. Uses FMEA to identify how the process can fail.
Kepner–Tregoe	This problem-solving approach enables root cause analysis (RCA) on complex problems and enables the understanding and management of risks and opportunities.

Risk management can be incorporated into holistic improvement in two ways. First, and perhaps most obviously, the organization can make risk considerations part of the accepted use of each improvement method. This is accomplished in the following way:

- Ensuring that risk considerations, quantitative or qualitative, are identified during each improvement project.

- Asking during each project, "How can this process fail?" In effect, this results in doing a formal or informal failure mode and effects analysis (FMEA). We know of a CEO who made FMEA an integral part of evaluating all strategic plans.

Second, the company can incorporate risk management projects as candidates in the project improvement hopper, to be prioritized in conjunction with other candidate projects. These projects would specifically focus on identifying and managing risk, such as re-evaluating the organization's computer security systems (perhaps by hiring professional "hackers" to try to break into the system) or determining the organization's response system for a terroristic attack (perhaps from a disgruntled employee potentially bringing a gun on the premises to seek revenge for perceived mistreatment). Most universities and high schools now have formal plans for addressing active shooters on campus, for obvious reasons.

At first glance, it might seem that such risk management projects are too important to be jointly prioritized along with process improvement projects. This is our point, however. All projects should compete for selection and resourcing on an equal playing field, without organizational boundaries or politics influencing the process. We argue that such critical risk management projects will swiftly rise to the top of prioritization if there is an equal playing field. However, if risk management is a separate organization, there is a distinct possibility that it will not receive the funding it needs to be effective, while perhaps other improvement groups remain overfunded.

Don't Forget About Process Control

Quality and process management is obviously a broad category, as we have shown. A key element of this category, and one that we have not addressed in detail up to this point, is process control. Process control makes adjustments to the process, often in real time, to maintain the performance level. It can be accomplished manually, by human intervention, or through automated control systems. Process control addresses problems that have caused deterioration in performance and returns the process to standard conditions.

Process control is often confused with process (breakthrough) improvement, which makes fundamental changes to the process itself or the way it is operated, to achieve higher levels of performance than have been achieved in the past. For example, most Six Sigma projects focus on process improvement instead of process control.

It should be clear from these definitions that excellence in process control does not, in itself, produce breakthrough improvement. However, poor process control inevitably produces a sequence of crises and unexpected problems. This results in constant firefighting, which pushes true improvement to the back burner. Process improvement works best on a solid platform of good process control, which is also required to sustain the gains of the improvement projects over time. Therefore, a holistic improvement system needs a balance of process improvement and process control, as well as new product and process innovation (quality by design).

We have already mentioned a number of tools that are often included in Six Sigma or other types of projects for use in process control. Control charts and mistake proofing are two examples. Furthermore, having employees who are trained in formal approaches to routine problem solving (using methods such as Kepner–Tregoe, for example) is helpful in ensuring good process control. When employees can handle routine problems as they occur, these routine problems don't become serious problems.

A few guiding principles for process control are helpful:

- Focus control efforts on key processes.

- Ensure that these key processes produce the right data to allow effective monitoring and control.

- Obtaining the right data might require putting new measurement systems into place.

- Have people at various levels in the organization routinely analyze process data using relevant tools and take appropriate actions; improvement is everyone's responsibility.

- Often the people who work within the process understand the data best, not necessarily Black Belts or other technical resources.

Figure 9.2 (Snee, 1999b) depicts a high-level schematic of how routine data can be utilized for process improvement and control. The organization should collect data from the process on a routine basis. Various levels of management should review this data on a regular basis to decide what, if any, process actions should be taken. Typical review groups for high-throughput environments (manufacturing, billing, hospitals, logistics, and so on) are as follows:

Review Team	Review Timing
Process operators	Continuously and daily
Process managers and staff	Weekly
Site manager and staff	Monthly
Business manager and staff	Quarterly

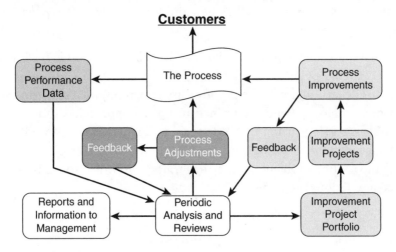

Figure 9.2   Schematic of data-based process improvement and control system

Process operators can be assembly line workers, accountants, nurses changing over beds in a hospital, or salespeople. Each should review the process performance data continuously, to look for out-of-control situations, and should review daily summaries to detect other sources of problems. Analysis tools such as run or control charts and Pareto charts are often used here.

We noted in Chapter 7 that management review is a critical success factor for holistic improvement. Regular management review keeps the effort focused and on track. We know of no successful holistic improvement deployment, or even Lean Six Sigma implementation, in which management reviews were not a key part of the deployment process. We refer to management reviews as the "secret sauce": Done regularly and at numerous levels, they significantly enhance the probability of success. Regular reviews not only ensure the success of a particular effort at a particular point in time, but they also help sustain the effort over time.

The process control plan, developed in the Control phase of the DMAIC framework of an improvement project, documents for the operators what to look for, what actions to take, and whom to inform when additional assistance is needed. The control plan typically details the process adjustments needed to bring the outputs back to the desired target and range. Typical control tools that the operators use for troubleshooting include process maps, control charts, histograms, and Pareto charts. We discuss the proper role of the methods and tools in more detail in Chapter 10, "Final Thoughts for Leaders."

As depicted in Figure 9.2, there is a short feedback loop between analyzing process data and making adjustments. This inner loop is intended to represent process control efforts, including routine problem solving. This activity should occur in near real time and not be based on a formal project. Examples of such process adjustments are changing the pressure setting on a piece of stamping equipment to eliminate bad stamps, calling in additional accountants to close the books on time, and having a salesperson work overtime to meet a sales quota. However, such efforts are primarily aimed at sustaining current performance levels, not improving to new levels.

Improving to new performance levels often requires involving additional people with specialized skills, such as engineers in manufacturing or experienced underwriters in insurance. True improvement is usually achieved through project teams that include process operators, technical specialists, and perhaps someone trained in the improvement methodologies we have discussed.

The improvement project feedback loop is an outer loop in Figure 9.2, in that it requires more time and is utilized only when routine problem solving will not solve the problem. Occasionally, the team determines that breakthrough improvement is not sufficient and that a fundamentally new process needs to be designed (for example, automating a manual billing process). In such cases, a quality by design project, perhaps using DFSS, needs to be chartered. Note that all of this activity is part of the holistic improvement system, so there are no organizational boundaries between process control efforts, improvement efforts, and innovation efforts, as is often the case in traditional organizations.

As we have seen, process control and routine problem solving activities should occur in real time—they generally don't require a formal project. However, process control still fits within a holistic improvement system, for three main reasons. First, the improvement organization should oversee the use of process control and problem-solving tools. That is, the improvement organization is responsible for determining the best set of tools that should be utilized and for ensuring that a training system is in place to develop the needed skills in these tools. Second, formal projects are needed to initially put these control systems into place. For example, if an organization decides to utilize control charts for process control, the employees will need training in control charts and some help in deploying them in the workplace. This will require a project.

Third, recurring process control issues often indicate that the process control system is not working properly and needs to be upgraded. This typically requires a breakthrough improvement project, to put in place a more effective control system. Although the project focuses on process control, not improvement, fundamentally upgrading the process control system should produce true improvement: levels of performance not previously seen. Therefore, we consider this a breakthrough improvement project.

Don't Forget About Managerial Processes

For true holistic improvement, process management and control systems must be developed for managerial processes. These can include budgeting, planning, employee selection, training and development, financial reporting, project management, performance management, communication, and recognition and rewards. Chapter 7 defined managerial systems and processes and discussed them in more detail.

The approach for developing control systems for managerial processes is essentially the same as for operational processes: integrating holistic improvement concepts, methods, and tools with the process management systems for these managerial processes. The key steps follow:

1. Recognize that all work (even managerial work) occurs through processes.

2. Identify a key managerial process.

3. Select a set of performance measurements.

4. Collect data on the process and review it at appropriate levels of management, as discussed previously.

5. Take action to make process adjustments.

6. Make fundamental improvements to the process by defining and completing improvement projects as needed.

In the ongoing effort to collect the process data, analyze the data, and take action based on this data (as well as subsequent improvement projects), holistic improvement concepts, methods, and tools become part of your daily work. Process management and control might not be the sexiest aspect of a holistic improvement system, but it is most critical in terms of making improvement a normal part of everyone's job. This is because it defines the routine procedures that the organization will use in its daily work. Therefore, if holistic improvement concepts, methods, and tools are embedded into process management and control systems, holistic improvement will become the way we work, both in operations and in management.

Admittedly, unique challenges arise in deploying process management systems for managerial processes. Perhaps the most challenging aspect is selecting the right process metrics. As we noted in Chapter 6, "Launching the Initiative," the key metrics for nonmanufacturing processes are typically accuracy (correctness, completeness, errors, defects, and so on), cycle time, cost, and customer satisfaction. However, many managerial processes do not have existing measurement systems that provide useful data for improvement. For example, few companies measure and analyze metrics on the effectiveness of their budgeting processes. Table 9.4 shows an example set of metrics used to measure the performance of a Lean Six Sigma training process (Snee, 2001). As in any important work activity, leadership (including regular reviews by various levels of management) is the key success factor.

Table 9.4 Lean Six Sigma Training Metrics

Participants like the training experience	■ Survey of participant evaluations of content, exercises, delivery, materials, instructors, facilities, food, and so on ■ Participant evaluation of each day: What went well? What needs to be done differently?
Participants learn the methodology	■ Score on weekly quiz on tools used ■ Written exam at the end of the training as part of the certification requirements
Participants use the methodology	■ Number of tools used per project ■ Percent of tools used appropriately ■ Project completion cycle time ■ Projects completed per training session (%) ■ Number of persons certified as BB ■ Other tools used for success ■ Time devoted by BB to project work ■ Number of meetings per month between Champions and BBs
Participants get results	■ Project results, for individual projects and for business and functional groups ■ Improvement in key process metrics ■ Improvement in bottom-line results ($$)

Another challenge in many managerial processes is that the data is often sparse. One company wanted to improve its annual college campus recruiting process. However, once a Green Belt got into the project she realized that the most important data for improvement purposes was generated only once a year, after each wave of campus recruiting.

A less obvious challenge is resistance to the introduction of process management and control systems for managerial processes because some people view them as threatening. As noted in Chapter 7, when we introduce formal metrics and reviews to manage these processes, the process owners, such as human resources (HR), finance, information technology (IT), and so on, might feel that Big Brother is watching them or that they will be micromanaged. As long as the emphasis remains on improving the process and not on assigning blame, this concern will be quickly seen as groundless.

Motorola Financial Audit Case

Stoner and Werner (1994) present an example of using Lean Six Sigma in the management and control systems for of a managerial process: Motorola's internal financial audit process. The first step, and a major breakthrough in thinking, was to view each internal audit not as an event, but as a process with five key steps:

1. Schedule the audit.
2. Plan the audit.
3. Perform the audit.
4. Report the results.
5. Perform the post-audit check.

Motorola developed performance measurements for the process, including internal errors, cycle time required to complete the audit, customer feedback on the audit, and cost in terms of person-hours to do the audit. Additional audit process measures included the time and cost for the audit of the corporate books by an external auditor. Accuracy of the external audit was the responsibility of the external auditor. To maintain independence, Motorola could not be involved in evaluating accuracy.

Impressive results were obtained through this approach. The process measures led to several breakthrough improvement projects in internal auditing. Within three years, Motorola reduced internal errors from 10,000 ppm to 20 ppm (parts, or errors, per million opportunities).

The company reduced its report cycle time from 51 days to 5 days. The quality of the customer feedback report was 21 times better in two years. Audit person-hours dropped from 24,000 hours to 12,000 hours, while annual sales increased from $4.8 billion to $11.3 billion during the same time period.

Clearly, higher-quality work was being done in less time and at less cost. Additionally, the external audit cycle time dropped by 50 percent because of better internal audit information from the process management system, producing $1.8 million cost avoidance per year. Unfortunately, many companies cannot achieve this same level of improvement because they still view internal auditing as an event instead of a process that can be managed and improved.

Accounting scandals at major corporations such as Enron, WorldCom, and Arthur Anderson have only reinforced the need for rigorous process management and control systems in finance in general and auditing in particular. Such systems could be considered part of the organization's risk management system.

The Long-Term Impact of Holistic Improvement

Chapter 5, "How to Successfully Implement Lean Six Sigma 2.0," presented the typical deployment phases of Lean Six Sigma 2.0, as shown in Figure 9.3, from initial deployment to expansion to holistic improvement. The first major transition is from business as usual to a Six Sigma approach. Most organizations launch Six Sigma or perhaps Lean Six Sigma in operations. Shortly thereafter, it becomes important to formally manage the initiative. This requires involving top talent and creating a formal infrastructure. Next, the organization typically expands the areas of application and the improvement portfolio in the third phase, sustaining momentum and growing the effort. New product development and other quality by design methods should also be integrated into the initiative at this point.

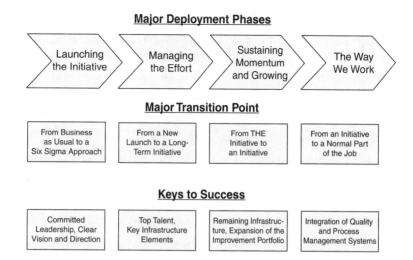

Figure 9.3 Roadmap for Lean Six Sigma 2.0 deployment

However, to achieve Lean Six Sigma 2.0, true holistic improvement, the organization still needs to make a major leap. This involves creating an overall organizational improvement system, incorporating multiple improvement methodologies, and integrating them within one improvement organization, as discussed earlier. Integrating quality and process management systems into this overall improvement system is typically the last major transition. Once this has been successfully accomplished, the organization has made improvement the way it works.

Top management has fueled the deployment through its leadership, evidenced by such things as clear goals, resources, breakthrough expectations, and a deployment plan. Of particular importance is the clear communication of very high expectations—what we need to do to be successful, how we are going to do it, and what will happen when we are successful. Without these expectations the organization will remain confused about what is expected and what will happen. Results rarely exceed leadership expectations. Let's take a closer look at this gradual evolution of the Lean Six Sigma initiative as it progresses to holistic improvement, or Lean Six Sigma 2.0.

The work done in the first 12 to 18 months, in the early phases of deployment, typically produces many useful results, including some worthwhile byproducts. Most important are business results in the form of improvement to the bottom line and increased customer satisfaction. This helps Lean Six Sigma build credibility, pay for itself, and provide fuel for continued growth. The capability of the organization is thereby greatly increased, including enhanced teamwork and cross-functional cooperation. Most important, the organization begins to believe that Lean Six Sigma will work here and that each person can personally benefit from Lean Six Sigma.

At about the 18-month time point, toward the end of the second phase of deployment, a move toward holistic improvement should be underway or at least initiated. Important considerations to include follow:

- Work to involve all aspects and functions on the organization including operations, R&D, finance, and sales and marketing.

- Address all aspects of organizational performance: flow of materials and information, product quality, and customer satisfaction.

- Put management systems in place to guide and sustain the improvement initiative over time.

- Integrate systems for quality by design, breakthrough improvement, and quality and process management.

- Use a more diverse portfolio of improvement methodologies, each chosen to fit the needs of particular projects.

- Use improvement as a leadership development tool.

When Lean Six Sigma deployment is off and functioning, the evolution toward holistic improvement should be initiated, evolved, and nurtured.

Two to three years into the initiative, typically during the phase of sustaining momentum and growing, the longer-term benefits begin to appear. The leadership team bench strength begins to increase as the Lean Six Sigma experience provides the organization with a larger number of highly skilled leaders. Organizations typically see greater use of scientific thinking in how they manage, including focusing on processes, using data to guide decisions, and understanding the effects of variation on the decision making process. The transition to one improvement organization becomes a more natural process.

Holistic Improvement Drives Culture Change

The financial benefits from holistic improvement are certainly welcome, but these will dry up gradually if the organization does not maintain a focus on improvement as a cultural value. This is analogous to someone who goes on a strict diet as a New Year's resolution and loses 30 pounds. If that individual declares success and gradually returns to his or her normal lifestyle and eating habits, the pounds will return. Only if the person makes a permanent change in lifestyle will the pounds stay off. Nutritionists and personal trainers generally agree that no one else can force or pressure you to keep weight off; it has to be something that you believe in and commit to for the long term. In other words, it must become part of who you are—your culture.

Similarly, we argue that if holistic improvement is truly going to become how you work, it must become part of your culture. Culture change cannot be implemented by edict or driven from PowerPoint charts; it must be led (including through leading by example). Fortunately, when organizations make the changes noted in this book (especially the ones in this chapter, such as integrating holistic improvement concepts, methods, and tools into quality and process management systems), the culture naturally changes. Improvement becomes integral to how we work on a day-to-day basis.

Consider an illustration of this new type of thinking. Jack Welch, former CEO of GE, wrote a discussion of the impact of statistical variation on customer satisfaction in the 1998 GE Annual Report. This prompted people to begin working in a new way, and a new culture began to emerge. This solid foundation enhances the organization's ability to expand and grow. The cadre of MBBs, Black Belts, and other experienced improvement leaders that has emerged, along with a focus on improving all processes, creates a better climate for rapid assimilation of new acquisitions. This climate also makes it possible to move acquired processes to new locations and get them productive in record time.

The following list summarizes some of the cultural changes seen in the organization along the way.

- Improvement is seen as a normal part of the job for everyone; improvement is not a special initiative.

- Leadership understands that financial and other desired results are produced by effective and efficient processes: The process produces the results.

- Improvement methodologies are seen as the *how*, not the *what*. Neither leadership nor rank-and-file employees fall in love with specific methodologies.

- The organization never declares success; everyone understands that improvement is a permanent commitment.

- Decision making at all levels is guided by data whenever possible: "In God we trust—all others, bring data."

- Data has intrinsic value; database systems are viewed as gold mines instead of nuisances to be avoided.

- Hiring processes search for people who will be successful in the new culture; no employee, no matter how talented, is more important than the organization.

- Because of ongoing opportunities to improve their workplace, employees feel empowered, respected, and energized; there is no *we* and *they*.

People begin to believe that a focus on process improvement is the way to improve business performance and growth. They see that this improvement comes not simply by demanding it, but by having methods and tools available to improve the processes that generate the results. Their focus remains on improvement itself, not on individual methods or tools. They realize that just as making weight loss permanent requires a fundamental change in lifestyle, organizational excellence requires a permanent commitment to improvement.

Process improvement rises to a new and higher level of importance, a part of how you run the business. Using data and facts as a guide to decision making becomes the norm. "Please show me the data that led to this recommendation" is a common request when evaluating proposals and recommendations. Instead of avoiding clunky, antiquated databases, employees have modern and agile data systems that they view as opportunities waiting to be mined. A new way of working evolves and higher levels of performance results are expected and achieved.

Recruiting efforts take culture seriously, realizing that some interviewing candidates, potentially some with outstanding credentials, might not want to work in such a collaborative environment. As the president of a Silicon Valley tech company is rumored to have said, "I don't hire *jerks*, no matter how smart they are." (We substituted the word *jerks* here for his more vulgar term.)

Improvement As a Leadership Development Tool

Holistic improvement has another positive side effect that warrants further discussion: leadership development. This has obvious connections with making holistic improvement the way we work. Jack Welch (2005) reminds us, "Perhaps the biggest but most unheralded benefit of Six Sigma is its capacity to develop leaders." Companies such as Honeywell, GE, DuPont, 3M, and American Standard require managers to achieve Lean Six Sigma Green Belt certification and, in some instances, Black Belt certification for management promotion.

Welch (2001) further states:

> We've always had great functional training programs over the years, particularly in finance. But the diversity of the company has made it difficult to have a universal training program. Six Sigma gives us just the tool we need for generic management training since it applies as much in a customer service center as it does in a manufacturing environment.

Why is leadership development so important to make holistic improvement the way we work? The answer is straightforward: Today's talent will likely become tomorrow's leaders, and we need to ensure that these leaders fully understand and embrace holistic improvement. Having ex–Black Belts and Master Black Belts (MBBs) in senior leadership positions ensures that the culture change is permanent, which is a major element of making the transition from an initiative to the way we work.

One of the most important leadership skills that can be developed through holistic improvement is to help an organization move from one paradigm of working to another paradigm—this is cultural change. Changing how we work means changing our processes. Holistic improvement provides the concepts, methods, and tools for improving processes. Thus, holistic improvement gives leaders the strategy, methods, and tools to change their organizations. This is a key leadership skill that has been missing from most organization's approaches to leadership development. Such change-management skills will likely be critical in addressing future organizational change. As we discussed in Chapter 1, the world is changing rapidly, and the ability to learn and change rapidly is virtually the only lasting competitive advantage.

Some other leadership skills also can be developed through holistic improvement:

- Linking improvement needs to business strategy and goals
- Leading a team effectively
- Identifying opportunities for improvement
- Matching improvement methodologies to specific problems
- Delivering bottom-line results consistently
- Using data to guide decision making
- Using DMAIC as a general-purpose problem solving model

Summary and Looking Forward

Deploying Lean Six Sigma is a major organizational initiative that requires a lot of effort and resources. To expand to true holistic improvement (Lean Six Sigma 2.0), maintain the gains over the long term, and continuously improve, organizations need to integrate holistic improvement into the way they work. In other words, they need to institutionalize it. In this way, they can retain the benefits without retaining a separate infrastructure permanently.

Of course, without integrating holistic improvement into the way you work, the benefits will disappear with the separate infrastructure, and holistic improvement will have been just another fad that offered temporary benefits. As the old saying goes, "It's easy to quit smoking. I've done it dozens of times." Successfully transitioning is therefore the key to making the financial and organizational benefits permanent.

In this chapter we discussed ways of making the transition and integrating holistic improvement into the way we work. The three main approaches were: (1) creating and managing an overall improvement system that guides and integrates all three types of organizational improvement; (2) integrating holistic improvement concepts, methods, and tools with your quality and process management systems; and (3) changing the culture by utilizing holistic improvement as a leadership development tool.

Quality and process management systems, including process control systems, are extremely important and valuable with or without holistic improvement. They are particularly critical when transitioning from an improvement initiative to the way you work because they replace much of the holistic improvement infrastructure while maintaining the gains. If holistic improvement is embedded within the quality and process management systems, it becomes the normal way work gets done. One key aspect of any quality and process management system is the process control system, which often triggers the creation of improvement projects within the holistic improvement system.

The important role of leadership continues and becomes even more important—and, of course, leadership never ends. In our view, organizations that publically declare success with Lean Six Sigma or other improvement initiatives and then move on to something else have dropped the ball and walked away from future benefits. In the next chapter, we provide some thoughts for leaders that will enhance their abilities to provide effective leadership of holistic improvement into the future.

References

Baldrige National Quality Program. (2017) *Criteria for Performance Excellence.* Gaithersburg, MD: National Institute for Standards and Technology.

Hoerl, R. W., and R. D. Snee. (2012) *Statistical Thinking: Improving Business Performance.* Hoboken, NJ: John Wiley and Sons.

Snee, R. D. (1999a) "The Impact of Six Sigma: Today and in the Future," Presented at the Quality and Productivity Research Conference Sponsored by the American Statistical Association and American Society for Quality, General Electric Corporate R & D Center, Schenectady, NY, May 19–21, 1999.

Snee, R. D. (1999b) "Statisticians Must Develop Data-Based Management and Improvement Systems As Well As Create Measurement Systems." *International Statistical Review* Vol 67, No 2: 139–144.

Snee, R. D. (2001) "Make the View Worth the Climb: Focus Training on Getting Better Business Results." *Quality Progress*. (November): 58–61.

Stoner, J. A. F., and F. M. Werner. (1994) *Managing Finance for Quality*. Milwaukee, WI: ASQ Quality Press.

Welch, J. F. (2001) *Jack: Straight from the Gut*. New York: Warner Business Books.

Welch, J. F. (2005) *Winning*. New York: Harper Collins.

10

Final Thoughts for Leaders

"The ability to learn faster than your competitors may be the only sustainable competitive advantage."
—Arie DeGeus, Royal Dutch Shell

I n this final chapter, we discuss three issues that are particularly important to leaders: understanding and using the individual methods and tools, ensuring that the project succeeds, and ensuring that the overall initiative succeeds.

Our discussion of how leaders should think about the methods and tools is not intended as a technical reference, since this is not the primary need for leaders. Instead, it is motivated by our belief that the continuous improvement literature has provided conflicting advice on what level of knowledge, understanding, and competency leaders need to have with the methods and tools the organization is deploying. Our goal is to clarify leaders' responsibilities in that area.

First, we should explain our terminology. When we use the word *method*, we refer to an overall improvement approach, such as Six Sigma, Lean, or Work-Out. Conversely, when we use the word *tool*, we refer to a specific technique, perhaps one of many within an overall method. For example, control charting is a specific tool used in Six Sigma, and value stream mapping is a specific tool used in Lean.

Some publications seem to indicate that leaders need to become mini-statisticians and make themselves experts in every tool within Lean Six Sigma. Other articles give the impression that no familiarity with tools is needed at all because leaders can delegate the technical details of methods to others, such as Master Black Belts (MBBs) or Black Belts. The actual truth lies somewhere in between.

First, we provide a case study of a Six Sigma DMAIC Black Belt project. It represents neither the most technical Black Belt project nor the project with the greatest financial return. Instead, it is an excellent example of the appropriate level of knowledge needed for methods and tools. Furthermore, it relates to newspaper publishing, an industry whose issues virtually anyone can grasp. After the case study, we discuss what leaders need to know about the methods and tools, and we look at how they fit into the bigger picture of holistic improvement, using the case study for illustration.

Understanding the Role of the Methods and Tools: A Case Study

Successfully deploying Lean Six Sigma 2.0 depends on leaders understanding both the methods involved (the overall approaches to improvement included in a holistic improvement system) and the individual tools employed (such as 5S or regression analysis). Leaders don't need to be experts, but they do need to understand what the methods and tools are, when they are used, when they work, and when they don't work. Certainly, the more leaders know about the methods and tools, the better, although familiarity is more important than a high degree of technical expertise.

The case study we discuss is an elaboration of the Newspaper Accuracy case from Hoerl and Snee (2012). This case is about reducing errors specifically in newspaper publishing, but it can be extended to the idea of generally reducing errors in processes. This is a traditional Six Sigma project, but we think it illustrates the proper role of individual tools in general, regardless of whether the project is a Six Sigma project, a Lean project, or a Big Data analytics project.

One of the first questions leaders should ask is, "Is this problem important?" The answer here was a clear yes. Nothing is more important to a newspaper than the accuracy of the names, facts, figures, and other information it publishes. In this case, the newspaper reported the promotion of a new CEO in a major U.S. corporation and misspelled the new executive's name. The newspaper received a call from an unhappy reader—not the new CEO, the company's public relations department, or the CEO's spouse, but the CEO's mother! This points out that accurate information can come from many different sources, some of which are not necessarily anticipated.

Define Phase

In the Define phase, we select a project to work on and define both the specific problem to be solved and the process to be improved. We use key process metrics to guide project selection and identify the goals, and we summarize the resulting project and its objectives in the project charter. The project charter is a key tool of the project definition phase.

A common cause of failure in improvement projects is lack of a common understanding of what the projects will do and accomplish. This can lead to disappointment and finger pointing at project closure. Regardless of the methodology chosen, all projects should develop a charter at the very beginning.

In the newspaper accuracy study, leadership established error reduction as an important issue. For a Black Belt to work on this issue, the newspaper needed a project charter. As discussed in Chapter 6, "Launching the Initiative," this charter defines the work to be done, including the process involved, the problem statement, the metrics (process baseline, project goal, and process entitlement) associated with the problem, the project objective, the financial impact of the project, the team members, and the project scope.

We looked at common problems encountered in constructing an effective project charter in Chapter 6. Leadership must ensure that, for each project, a charter is created by the project Champion, is refined by the Champion and Black Belt, contains all the relevant metrics, defines the proper scope, specifies all the metrics, names the team members, and so on.

In short, the charter must be complete, with no shortcuts taken. It then serves as an internal contract among all project stakeholders. The project scope is important because it defines the boundaries of the project. The scope of the newspaper accuracy project was the editorial process, beginning with assignment of the story and ending with transmission of the story to production. Anything before or after these boundaries was considered out of scope for this project.

Some baseline data showed that although the copy desk might catch and fix as many as 40 errors per day, the rate on a typical day was 20 errors. Each error caused significant problems in the production process, so improvement was needed. A goal was set for this project to reduce the errors by 50 percent, to less than 10 per day.

The financial impact of an error was established as $62 if it was caught at the copy desk, $88 if it was caught in the composing room, $768 if a page had to be redone, and $5,000 if the presses had to be stopped and restarted. Of course, the cost of an error being published is unknown and unknowable.

The team developed an operational definition for an error before any data was collected, to ensure that the data would be accurate and that everyone would be talking about the same thing when discussing errors. It defined *error* as (1) any deviation from truth, accuracy, or widely accepted standards of English usage, or (2) a departure from accepted procedures that causes delay or requires reworking a story or a graphic. The team also divided the errors into nine categories: misspelled words, wrong number, wrong name, bad grammar, libel, word missing, duplicated word, fact wrong, and other. Obviously, not all of these errors are equally serious.

The 11-person team consisted of the Black Belt, the editor, two copy editors, two graphics editors, one reporter, and four supervisors. This team was large (we recommend teams of four to six), but it was effective. Larger teams have difficulty finding mutually agreeable meeting times, reaching consensus, and making decisions. Fortunately, team size turned out not to be a problem in this case.

Measure Phase

The Measure phase is intended to ensure that we are working on improving the right metrics (the ones we truly need to improve) and that we can measure well. This phase focuses on selecting the appropriate process outputs to be improved, based on the objectives of the project and customer needs. We determine what is acceptable performance and gather baseline data to evaluate current performance. This work includes evaluating the performance of both the measurement system and the performance of the process being studied.

As we discussed in Chapter 3, "Key Methodologies in a Holistic Improvement System," tools used during the Measure phase include the process map, cause-and-effect diagram or cause-and-effect matrix, measurement system analysis, capability analysis, and a control chart analysis of the baseline data on the process output. Quality Function Deployment (QFD) can also be used to refine and validate the output metrics (often referred to as CTQs).

Process mapping, cause-and-effect diagrams, capability studies, and control charts are popular improvement tools discussed by Hoerl and Snee (2012) and other authors. For more detailed discussions on analyzing measurement systems, see the Automotive Industry Action Group (AIAG, 2010) and Wheeler and Lyday (1989). Breyfogle (2003) elaborates on the use of the cause-and-effect matrix.

The process map is prepared by the team, not the Black Belt alone. It provides a picture of the process and identifies non-value-added work and the hidden factory where the reworking is done. Reworking refers to redoing substandard work done previously, such as finding and correcting errors in financial reports. Non-value-added work refers to work that adds no value to the product or service but that is currently required because of inefficiencies in the process. For example, warehousing finished goods adds no value from a customer point of view, but some level of warehousing is typically needed to maintain a supply chain.

The first process map is typically prepared at a macro level and usually consists of five to ten steps. If the team needs further detail for some key steps, it can map them further, creating substeps for each macro step.

The team usually identifies important process input and output variables during the process mapping work. Figure 10.1 shows the newspaper five-step process map for writing and editing. Note that the revision cycle can be a source of both non-value-added work and rework. The team identified the size of the paper (number of pages), the number of employees absent each day, and the need for a major change in a front-page (cover) story (yes, no) as variables that could have an effect on errors.

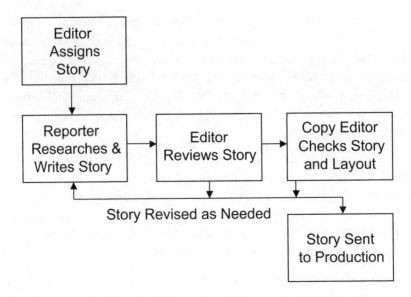

Figure 10.1   Newspaper writing and editing process

The purpose of both the cause-and-effect diagram and the cause-and-effect matrix is to enable the Black Belt and the team to study the relationships between the process input variables and the process output variables. In the case of the newspaper accuracy study, the key output variable was errors. The diagram serves as a visual display of the effect, or output variable, and its important causes or input/ process variables.

Figure 10.2 shows the cause-and-effect diagram for errors. The cause-and-effect matrix rates the process input variables in terms of their relative impact on the process output variables. It is actually one of the houses (typically the third house) created in a full-blown QFD analysis (Breyfogle, 2003).

For this project, the cause-and-effect diagram was adequate and the cause-and-effect matrix was not needed. As a general rule, we do not have to use every tool on every project; we simply use whatever tools are needed to successfully complete each phase of the DMAIC methodology. Recall that the DMAIC approach can be applied with a wide array of improvement methodologies, not just Six Sigma. Note also that both the cause-and-effect diagram and the matrix are examples of knowledge-based tools;

they are developed based on our existing knowledge of the process instead of on objective data. Eventually, we need objective data to ensure that our current understanding is correct and to enhance this understanding.

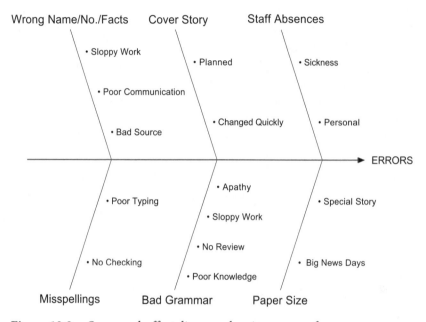

Figure 10.2   Cause-and-effect diagram showing causes of newspaper errors

In this case, the measurement system analysis consisted of developing the measurement system and errors collection scheme and then validating it. In other instances, particularly in manufacturing, gage repeatability and reproducibility studies (AIAG, 2010) are used to evaluate the adequacy of the measurement system. Gage repeatability and reproducibility (Gage R&R) studies evaluate your ability to replicate results when you take multiple measurements (repeatability), as well as the ability of several people or pieces of measurement equipment to obtain similar measurements (reproducibility). Such analysis is a particularly important step because, in our experience, as many as 50 percent of the measurement systems in use need significant improvement. Of course, measurement issues also extend beyond repeatability and reproducibility, such as those dealing with accuracy (ability to achieve the correct average measurement) and stability over time.

In Six Sigma projects outside manufacturing, such as the newspaper study or projects in finance, most of the measurement system work focuses on the creation of the measurement system and the construction of the data collection process. Most measurement systems in finance, for example, were created for accounting purposes, not for improvement.

A process capability study is often conducted to measure how well the process is capable of meeting the customer specifications. Typical outputs of these studies are short-term capability indices (short-term sigma level, Cp, Cpk) in the Measure phase and long-term capability indices (long-term sigma level, Pp, Ppk) in the Control phase. See Automotive Industry Action Group (AIAG, 2005) for definitions of these capability indices. Black Belts often conduct such studies using control charts (AIAG, 2005, Montgomery, 2012), which are graphical depictions of performance level and variation over time. A control chart analysis of 44 days of baseline data for the newspaper study showed that the errors were being produced by a stable process with an average value of approximately 20 errors per day, with daily variations from just below 10 to just below 40.

A control chart is a plot of data over time with statistically determined limits of normal variation. A run chart is analogous to a control chart but does not have the statistically determined limits. Figure 10.3 shows a run chart of this data, illustrating the degree of stability, average level, and variation of the process.

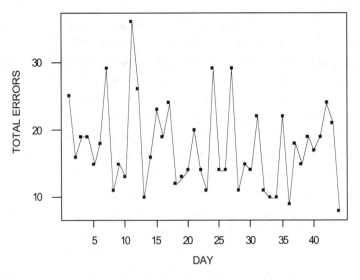

Figure 10.3 Run chart of newspaper errors March–April

Analyze Phase

The Analyze phase helps us avoid the ready, fire, aim approach by accurately diagnosing the root causes of problems. In this phase, we evaluate the baseline data to further document current performance and to identify root causes of the observed variation and defects. Additional data can be collected as needed.

Two improvement tools commonly used in the Analyze phase are multi-vari studies and failure mode and effects analysis (FMEA). *Multi-vari studies* is a generic term for any process study in which we collect data on the key process and input variables, as well as on the key outputs. We then analyze the data using graphical and statistical tools such as regression analysis and hypothesis testing, to identify the variables that have the most significant impact on the output variables. FMEA is a disciplined methodology for identifying potential defects and taking proactive steps to avoid them. More detailed explanations of these tools are given in the references at the end of this chapter.

When we evaluate data on discrete errors, we often use Pareto analysis to determine which categories of errors are the biggest problems. A Pareto chart (see Figure 10.4) is basically a bar graph whose bars are ordered by number or magnitude of occurrence. The theory is that a few categories will account for the majority of the errors. This is the case in the newspaper errors study. In Figure 10.4, we see that the majority of the errors during the March–April time period were due to misspelling; wrong names, numbers, and facts; and poor grammar.

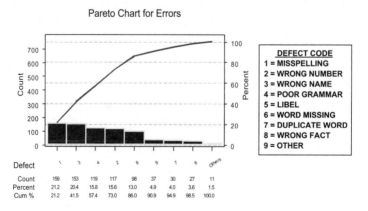

Figure 10.4   Pareto chart of newspaper errors March–April

The team initially focused its attention on addressing these categories and identified a major root cause: Reporters were not using the spell checker. The typical attitude was, "I don't have time to spell-check. Besides, the copy editors will catch the errors anyway." The reporters were also not routinely checking their facts and their sources, which was a job requirement. We address how to deal with these root causes in the improve phase.

A multi-vari study is often conducted to identify variables that could be producing the errors. The variables studied in the newspaper case were identified in the Measure phase: the size of the paper, the number of employees absent, and major changes made to the front-page story. The size of the paper was controllable, but the other two variables were not. The team also studied days of the week and months of the year. Work teams often perform differently on Mondays and Fridays than on the other days of the week. Analysis of the data indicated that the only variables with a clear effect on errors were the size of the paper (more pages leads to more errors) and changes in the front cover story (new stories had to be created under very tight schedules, increasing the error rate).

Improve Phase

In the Improve phase, teams figure out how to change the process to address the root causes identified in the Analyze phase, thereby improving the performance of the process. Each process change should be tested with a confirmatory study to verify that the predicted improvements actually happen. Several rounds of improvements might be needed to reach the desired level of performance. Note that this is the only phase in the DMAIC process that actually makes improvement. The other phases are intended to properly set up (DMA) and maintain (C) the improvements from this phase.

At this point in the newspaper case, management reaffirmed that reporters were responsible for checking the accuracy of their articles. Three job aids were also created: a "Spell Check How-To," a list of "10 Rules of Grammar," and the "Pyramid of Trust," which detailed the sources that can be trusted to produce accurate names, facts, and numbers.

These new working methods were communicated in an all-hands meeting in July. Management also discussed the importance of being careful when the front cover story changed with little notice and called attention to problems associated with large editions of the newspaper. The interim goal of letting less than 10 errors reach the copy desk per day was also reviewed and reaffirmed.

One month went by, and it was then time to test whether the changes were having an effect. Data for the month of August was analyzed, which found that the total errors had not changed! The leadership team assembled and reviewed the situation. Why were errors still high? Leadership learned that the new procedures were simply not being used. Many employees did not feel that leadership was serious about the changes and, therefore, did not take them seriously. This emphasizes the point that deciding on improvements and actually implementing them effectively are two different things. The editor reiterated that the new procedures were to be used and that the leadership team was expected to lead this new way of working. Another all-hands meeting was held to address the issue.

One month later, when the latest data was analyzed, total errors had dropped significantly (see Figure 10.5). In another month, the total errors had dropped by approximately 65 percent, compared to the goal of 50 percent. The new procedures were clearly working.

It is not uncommon to find that new procedures are not being used. It is the leadership's responsibility to ensure that the new way of working is put into practice. Otherwise, the benefits of the project will not be realized. Project reviews, confirmatory studies, and process audits are effective ways to identify whether the process changes are being used and are effective.

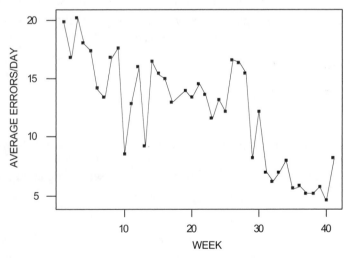

Figure 10.5   Run chart of weekly average newspaper errors March–December

In some instances, particularly in manufacturing processes, additional work needs to be done in the Improve phase to obtain the desired process performance. Typical studies include verifying cause-and-effect relationships identified in the Measure and Analyze phases, identifying optimum operating conditions, and defining process specification limits. The tools of statistical design of experiments (DOE) and response surface methodology can be helpful in these instances (Box, Hunter, and Hunter, 2005; Myers et al., 2016). Designed experiments have been successfully used in nonmanufacturing studies, and their use continues to grow in this important area of improvement (Koselka, 1996).

Control Phase

In the Control phase, we implement a system to ensure that the improved performance of the process is sustained after the team has completed its work and moved on to another project. The key tools of this phase are the control plan (AIAG, 2008), including control charts (part of statistical process control—Montgomery, 2012; AIAG, 2005) and long-term capability studies.

Returning to our newspaper case, we see that although the errors were significantly reduced, errors were not yet at zero. More work was needed to achieve further improvement. In the meantime, a control plan was put in place to hold the gains of the work done to date and to keep the errors at the level obtained. This is the purpose of the Control phase in Six Sigma: to hold the gains. The control plan specified that the following measures would be monitored using control charts:

- Total errors

- Errors by category

- Percent of articles checked by the author

- Percent of articles spell-checked

The latter two measurements were particularly useful in detecting when the reporters were not following procedures and thus when errors would likely be a problem.

The team created checklists (Gawande, 2009) and defined roles and responsibilities, including backups, to reduce handoff problems between departments. This approach enabled people to view their work processes as part of an overall system. To obtain further improvements, another team was chartered to find the sources of errors in the newspaper graphics and eliminate them.

Results

In addition to reducing the errors by 65 percent, the new way of operating had other benefits:

- Fewer missed deadlines, including the ability to deal effectively with extremely tight deadlines.

- Improved morale at the copy desk. Copy editors' time was freed up to make better use of their talents and training.

- Reduced re-entering of names (rework).

- Identification of more efficient and less costly sources of information, resulting in reduced errors and lower input time (less manual input of data). News assistants' time was freed up to do more valuable work.

Fewer errors resulted in less non-value-added work and a more streamlined and effective process. Such effects are characteristic of what happens when the errors and defect levels of business processes are reduced. The processes work more effectively and efficiently, costs are reduced, employee moral improves, and customer satisfaction increases.

It is not uncommon for a project, when completed, to achieve improvements to the process that were not anticipated initially. Leaders should be on the lookout for these situations and make sure that all the benefits are included in the financial impact calculation of the project. It is also important that the benefits of the project be communicated widely and that the success of the project be appropriately celebrated.

We also note that two commonly applied improvement tools, FMEA and DOE, were not used in this newspaper accuracy project. This is not unusual. In any given project, some tools are not needed; in other cases, the work might have already been completed in a previous phase. Leaders should assess whether the proper tools were used and provide input to the Black Belt as appropriate. Sometimes the unused tools are needed in subsequent studies. In the newspaper accuracy case, the error rate was reduced to less than 10 per day, which is not 0, the desired state. FMEA and DOE might prove useful in subsequent projects intended to make further improvements.

How to Think About the Methods and Tools

The methodologies incorporated into an organization's improvement methodology portfolio, as well as the individual process improvement tools utilized by each, are clearly an integral part of holistic improvement. As illustrated in the newspaper case study, without selecting an appropriate methodology to fit the specific problem, and without including powerful technical tools within it, Lean Six Sigma 2.0 would regress into a collection of vague concepts, slogans, and other fluff. The methodologies and underlying technical toolsets bring rigor to holistic improvement. The MBBs, Black Belts, and Green Belts are the resources primarily responsible for using the methodologies and subsequently the tools. This raises the question, "How should leaders such as executives, business unit leaders, and Champions think about the methods and tools?"

First, it is important to understand that these leaders do not need to become professional statisticians or even develop particular skills in using each methodology and tool. Of course, we can never have too much knowledge, but forcing leaders to become technical experts (as some executives have attempted to do) is a misguided approach. They simply don't need this expertise to do their job. After all, in the vast majority of projects, such as the newspaper case study, these leaders will not be the ones directly applying the tools. On the other hand, we recommend that leaders study and learn the methods and tools well enough to complete good Leadership Green Belt projects, as discussed in Chapter 8, "Sustaining Momentum and Growing." These might be Six Sigma projects, Lean projects, or some other methodology known by the specific individual.

At a minimum, leaders should understand the basics of Lean and also Six Sigma (for most organizations, the initial deployment will be Lean Six Sigma instead of holistic improvement). During Green Belt training, leaders should actually complete their own projects instead of relying on

MBBs or Black Belts in their organizations to do this for them. There's no substitute for personal experience with the tools and the overall DMAIC process. As we have discussed previously, DMAIC is a generic process and will work as a framework for most improvement methodologies.

Two extreme viewpoints that leaders should avoid are, at one end, feeling that they need to become experts in all the methodologies and all the tools, and, at the other end, refusing to study the methods or tools at all. For example, when the topic of the technical tools comes up, some leaders will joke, "I was never good at math!" Such an attitude belittles the importance of the tools and diminishes this leader's ability to hold meaningful project reviews.

The more appropriate middle ground is for leaders to study and struggle with the methods and tools like everyone else in the organization and to apply them to their own projects. They should understand what the key methods are and what type of projects might be most appropriate for each. For at least Lean and Six Sigma, they should know the typical tools utilized, when they should be applied, and what information each produces. This understanding will help leaders hold useful project reviews and overall initiative reviews.

Leaders don't necessarily need to understand the mechanics of how each method works, or the underlying mathematics of each tool. They do need to understand how the methods integrate in a portfolio that will address the vast majority of problems facing the organization. Additionally, leaders should avoid having a favorite methodology, whether it is Six Sigma, Lean, Work-Out, Big Data analytics, or something else. Individuals in their organizations might be tempted to defer to the boss's favorite approach instead of selecting it based on the specifics of the problem at hand.

Leaders should understand and publicly reinforce some key principles, listed next. Following this list, we elaborate on a few of the given points.

- Methodologies should be selected objectively, based on the problem; never pick the methodology first and then restate the problem to fit the preselected approach. Recall that holistic improvement is method agnostic.

- The individual statistical and process improvement tools provide the rigor in holistic improvement, when properly linked and integrated within an overall methodology.

- The methods and tools themselves don't make improvements; the action taken by people applying the methods and tools generates improvement.

- No single individual will have expertise in every method and every tool; a team is needed to cover all the bases.

- If the leadership aspects of holistic improvement are not in place, the methods and tools will not have lasting effect.

- Within each methodology, the improvement tools should be combined with subject matter knowledge in an iterative cycle of generating, testing, and revising hypotheses.

Tools Themselves Don't Make Improvements

Notice from the newspaper case study that all improvements to the publishing process came about from actions taken by people, not from Six Sigma or the individual tools. For example, implementing (and actually using) well-designed job aids significantly improved accuracy. Of course, use of the tools helped identify the root causes of inaccuracy and determine the best countermeasures to deal with these root causes. Pareto analysis was a key tool in this project. As with most Black Belt projects, rigorously defining the appropriate metrics to be improved and then obtaining relevant data for improvement purposes were key challenges. In this case, developing a precise definition of an accuracy error was critical for progress.

The key point here is that the tools help identify the root causes of problems and potential solutions, but for improvement to occur, people need to take action based on the tools. For example, numerous investment organizations lost large sums of money when the U.S. economy nosedived in late 2008, resulting in numerous bankruptcies and other financial defaults. Interestingly, many of these investment companies had sophisticated tools designed to predict such defaults. No doubt some of these tools were poorly constructed, but it is clear that many investment firms lost money not because of tool inadequacy, but rather because of lack of prompt action based on the tools.

Tools Must Be Properly Sequenced

The tools must also be properly sequenced and integrated within the overall methodology to be effective. Figure 10.6 illustrates how the most commonly used tools are typically sequenced and integrated by the DMAIC process during Six Sigma projects. There is a logical progression, with the input of one tool often being the output from a previously used tool. As discussed earlier, the sequence of tool application is based on the sequence of DMAIC; Figure 10.6 simply highlights the way the tools used in the various steps of DMAIC link to one another. Of course, the specific tool linkage depends on the individual methodology. For example, in Lean, the 5S process follows a similar logical sequence with tool linkages.

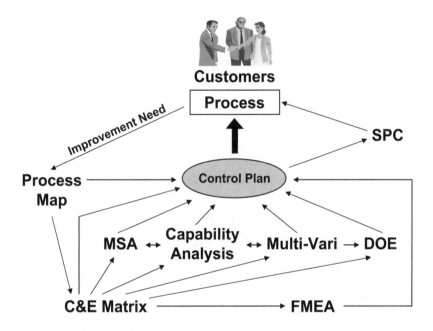

Figure 10.6   Six Sigma tool linkage

The process map, or flowchart, is typically the first formal tool used in Six Sigma. The process map sets the stage for subsequent tools by carefully documenting a common view of the process. This map enables people to see their piece of the process in the context of the bigger picture. The cause-and-effect (C&E) matrix naturally follows the process map.

After the team agrees on the major steps in the process, it is logical to determine which steps and process variables are most critical to achieving our critical to quality metrics (CTQs). The C&E matrix does this by noting how strongly each process step and variable impact each CTQ. The process map and C&E matrix also provide input to the control plan by documenting the process steps and variables that need to be included.

When the C&E matrix identifies the priority steps, the team needs to ensure that it can accurately measure the key variables at these steps, utilizing a measurement system analysis (MSA). In addition, the team might begin a formal failure mode and effects analysis (FMEA) to identify potential failures in the prioritized steps and variables and then begin proactive countermeasures to prevent them. When the team is convinced that it can accurately measure the key variables, it will likely evaluate process capability using capability analysis tools. Assuming that the capability is insufficient, the team can use a multi-vari analysis to identify the key process variables that are causing the bulk of the variation in the process outputs (CTQs). Formal design of experiments (DOE) provides additional power to resolve ambiguities and quantify cause-effect relationships.

A key characteristic of the Six Sigma methodology is that the output of each of these tools provides input to the control plan by determining the most important aspects of the process that need to be controlled to maintain improvements. This approach greatly simplifies development of the control plan because much of the hard work has already been done. Statistical process control (SPC), the other commonly used tool depicted in Figure 10.6, is then utilized by the control plan to quickly identify abnormal behavior in the process so that root causes can be found and addressed. Statistical process control uses control charts to document the range of normal behavior in the process, allowing early detection of potential problems before they become major issues.

This logical integration of tools into an overall improvement process is a major contribution of the Six Sigma methodology. Statistical and process improvement tools have been around for a long time and have been promoted by many other initiatives, such as Total Quality Management (TQM). However, instructors have generally taught practitioners a collection of tools without providing guidance on how to properly integrate or sequence them to solve a real problem. This approach often left people confused on how to start or where to go next after applying one tool. Of course, other improvement approaches also link and integrate individual tools in logical ways; these include DFSS, statistical engineering, and Kepner–Tregoe.

Leadership Is Still Required

We have attempted to stress throughout this book that leadership is the key to success with Lean Six Sigma and especially holistic improvement. This is also true for effective use of the tools. If the leadership component is lacking, no amount of tool usage can overcome this deficiency. For example, when the job aids were originally rolled out to the newspaper organization, subsequent data revealed no improvement. Why? People did not think management was serious, so they did not use the job aids. If this situation had been allowed to continue, the project would have ended in failure. Fortunately, the editor exerted leadership by directly addressing the problem and insisting that the job aids be utilized. Errors decreased dramatically in the next few months. There is no substitute for leadership.

Leaders should be continuously looking for similar situations in their own organizations where effectiveness of tool applications is being hampered by leadership issues (bureaucracy, politics, lack of clear direction, and so on). These issues tend to be the ones the Black Belts and even MBBs are unable to address on their own, and they are one reason for having a formal Champion role. Effective use of tools should be another area of focus at both project reviews and overall initiative reviews.

Incorporate Subject Matter Knowledge

Keep in mind that the methods and tools work best when they are combined with good subject matter knowledge in the technical area of the project, whether it is engineering, finance, or marketing. This is why it is helpful to have Black Belts who are knowledgeable in the areas in which they are doing projects. Furthermore, it is always helpful to have subject matter experts on the team.

Subject matter knowledge provides the theory to guide initial use of the tools. The information gained from the tools then helps refine, augment, or revise the original theories. This sequence continues from phase to phase, and tool to tool, resulting in greater and greater process knowledge. This is essentially applying the scientific method to organizational problems. A more detailed discussion of the proper integration of data-based tools and subject matter knowledge can be found in Hoerl and Snee (2012).

In the newspaper accuracy case, it was necessary to have the editor, copy editors, graphics editors, reporters, and supervisors on the team to cover all the key areas of subject matter knowledge. If such subject matter knowledge were not critical, you wouldn't need such diverse teams. Data and statistics can augment and sometimes even contradict subject matter knowledge, but they are certainly no substitute for such knowledge.

For example, it would likely have been impossible to determine the costs of finding errors at various stages of the publication process without such expertise. Subject matter knowledge also helped guide the original data collection and interpret the results of the data analysis. Of course, the data analysis revised the team's original theories—for example, dispelling the theory that the number of absent employees was a key contributor to the accuracy problem. As is often the case, analyses of data and subject matter theory enhanced one another when properly integrated.

Leaders should ask questions about what new knowledge the organization has learned from data analyses and how current theories about the process need to be revised based on them. In short, we should have data to validate all our theories, and theories should properly interpret all our data.

In this arena, there are again extreme positions that can inhibit project success. For example, some proponents of Big Data analytics might become enamored with the statistical tools and feel that volumes of data and sophisticated analyses are a replacement for process knowledge. Such analysts tend to skip over the step of interpreting the data in light of subject matter theory, resulting in invalid conclusions (Hoerl et al., 2014). Conversely, some purists might believe that all problems can be solved based on first principles (fundamental laws) of engineering, physics, or finance, and thus resist data collection and analysis. Leaders must push back on both extremes and insist on the proper integration of subject matter knowledge and data analysis. History has proven that the scientific method works best with both.

If leaders understand these key concepts about the methods and tools and also can properly audit for them during project and overall initiative reviews, they will add significant value to their organization's deployment. Conversely, those who either try to become professional statisticians or totally avoid discussion of the tools will significantly diminish their value-add.

Summary and Looking Forward

Merely launching a Lean Six Sigma or holistic improvement initiative does not guarantee success. The initiative must be properly led and managed to succeed. We believe that the material in this book will help leaders do just that. As we have noted elsewhere, holistic improvement works if you follow the process. If it is not working, you are not following the process.

Certainly, anything can be improved and streamlined. However, readers should be wary of claims of instant success with no significant investment or effort required. The saying "No pain, no gain" holds true in both weight loss and improvement. Lasting success requires both financial and personal commitment. Committed leadership is the single most important key to success.

We have provided an overall process for Lean Six Sigma deployment that goes from initial decision to launch, through expansion to holistic improvement. This process uses Lean Six Sigma 2.0, which ingrains improvement into the fabric and culture of the organization. Previous chapters of this book described each major phase in this process. Although the process does not need to be followed religiously, every organization we know of that has followed it closely (about 30 organizations) has achieved significant success. Leaders need to monitor the success of both the set of individual improvement projects and also the overall initiative itself, until it becomes the way we work instead of merely an initiative. Good luck with your deployment!

References

Automotive Industry Action Group. (2005) *Statistical Process Control Reference Manual*, 2nd ed.

Automotive Industry Action Group. (2008) *Advanced Product Quality Planning and Control Plan*, 2nd ed.

Automotive Industry Action Group. (2010) *Measurement System Analysis Reference Manual*, 3rd ed.

Box, G. E. P., W. G. Hunter, and J. S. Hunter. (2005) *Statistics for Experimenters*, 2nd ed. Hoboken, NJ: John Wiley and Sons.

Breyfogle, F. W. (2003) *Implementing Six Sigma: Smarter Solutions Using Statistical Methods*, 2nd ed. Hoboken, NJ: John Wiley and Sons.

Gawande, A. (2009) *The Checklist Manifesto: How to Get Things Right*. New York: Henry Holt and Company.

Hoerl, R. W., and R. D. Snee. (2012) *Statistical Thinking: Improving Business Performance*, 2nd ed. Hoboken, NJ: John Wiley and Sons.

Hoerl, R. W., R. D. Snee, and R. D. De Veaux. (2014) "Applying Statistical Thinking to 'Big Data' Problems." *Wiley Interdisciplinary Reviews: Computational Statistics* (July/August): 221–232.

Koselka, R. (1996) "The New Mantra: MVT (Multivariable Testing)." *Forbes* (March 11): 114–118.

Montgomery, D. C. (2012) *Statistical Quality Control*, 7th ed. New York: John Wiley and Sons.

Myers, R. H., D. C. Montgomery, and C. M. Anderson-Cook. (2016) *Response Surface Methodology*, 4th ed. Hoboken, NJ: John Wiley and Sons.

Wheeler, D. J., and R. W. Lyday. (1989) *Evaluating the Measurement Process*, 2nd ed. Knoxville, TN: SPC Press.

Ensuring Project and Initiative Success

We have provided a great deal of advice on how to launch a holistic improvement initiative, lead it, and ensure its long-term success. In this appendix, we summarize our advice for ensuring the success of projects, including pitfalls to avoid. This is followed by guidance on pitfalls and success factors for the overall holistic improvement initiative. We trust that this concise listing of advice and questions to ask will prove helpful in your deployments.

Advice for Ensuring Project Success

In this section, we summarize key points made throughout this book that relate to achieving success with holistic improvement projects.

Key Project Success Criteria

Improvement initiatives produce tangible results primarily project by project, although the resulting cultural change adds benefits beyond formal projects. We must ensure that these projects succeed in order for the organization to fully benefit from holistic improvement. The following guidance is intended to relate generically, regardless of project methodology—that is, it is appropriate for Six Sigma projects, Lean projects, Work-Out projects, and so on. Note that, in Lean Six Sigma 2.0, we still use the infrastructure from Six Sigma such as Black Belts (BBs), Master Black Belts (MBBs), the DMAIC and DMADV frameworks, and so on. Although this infrastructure was originally developed through Six Sigma initiatives, it is certainly not limited to Six Sigma projects.

The primary keys to project success (discussed in Chapter 6, "Launching the Initiative," and Chapter 7, "Managing the Effort") include the following:

- Good projects that connect to organizational objectives

- The most appropriate improvement methodology, based on the specifics of the problem

- A talented Black Belt and Champion assigned to the project

- Proper support, such as from functional support groups (information technology [IT], finance, human resources [HR], legal, and so on)

- Regular, well-structured project reviews

- Clear project close-out criteria

Chapter 6 recommended criteria for project selection and provided an example of criteria used by one organization. The key points are that you should be working on important projects that are supported by management, that can be completed within a reasonable amount of time (three to six months for Six Sigma, less for Lean or Work-Out, and more for quality by design initiatives), and that have clear measures of success. To gain such projects, organizations need to develop a rigorous project identification and prioritization process, as discussed in Chapter 9, "The Way We Work." Prioritized projects are then placed into an improvement project portfolio, to await the assignment of a Black Belt.

Some pitfalls to avoid in project selection include the following:

- Fuzzy objectives

- Poor metrics

- No tie to financials

- Overly broad scope

- Lack of connection with strategic or annual plans

- Projects with too many objectives

Use of top talent in key holistic improvement roles is a theme running throughout the initiative, but it is perhaps most critical in the Black

Belts leading the individual projects. We have seen huge variation in success rates between projects that were led by true top talent and projects that weren't. It is also important that projects have access as needed to resources from support groups, such as IT, finance, and maintenance. This often is critical in the Improve phase of Six Sigma projects or whenever an identified improvement needs to be implemented in other methodologies. If the improvement calls for a process step to be digitized, for example, the prompt support of the IT organization will be necessary.

Well-structured project reviews serve several purposes. First, scheduling project reviews indicates leadership's seriousness and sets the expectation of tangible results. In addition, reviews identify issues or roadblocks hindering projects so that they can be addressed by Champions or others in leadership roles. Projects with regular, formal reviews rarely drag on past the expected completion date. A fringe benefit is that as leaders see more success in improvement projects firsthand, they become stronger proponents of the initiative.

Clear close-out criteria keep perfectionist Black Belts from continuing on a project past the point of significant return, overlooking other processes in critical condition that urgently need a Black Belt. Conversely, these criteria also prevent Black Belts from prematurely jumping from one project to another before ensuring success. Well-thought-out criteria help Black Belts move crisply from one project to the next, maximizing the overall benefit to the organization.

Common Pitfalls to Avoid

Project pitfalls that can derail success are almost mirror images of the key success criteria; omission of success criteria is itself a pitfall. However, some pitfalls are more common than others, so we briefly list the most common ones here in order of frequency, based on our experience. In each case, one or more success criteria will help address the pitfall:

- Poorly scoped projects, which typically attempt to "boil the ocean" or "solve world hunger," for example. Proper project selection and scoping are the key solutions to this pitfall. Frequent project review also can catch problems early.

- An inappropriate improvement methodology. As discussed in earlier chapters, no single methodology is universally best; we must start with understanding the problem and only then select the method. An inappropriate methodology typically leads to team frustration and lack of progress. A good project selection system that is objective and carefully considers the uniqueness of the problem can circumvent this pitfall.

- Lack of available data to study and improve the process. Insufficient data is generally an indication that a project should have been weeded out before this point. A good project identification and prioritization process minimizes this pitfall.

- Failure to follow the DMAIC, DMADV, or other project management process. In some cases, poorly trained or led Black Belts might haphazardly attack the problem using Six Sigma tools instead of following the DMAIC process in a disciplined manner. The DMADV framework is typically more useful for quality by design projects. Proper training and frequent project reviews address this pitfall.

- A weak Black Belt or Champion. Selecting Black Belts and Champions from the top talent pool prevents this problem.

- Dysfunctional improvement teams. This can result from poorly trained Black Belts, lack of a team culture, or missing leadership support (especially intervention from the Champion). The combination of an active improvement organizational structure (including functional Champions), proper training of Black Belts, and a formal project review process help nip this problem in the bud.

Good Questions to Ask in Project Reviews

Of course, the best questions to ask in a project review depend on the specific methodology used for the project, the experience of the Black Belt, and many other factors. Therefore, we cannot provide a generic list of the questions that apply in all situations. However, the types of questions leaders ask in project reviews are extremely important because they set the tone for the projects. As you can see here, few of these questions can be answered as "yes" or "no." Instead, they lead to a dialogue about the problem and how it is being attacked.

We provide sample questions that might be appropriate to ask in some reviews, particularly if the Black Belt has not already raised the subject during the review. The questions are organized according to the specific phase of the DMAIC framework to which the question would most likely pertain.

Define

- Why are we working on this project instead of others we could be doing?

- How does this project relate to key objectives or initiatives of the organization?

- What specifically are we trying to accomplish with this project? How will you measure success?

- What improvement methodology was selected for this project, and why do you feel that was the right choice?

Measure

- Can you show me a map of the process in question?

- Did customers validate these CTQs? If not, how were they validated?

- How did you evaluate the measurement system? Where is the data?

Analyze

- What data and analyses do you have to corroborate that conclusion?

- Did you plot the data? May I see the graph?

- What hypotheses do you have about the process that would explain the data?

Improve

- What other options for improvement did you consider? Why were they not selected?

- How do the proposed improvements relate back to the root causes found in the Analyze phase?

- Have you piloted the improvements to make sure they work?

Control

- What makes you confident that this control plan will maintain improvement?

- Is the process owner comfortable with this control plan, and has he or she committed to using it going forward?

- To what extent does this control plan consider key process variables (input, controlled, and uncontrolled) as well as key process outputs?

Advice for Ensuring Long-Term Success of Holistic Improvement

Not every organization that has launched a Lean Six Sigma or other improvement initiative has achieved the financial benefits it anticipated. Among those that have gained significant financial benefits, some have certainly done better than others. In addition, the improvement initiatives that have truly become the way we work have been few and far between. There are logical reasons for this: Improvement is hard, and maintaining behaviors over time is even harder. In this section, we provide guidance on steps to take to ensure long-term success in making holistic improvement the way we work.

Key Criteria for Long-Term Success

In Chapter 4, "Case Studies in Holistic Improvement," we reviewed three specific companies' experiences with holistic improvement; in the first edition of this book, we also reviewed several others. Based on this information, as well as our collective experience with many other organizations, we identified four key long-term success criteria (see Chapter 5, "How to Successfully Implement Lean Six Sigma 2.0"):

- Committed leadership
- Top talent
- Supporting infrastructure
- Improvement methodology portfolio

Each successful deployment of holistic improvement that we are aware of has included these criteria. Successful Six Sigma, Lean, or other one-methodology initiatives have included the first three. Similarly, the root causes of each less successful deployment that we are aware of can be traced back to the lack of one or more of these four criteria. There is simply no substitute for any of them.

Committed leadership is perhaps the most critical success criterion. Remember that there is a big difference between supportive leadership and committed leadership. Committed leadership is determined to make holistic improvement successful; it will spend the necessary time and take whatever actions are required to make this happen. Supportive leadership thinks this is a good idea but is not necessarily willing to devote personal time to the deployment or change management style to ensure success. We know of no committed leaders who have not achieved significant success for their organizations.

Committed leaders must be backed up by top talent in the operational roles in holistic improvement, such as Black Belts and Champions. These are the people who will lead the individual projects that produce the tangible results, so the organization's most talented people are needed. Committed leaders with less talented Black Belts, MBBs, Champions, and so on can achieve only so much because they can't do everything themselves.

One reason many improvement initiatives are not assigned top talent is that these people are typically quite busy doing important things. Freeing them from their current duties and reassigning them to improvement is painful and sometimes difficult. This is why committed leadership is necessary, to take the more difficult (but also more fruitful) path instead of the path of least resistance, which would assign whoever was available to key improvement roles.

Supporting infrastructure is perhaps a more subtle success factor. The supporting infrastructure is the organizational structure and systems that provide support to the improvement initiative, along with legitimacy and formality. Some of the typical elements in this infrastructure follow (see Chapter 7):

- An organizational structure that includes overall leadership of the effort. This might initially be a Lean Six Sigma Council, for example, which would eventually be replaced with an overall improvement organization and dedicated positions for key roles (MBBs, Black Belts, and so on).

- Improvement planning systems. This includes development and managerial review of implementation plans, budgets, human resources plans, and so forth done at least annually. This is nothing more than the routine planning done for each business unit in a major corporation, but it is often overlooked for improvement initiatives.

- Support from functional groups, such as finance, HR, engineering, and purchasing.

- Project selection and review processes.

- Training systems for key roles.

- Modification of human resources, reward and recognition, business planning, financial, and other business systems to support holistic improvement as needed.

We've previously noted that no major corporation operates its finance department without a designated leader or finance committee, with unclear roles, or with resources addressing finance in their spare time. If this type of unorganized approach doesn't work for finance, why would we expect it to work for improvement? Without such an infrastructure, Champions, MBBs, Black Belts, and others have to spend considerable time and effort justifying every training class, begging for money for each project selected, trying to track down needed resources, and competing for managerial attention. This leaves little time and energy to actually complete projects that will benefit the bottom line.

A good infrastructure gives the initiative legitimacy, resolves personnel and budgetary issues at a strategic level, and provides formal mechanisms for such actions as project selection and training. In other words, this infrastructure allows us to manage the effort instead of having it just happen. Including a supporting infrastructure is one of the true enhancements Six Sigma brought to previous improvement initiatives, such as Total Quality Management (TQM) or reengineering. Contrary to popular opinion, it is possible to add organizational structure and processes without adding a lot of bureaucracy. The key is to ensure that the focus is always on achieving the objectives of the infrastructure (tangible results) instead of religiously adhering to the infrastructure processes.

As discussed throughout this book, creating an improvement methodology portfolio is the single most important step an organization needs to take to advance from Lean Six Sigma (or some other improvement initiative) and achieve true holistic improvement. Organizational problems are simply too diverse to solve with any one method—or even two or three methods. Furthermore, to integrate all improvement activities under one umbrella, organizations need to incorporate quality by design efforts, as well as quality and process management systems, into the holistic improvement organization. This is the only way to avoid the common pitfall of islands of improvement, in which different organizations create unhealthy internal competition for improvement resources.

Recall that no organization can realistically incorporate all known improvement methodologies into its portfolio. Therefore, organizations need to carefully consider the proper balance and mix of methodologies that it feels is most appropriate for its unique problems. The mix at a financial institution might look different from that of a hospital network or tech company. Although we do not feel that a "perfect" portfolio exists, we identified key methodologies to consider in Chapter 3, "Key Methodologies in a Holistic Improvement System," and Chapter 8, "Sustaining Momentum and Growing." Other methodologies might be needed as well. It should also be clear that the portfolio needs to be dynamic; new methods will need to be incorporated, and some older ones might become less useful over time.

Common Pitfalls to Avoid in Holistic Improvement

As with project pitfalls, the vast majority of pitfalls for the overall holistic improvement transformation have root causes that relate to the absence of one or more of the success criteria noted earlier. Again, we provide the pitfalls in the order of frequency based on our experience, and we offer suggestions for avoiding them.

- Lack of true commitment from senior leadership. Unfortunately, this pitfall has no solution. Our recommendation is to hold off on deployment until such commitment exists and, in the meantime, try to obtain this commitment by sharing improvement success stories.

- Lack of dedicated resources—that is, an attempt to do holistic improvement in people's spare time. Who has spare time in today's business world? Such an approach will slow, if not derail, deployment. The solution is to implement a proper improvement organization, including full-time resources.

- Assignment of less than top talent to key positions. This pitfall is similar to the previous one: Both relate to providing the required human resources to achieve holistic improvement. We can appreciate that it is very tempting to merely assign resources that are available, even if they do not represent top talent in the organization. However, this will not only hinder current success, but it might convince top talent in the organization that improvement is not for them. The solution is to ensure that only top talent is assigned to key leadership positions. Referencing annual employee evaluations, where relevant, can help here.

- Ad hoc deployment of Lean Six Sigma (initially) or holistic improvement (later) without the proper supportive infrastructure. This pitfall might not become obvious until a year or two into deployment, but it will prevent improvement from having a lasting impact. The key to avoiding this pitfall is for those leading deployment (overall Champion or leader, Six Sigma Council, improvement organization, and so on) to prioritize development of the key elements of the supportive infrastructure (see Chapters 6 and 7).

- A bureaucratic focus for the initiative. This can occur when such factors as the number of Black Belts trained, the number of projects completed, the percentage of employees Green Belt certified, and so on become the emphasis of the organization's improvement effort. In other words, the focus is on the effort itself, not on the results it is supposed to generate. Certainly, there is no harm in measuring these internal metrics, but you must always keep in mind that the purpose of implementing Lean Six Sigma, and eventually holistic improvement as a whole, is to better satisfy customers and generate financial benefits. Therefore, the solution to this pitfall is to make financial benefits and direct measures of customer satisfaction (such as retention and attainment of additional business) the overall measure of success.

Good Questions to Ask in Initiative Reviews

In Chapter 8, we discussed the need to hold periodic management reviews of overall deployment, as well as project reviews. We emphasized that management reviews are the "secret sauce" for success. Initially, these reviews would typically be for a Lean Six Sigma initiative; they would eventually move to a holistic improvement initiative. Once we have truly made holistic improvement the way we work, it is no longer an initiative: At that point, initiative reviews would be replaced with regular reviews of the status of improvement, just as there are regular financial reviews, regular staffing reviews, and regular reviews of other major functions.

Project reviews help ensure success of the improvement projects, but they are not designed to evaluate the overall initiative from a strategic perspective. This is the purpose of the reviews of the overall initiative. A key similarity with project reviews is that the questions leaders ask in the initiative reviews also help set the tone; they establish expectations, determine direction, create a mind-set, and so on. Therefore, it is important for leaders to ask questions that create the desired tone. Again, no single list of "correct" questions exists, but the following list can prove useful in setting the tone needed to make holistic improvement successful in the long term. Leaders can ask the questions at any time, but they are typically most relevant during the deployment phase noted.

Launching the Initiative

- How often are the Lean Six Sigma projects reviewed by their Champions? By you and your staff?

- What percentage of your time and your leadership team's time will be allocated to Lean Six Sigma deployment over the next year?

- May we review your overall deployment plan?

Managing the Effort

- What level of incremental operating profit from Lean Six Sigma do you feel confident committing to this year? What is your basis for this number?

- May I see your project selection criteria and your current project portfolio? Please describe your project prioritization process.

- May I review some projects in your project tracking and reporting system?

Sustaining Momentum and Growing

- Can you show me your overall financials for the Lean Six Sigma initiative so far (expenses and returns)?

- Can you show me the status of each element of your Lean Six Sigma deployment plan?

- What are your deployment plans for extending Lean Six Sigma across your entire business unit?

- How are you expanding your improvement project portfolio toward holistic improvement?

The Way We Work

- Can you show me your organizational chart for the integrated improvement group?

- How do you manage differently now versus before holistic improvement?

- How have you embedded improvement into quality and process management systems?

B

Glossary

> *"An operational definition puts communicable meaning into a concept. ... It is one that reasonable people can agree on."*
> —W. Edwards Deming

5S   An acronym for Sort, Set in order, Shine, Standardize, and Sustain. This approach is often used in Lean enterprise to clean and organize the workplace.

baseline   The level of process performance when a project is initiated.

Big Data analytics   The statistical analysis of very large data sets, in hopes of finding opportunities for improvement.

Black Belt   A process improvement project team leader who is trained and certified in specific improvement methodologies and tools, such as Six Sigma, and who is responsible for project execution.

capability   The total range of inherent variation in a stable process. It is determined using data from control charts.

capability index   A calculated value used to compare process variation to a specification. Examples are Cp and Cpk. A capability index can also be used to compare processes to each other.

cause and effect matrix   A prioritization matrix that enables you to select the process input variables (X's) that have the greatest effect on the process output variables.

Champion   A business leader who facilitates the leadership, implementation, and deployment of the Lean Six Sigma initiative and breakthrough philosophies, and provides support to the Black Belts and Green Belts and their projects.

control plan   A process control document that describes the system for controlling processes in order to sustain improvement over time.

cost of poor quality Cost associated with poor-quality products or services. Examples include product inspection, sorting, scrap, rework, and field complaints.

critical to quality (CTQ) A characteristic of a product, a service, or information that is important to the customer. The characteristic must be measureable in either a quantitative manner (numerically) or a qualitative manner (for example, correct or incorrect).

defect Any characteristic that deviates outside of specification limits or customer requirements.

design of experiments An efficient method of experimentation that identifies, with minimum testing, factors (key process input [DOE] variables) and their optimum settings that affect the mean and variation.

entitlement The best level of performance a process can be expected to produce.

failure mode and effects analysis (FMEA) Analytical approach for preventing defects by prioritizing potential problems and their resolution.

first pass yield (FPY) The percentage of products or services that are successfully completed on the first attempt without requiring remedial action or rework.

gage bias The difference between the true or reference value and the observed average of multiple measurements of the identical characteristic on the same part. Also known as accuracy.

gage repeatability The variation in measurements obtained with one measurement instrument when used several times by one appraiser while measuring the identical characteristic on the same part.

gage reproducibility The variation in the average of the measurements made by different appraisers using the same measuring instrument when measuring the identical characteristic on the same part.

Green Belt Someone trained in improvement methodologies, such as Six Sigma, who leads improvement projects working part time. A Green Belt typically completes one to two projects per year.

hidden factory The part of the process that handles defective product by reworking as appropriate and scrapping what cannot be reworked to meet specifications.

holistic improvement A paradigm of improvement that starts with the totality of improvement work needed and then develops a suite of methods and approaches to enable the organization to address all the improvement work identified. It is holistic in the sense that it can successfully create and sustain significant improvements of any type, in any culture, for any business or organization.

Internet of Things A building block to effective quality and process management in which physical devices instead of people or businesses communicate via the Internet.

JMP Statistical software package useful for doing statistical calculations.

Kaisen event A rapid, intense improvement project often used in Lean enterprise, with processes broken down and reassembled in a more logical layout.

Kepner–Tregoe An improvement approach that carefully documents an issue so that root causes (not the symptoms) can be addressed. Also referred to as Is–Is Not analysis.

Lean enterprise System of improvement based on the Toyota Production System. Lean emphasizes the broad application of known principles, such as line of sight, single-piece flow, and pull versus push inventory systems.

Lean Six Sigma The integration of Lean and Six Sigma. Lean Six Sigma is typically the improvement approach initially deployed today. It is a major step toward true holistic improvement.

Lean Six Sigma 2.0 The holistic improvement system integrating Lean and Six Sigma, as well as other improvement methodologies, while also retaining the infrastructure of Lean Six Sigma (Black Belts, MBBs, project hopper, and so on). Lean Six Sigma 2.0 also integrates quality by design and quality and process management systems with breakthrough improvement.

Master Black Belt (MBB) A person who is an "expert" in specific improvement techniques, such as Six Sigma, and project implementation. MBBs play a key role in facilitating project selection and in training and coaching Black Belts.

measurement system The complete process used to obtain measurements. It consists of the collection of operations, procedures, gages and other equipment, software, and personnel used to assign a number or value to the characteristic being measured.

measurement system analysis Study of the measurement system, typically using gage R&R or nested variance component studies to measure the quality (repeatability and reproducibility) of the measurement produced by the system.

Minitab Statistical software package useful for doing statistical calculations

multi-vari chart A graphic way of depicting variation within a single part, machine, or process, or between parts (produced at the same time or over time). It facilitates the study of process inputs and outputs in a passive mode (natural day-to-day process).

multi-vari study A statistical study that samples the process as it operates and, by statistical and graphical analysis, identifies the important controlled and uncontrolled (noise) variables.

Nike project A relatively straightforward project that requires minimal planning (Just Do It!).

normal distribution A continuous, symmetrical, bell-shaped frequency distribution for variable data.

Pareto chart A way to display data graphically to quantify problems from most to least frequent so that the "vital few" can be identified. Named after Wilfredo Pareto, a European economist.

Pareto principle The 80/20 rule. Eighty percent of the trouble comes from 20 percent of the problems, the basis of the "vital few."

process The combination of people, equipment, materials, methods, and environment that produce output (a given product or service). It is the particular way of doing something.

process management and control The "third leg" of the holistic improvement stool. Process management and control consists of the routine, real-time operation and control of processes, without formal projects. ISO 9000 is one example of a process management and control system.

process map A step-by-step pictorial sequence of a process showing process inputs, process outputs, cycle time rework operations, and inspection points.

process variation The extent to which the distribution of individual values of the process characteristic (input or output variable) vary; it is often shown as the process average plus and minus some number of standard deviations. Other related measures of spread include the range and variance.

Project Champion A person skilled in improvement system deployment that has the responsibility of guiding improvement projects. Project champions are responsible for maintaining the business focus of the team, as well as keeping the project on schedule and removing roadblocks the team encounters.

quality by design The collection of concepts, methods, and tools that results in building quality into products and processes. The tools are typically an integration of technical (statistical) and nontechnical tools.

Quality Function Deployment A systematic approach to product and process design that was developed in the Kobe shipyard in Japan.

risk management The set of methods organizations use to first identify and then mitigate the major sources of risk (financial risk, terrorism, vulnerability to computer hackers, and so on).

rolled throughput yield (RTY)   Multiplying all of the individual first pass yields of each step of the entire process. RTY is equal to first pass yield.

Six Sigma   The improvement initiative that originated at Motorola, in which statistical methods and other improvement tools are integrated in a standard approach to breakthrough improvement.

specification   The engineering requirement or customer requirement for judging acceptability of a particular characteristic.

standard deviation   A measure of the spread of the process (width of the distribution).

statistical control   The condition describing a process from which all special or assignable causes of variation have been eliminated and only common or random causes remain. It applies to both the mean (location) and standard deviation (spread).

statistical engineering   The study of how to best utilize statistical concepts, methods, and tools and how to integrate them with information technology and other relevant disciplines to achieve enhanced results.

statistical process control   An approach to process control that makes heavy use of control charts.

variation   Difference between individual measurements. Differences are attributed to common as well as special causes.

Work-Out   An improvement approach developed at GE to make workplace enhancements driven by employee identified improvements.

Y = f(X's)   Symbol of a cause and effect model the relates process outputs (Y's) as a function (f) of process inputs (X's).

X's input variables   An independent material or element, with descriptive characteristic(s), that is either an object (going into) or a parameter of a process (step) and that has a significant effect on the output of the process.

Y's output variables   A dependent material or element, with descriptive characteristic(s), that is the result of a process (step) that either is or significantly affects the customer's CTQ.

Yellow Belt (YB)   A process worker trained in improvement tools (typically, the tools of the Measure and Control phases of DMAIC). YBs use these tools to monitor and control processes and also serve as team members on Black Belt and Green Belt teams.

C

Acronyms

"Everything should be made as simple as possible, but not simpler."
—*Albert Einstein*

5S   Sort, Set in order, Shine, Standardize, Sustain (method in Lean)

ACFC   "At the customer, for the customer" projects

ANOVA   Analysis of variance

AOP   Annual operating plan

ASQ   American Society for Quality

BB   Black Belt (person leading improvement projects)

BD   Big Data

C&E   Cause and effect

CAP   Change Acceleration Process

CEO   Chief Executive Officer

CFO   Chief Financial Officer

CIO   Chief Information Officer

CIMO   Chief Improvement Officer

CMMB   Chief Master Black Belt

COO   Chief Operating Officer

CQ   Commercial quality

CTQ   Critical to quality metrics

DFSS   Design for Six Sigma

DMADV   Define, Measure, Analyze, Design, Verify framework for DFSS

DMAIC   Define, Measure, Analyze, Improve, Control framework for breakthrough improvement

DOE   Design of experiments

FMEA   Failure modes and effects analysis

GAAP Generally Accepted Accounting Practices

GB Green Belt (person applying improvement methods part time)

GE General Electric Corporation

GR&R Gage repeatability and reproducibility (measurement system evaluation)

HIS Holistic improvement system

HR Human resources

IoT Internet of Things

ISO 9000 International Organization for Standards (9000-series quality standards)

IT Information technology

MBB Master Black Belt

MSA Measurement system analysis

P&L Profit and loss

PPM Parts per million

QbD Quality by design

QFD Quality Function Deployment

R&D Research and development

R&R Reward and recognition

RSM Response surface methodology

SE Statistical engineering

SMED Single-minute exchange of dies

SIPOC Process map identifying suppliers, inputs, process steps, outputs, and customers

SOP Standard operating procedures

SPC Statistical process control

TQM Total Quality Management

VOC Voice of the customer

WIP Work in progress

YB Yellow Belt (person trained to participate in improvement projects)

Index